AARON BURR

AARON BURR

Now reproduced for the first time from the original miniature by Inman in the possession of Dr. J. E. Stillwell.

AARON BURR

A BIOGRAPHY WRITTEN, IN LARGE PART,
FROM ORIGINAL AND HITHERTO UNUSED MATERIAL

By

SAMUEL H. WANDELL

and

MEADE MINNIGERODE

VOLUME TWO

" It will be a host of choice spirits."
AARON BURR.

With Sixty-four Illustrations

G. P. PUTNAM'S SONS
NEW YORK   LONDON
The Knickerbocker Press
1927

Republished by
Scholarly Press, Inc., 22929 Industrial Drive East
St. Clair Shores, Michigan 48080

Library of Congress Catalog Card Number: 78-145356
ISBN 0-403-01263-5

Copyright, 1925
by
G. P. Putnam's Sons

CONTENTS

vi

CONTENTS

ILLUSTRATIONS

ILLUSTRATIONS

FACING
PAGE

THEODOSIA BURR ALSTON 298

Now reproduced for the first time from the original portrait
by Vanderlyn, formerly in the possession of the Alston family,
now in the possession of Dr. J. E. Stillwell.

THE JUMEL MANSION 314

MADAME JUMEL 322

AARON BURR 328

From the original portrait by Van Dyke in the possession of
Dr. J. E. Stillwell.

WINANT'S INN, PORT RICHMOND, STATEN ISLAND . 336

PART VI

The Conspirator

1805–1806

"It is beyond question that there exists in this country an infinite number of adventurers, without property, full of ambition, and ready to unite at once under the standard of a revolution which promises to better their lot."

THE MARQUIS DE CASA YRUJO.

CHAPTER I

NUMBER THIRTEEN

I

MR. JEFFERSON was in a good deal of a quandary in the spring of 1805. "We want nothing of hers [Spain] and we want no other nation to possess what is hers," he was writing in April, to Mr. Bowdoin, his newly selected Minister to Madrid, "but she has met our advances with jealousy, secret malice and ill faith. Our patience . . . is now on its last trial, and the issue of what is now depending between us will decide whether our relations with her are to be sincerely friendly or permanently hostile." Of course, Mr. Jefferson did not really mean that—indeed, at the time, he particularly wanted something of Spain's, namely the Floridas—but he thought that he meant it. . . .

It all went back to the Treaty of Paris, in 1763, under the terms of which France had lost her American colonial empire, Canada to England, and Louisiana to Spain—the latter really by secret cession the year before. In place of the old French peril, there was now, to the Colonies, the threat of a new Spanish danger, to the southern Colonies and

3

to their opening Back Countries. For men were
seeping into the wildernesses; Daniel Boone and
other buckskin-clad adventurers were exploring the
unknown lands beyond the mountains; in 1775,
Richard Henderson was purchasing the "dark and
bloody ground" of Kentucky from the Cherokees;
in 1780, John Donelson and James Robertson were
establishing their Tennessee colony on the Cumberland, just a cluster of blockhouses which were to be
known as Nashville. And for these settlers, for these
growing communities, for the carriage and profitable disposal of their corn, and furs, and produce, the
free navigation of the Mississippi and an outlet at
its mouth were a necessity.

But the secret commercial diplomacy of France
and Spain—under their Bourbon kings—saw these
matters in a different light. At the close of the
Revolutionary War, whatever their official attitude
might have been during the conflict, the Ministers of
Foreign Affairs at Paris and Madrid were intriguing
with England to prevent the recognition of American independence; and when this failed, their efforts
became concentrated on a restriction of the new
republic within the boundaries of the Appalachian
Mountains. Kentucky and Tennessee must be
destroyed, or else terrorized into seeking a Spanish allegiance. The task was to be accomplished
by means of secret agents, well furnished with funds,
by means of a constant stirring up of Indian mas-
sacres—and by closing the Mississippi to the inhabitants of those precarious territories. It might mean
nothing to New England, but to Kentucky and Tennessee, to Virginia and North Carolina, the Span-

ish decree was a vital issue, then, and at all times
in the future.

2

Governor Mirò, of Spanish Louisiana, was an
enterprising gentleman who found himself, upon his
assumption of office, in 1785, entirely in accord with
these projects, and, while conducting an urbane correspondence concerning their misfortunes with the
settlers of Kentucky and Tennessee, looked around
him for suitable underlings.

And so he naturally turned, on the one hand,
to Alexander McGillivray, the dreaded "White
Leader" of contemporary Indian history; that astonishingly polished and educated son of a Scotch
trader and a Creek squaw—herself half French—a
Tory during the War, and now the implacable enemy
of all American colonists, and the Chief, for many
years already, of the ferocious Creeks. At a cost to
Governor Mirò of some fifty-five thousand dollars a
year, the Leader and his six thousand odd warriors
made a massacring ground of Tennessee until Mr.
Robertson and Mr. Sevier were almost ready to
place themselves under Spanish protection, since
North Carolina would do nothing for them. And,
on the other hand, for assistance in more delicate
tasks, the Governor of Spanish Louisiana turned to
"General" James Wilkinson, of the American army,
who, in 1787—but the fact was not discovered,
unfortunately for a great many people, until long
years later—took the oath of allegiance to Spain,
and became secret agent Number Thirteen on the
records of the Ministry of Foreign Affairs at Madrid.

One has already seen this gentleman for a moment, volunteering for Colonel Arnold's Quebec expedition; one has seen him again, an old army friend of the Vice President, appointed Governor of Upper American Louisiana by Mr. Jefferson, in 1805. One must now bring a more detailed observation to bear upon the incidents of his distinguished career. A Marylander—the State was not responsible for the accident of his birth within her confines— he had, after Quebec, found himself upon the staff of General Gates, from whom he brought to Congress the news of Saratoga, together with a recommendation for a brigadier generalship which he had obtained by the assumption on his part of a gallant act performed by another officer. Implicated, however, in General Conway's cabal against General Washington his imposture was discovered, and he resigned the commission, being permitted to serve in the clothier's department. In 1784, he had settled in Kentucky, near the Falls of the Ohio; in 1786, he was loud in his disparagement of General George Rogers Clark—who had just been defeated by the Ohio Indians—and took a vicious part in the villification of that officer which finally resulted in the latter's censure and downfall.

Such was the previous history of the personage who, in 1787, became the paid agent of Governor Mirò—on whose behalf the final slanders against General Clark may have been advanced, since the General was a famous Indian fighter, and Governor Mirò was well disposed towards Indians. At all events, "General" Wilkinson enjoyed an exclusive trading privilege at New Orleans; through his representatives—Philip Nolan, Thomas Power and others—he received payments from the Spanish authorities by what was afterwards to be described as the mule load; in 1788, he was openly proposing the separation of Kentucky in favor of Spain. And in 1791, having been reinstated in the army as a lieutenant colonel, he served under Generals St. Clair and Wayne, and, although involved in the instigation of mutiny and other scabrous undertakings, was made a brigadier general in 1792, and placed in command of the American army upon the death of General Wayne in 1796—for he had a way of concealing his duplicities and evading suspicion. But now the Spaniards had opened the Mississippi again temporarily, and the tangle of plots was for a while unravelled.

Evidently a dangerous gentleman, this General Wilkinson—a handsome, intelligent, plausible and somewhat verbose person, consumed with avarice, steeped in jealousy and malice, treacherous and crafty—against whom, in those days, little was known in America except that he had once committed a dishonorable act, for which he had been punished, and that he had been the object of certain rumors concerning his service under General Wayne, in spite of which he had been promoted. But a brave soldier, a leader, a good enough brigadier general. Yes . . .

3

The boon of the reopened Mississippi—and of a duty free warehouse at New Orleans for three years at least—had been granted, in 1795, through a

treaty made with the United States by another
astonishing personage, Don Manuel Godoy, Prince
of the Peace—a title earned as a result of his ter-
mination of the French war—and Prime Minister of
Spain under that long suffering monarch, Don
Carlos IV.

A gentleman of the royal guard, of no particular
extraction, he had, in 1792, at the age of twenty-five,
reached his exalted station through an assiduous
cultivation of the shameless favors of Maria Luisa
of Parma, Queen of Spain—a lady devoid of virtue,
whose deportment was the scandal of Europe. Un-
scrupulous and profligate in private life, a symbol
of vice and corruption, and grown wealthy beyond
words, the Prince Godoy was nevertheless an enlightened and courageous Minister, a devoted guardian of his country's interests. And if he had made
his compact with America to counteract Mr. Jay's
treaty with England, the document brought down
upon him the wrath of France, in the person of Mr.
de Talleyrand, Foreign Minister to the Directoire,
which was another way of saying General Bonaparte.
And Mr. de Talleyrand, for whom intrigue was as
the breath of life, disliked America which he considered hopelessly Anglophile, and dreamed of re-
establishing the lost French colonial empire upon its
shores.

And first, he must have Louisiana again; Spain
must be teased, bullied, coerced. She must be, and
was, forced into the war with England; her independence was threatened; her ports were filled with
French privateers attacking American commerce,
at the same time that Mr. de Talleyrand was in-

DON MANUEL GODOY

sulting Mr. Adams's envoys—until finally, in 1798, the Prince Godoy told his King that Spain must free herself from the French influence, or he must resign. He resigned.

But now there was to be war—Mr. Adams's War—between France and America; General Hamilton was second in command; with the help of an American squadron, Toussaint L'Ouverture—the great leader of the revolted blacks, the "Bonaparte of Santo Domingo"—was wresting that island province from its French allegiance; at New Orleans, the Spanish Intendant had threatened to close the Mississippi again; the Southwest was in a turmoil, and enlisting twelve regiments, ostensibly for the French war but really for the Spanish one for which the whole region was confidently praying; and Don Francisco de Miranda was writing curious letters to General Hamilton. . . .

4

Godoy, Talleyrand, Napoleon, Toussaint, Miranda—the romantic, portentous figures were gathering upon the American stage. . . .

He was a Spaniard, a South American, this Francisco de Miranda, a crusader for independence who aspired to become the liberator of his country. "During our revolutionary war," John Adams wrote to James Lloyd, in 1815, "General Miranda came to the United States, travelled through many, if not all of them, was introduced to General Washington and his aids and secretaries, and all the gentlemen of his family, to the other general officers and their families, and to many of the colonels. He acquired

the character of a classical scholar, of a man of universal knowledge, of a great general and master of
all the military sciences, and of great sagacity, an
inquisitive mind, and insatiable curiosity.

"It was a general opinion and report that he
knew more of the families, parties and connections
in the United States than any other man in them;
that he knew more of every campaign, siege, battle
and skirmish that had ever occurred in the whole
war than any officer of an army, or any statesman
in our councils. His constant topic was the independence of South America, her immense wealth,
inexhaustible resources, innumerable population, im-
patience under the Spanish yoke, and disposition
to throw off the dominion of Spain. It is most
certain that he filled the heads of many of the
young officers with brilliant visions of wealth, free
trade, republican government, etc., etc., in South
America.

"Hamilton was one of his most intimate friends
and confidential admirers, and Colonel Smith, I
presume, was another. Of Burr I will say nothing,
because I know nothing with certainty. Of Dayton
I will say but little. Of Wilkinson, nothing at all,
at present . . . General Knox was also one of
his intimates."

And now, in 1798, General Miranda—they were
all Generals—was in London, at the invitation of
Prime Minister Pitt, to lay before him certain interesting proposals. "South America must soon pass
through a revolution," Rufus King was writing
from the British capital in April. "We have an
immense interest in the event, as well as in the

manner in which it shall be effected." And General
Miranda's idea was simply this. England was to
furnish the money, and a fleet of not more than
twenty ships of the line; America was to supply an
army of five thousand foot and two thousand horse,
preferably under the command of General Hamilton; together they would descend upon the Spanish possessions in the West Indies and in South America. In return, America was to have the Floridas
and the territory east of the Mississippi; England
the control of the Isthmus, the West Indies and certain exclusive commercial privileges; and General
Miranda, presumably, an emancipated continent.
Owing to the lethargy and debility of the Spanish
giant, the plan was not as fanciful as might appear;
it had, in fact, occurred some five years before to
the French, and the arousing of America to its support had found its way into the confidential instructions of the Citizen Genêt, whose agents had over-
run Kentucky securing enlistments and issuing
commissions.

5

From the extracts published by Mr. Antepara in
1808, in the *Edinburgh Review*, one may obtain some
conception of the correspondence which passed
between General Miranda and General Hamilton
on the subject. "This letter will be handed you, my
dear and respected friend," General Miranda wrote,
on April 6, 1798, "by my fellow countryman . . .
who brings dispatches of the utmost importance for
the President of the United States; he will tell you
confidentially all that you wish to know on the sub-

ject. It seems that the moment for our emancipation approaches, and that the establishment of liberty throughout the entire continent of the new world
has been entrusted to us by Providence. The only
danger I foresee would be the introduction of French
principles which would poison liberty in its cradle,
and end by destroying yours in the near future."

To this General Hamilton replied, on August 22,
that "I have lately received, by duplicates, your
letter of the 6th of April, with a postscript of the
9th of June. The gentleman you mention in it
has not made his appearance to me, nor do I know
of his arrival in this country; so that I can only
divine the object from the limits in your letter.

"The sentiments I entertain with regard to that
object have been long since in your knowledge; but
I could personally have no participation in it, unless
patronized by the government of this country. It
was my wish that matters had been ripened for
a co-operation in the course of this fall, on the part
of this country; but this can now scarce be the case.
The winter, however, may mature the project and
an effectual co-operation by the United States may
take place. In this case I shall be happy, in my
official station, to be an instrument of so good a
work.

"The plan, in my opinion, ought to be a fleet of
Great Britain, an army of the United States—a government for the liberated territories, agreeable to
both the co-operators, about which there will probably be no difficulty. To arrange the plan, a competent authority from Great Britain to some person
here, is the best expedient. Your presence here will,

in this case, be extremely essential. We are raising an army of about 12,000 men. . . . I am appointed second in command."

And on October 19, General Miranda was writing back that "your wishes have been granted up to a certain point, since it is agreed here, on the one hand, that no English troops are to take part in the land operations, as the auxiliary land forces are to be entirely American; and, on the other hand, that the navy is to be solely English. Everything is straightened out, and we await only the decision of your illustrious President to start like lightning."

6

It is quite evident from all this that in 1798, under the pretext of the French war, preparations were going forward for a conflict with Spain, the outbreak of which was awaited with eager interest, not only in the Southwest which would undoubtedly have joined General Miranda's armada to a man, but in some of the highest military circles in the country—for it appears that General Pinckney and Secretary of War McHenry shared General Hamilton's enthusiasm, while President Adams was causing flat boats to be constructed at Fort Washington for the transportation of troops, in the event of a descent upon New Orleans. In view of not far distant events, it is interesting, surely, to observe that the notion of war with Spain was possessed of wide popular approval throughout the Mississippi Valley; and that the project of a glorified filibustering expedition enjoyed the sanction, and was to profit by the leadership, of so prominent and correct a person as General Hamilton.

But what General Hamilton, and all of them, could not possibly have realized at the time, was that the Spanish government was probably fully cognizant of these preparations, through its Number Thirteen. For in February, 1799, General Hamilton, whose relations with him seemed to have remained sufficiently cordial, sent for General Wilkinson to come to New York—which he did by way of New Orleans —for a consultation. They met in August, and General Hamilton gave him a memorandum of the points to be covered in future conferences, including "the disposition of our western inhabitants towards the United States and foreign powers; the disposition of the Spaniards in our vicinity, their strength in number and fortifications . . . the best mode (in the event of a rupture with Spain) of attacking the two Floridas, the troops, artillery, etc., requisite; the best method of supplying the western army with provisions . . . the best arrangement of command, so as to unite facility of communication with the seaboard . . . under the general commanding the western army."

And General Wilkinson told General Hamilton that "the imbecility of the Spanish government on the Mississippi is as manifest as the ardour of the gallant Louisianians is obvious. A single individual of hardy enterprize, presenting himself with directorial credentials, and hoisting the national standard at New Orleans, might depose the Spanish administration in one hour, and have the population of the country for any chivalrous enterprize." Such as, for instance, an invasion of Mexico? "Under such circumstances, will it be indecorous should I express my apprehensions that we repose in false security, and that if we are not seasonably aroused, the dismemberment of the union may be put to hazard?" And General Wilkinson was certainly in a position to know about that.

As for the rest, "let us," General Wilkinson suggested to General Hamilton, "let us contemplate the unmeasured range of the Mississippi, let us view its countless tributary waters which bathe the most extensive tract of luxuriant soil in the universe; let us reflect that the most valuable portion of this soil is ours of right, and that on the maintenance of this right must depend the national union: under such well founded reflections . . . I flatter myself we shall not hesitate . . . for the safety, the subordination and prosperity of our western possessions, the most cheap and conclusive plan would be the capture of New Orleans; but as this step is at present unwarrantable we must turn our thoughts to the defensive protection of these settlements."

Copy to the Prince Godoy—or rather, to his successor, Don Mariano de Urquijo—not to mention Don Carlos de Yrujo, Spanish Minister at Philadelphia. . . .

One has to rely for these matters on General Wilkinson's memoirs, a frequently imaginative work; how much better might one examine the correspondence of the two generals, now apparently destroyed, of which Mr. Edward Everett Hale said that "I have read the manuscript correspondence between Hamilton, the acting commander of the new army, and Wilkinson, the commander of the Ohio, with reference to the proposed attack on Orleans. Wilkinson himself made a visit to Hamilton to adjust the details of the campaign. This mine was ready to be sprung upon poor Spain, when the republic of the United States should make war upon the French republic."

They were all ready to "start like lightning," but as it turned out, President Adams never answered the proposals from General Miranda; and General Hamilton's sword was not placed upon the altar of South American liberty. . . .

CHAPTER II

MOUNTAINS OF SALT

I

In 1798, Mr. de Talleyrand had succeeded in driving out the Prince Godoy, but in 1799 he was himself out of power. But only for a while. Napoleon soon declared himself First Consul; the victory of Marengo made him master of Europe; and on September 30, 1800, he and Mr. de Talleyrand were signing a peace of sorts with the United States.

But in August they were negotiating a treaty of a vastly different nature. Marshal Berthier took it to Madrid, and with the Queen of Spain on his side, secured an agreement whereby, in return for the addition of Tuscany to the Duchy of Parma—and the daughter of the Queen of Spain was Duchess of Parma—Spain undertook to cede Louisiana to France. It was Mr. de Talleyrand's old idea of the French colonial empire, although as they explained it to Spain, it was to provide an efficient protection for her unwieldy dominions in the new world. The treaty was signed at San Ildefonso, on October 1, 1800, and the fact that its clauses were to all intents incompatible with the covenants signed

exactly twenty-four hours before with the United
States was a matter of small concern to Mr. de
Talleyrand. In February, 1801, while Mr. de Talleyrand was still vigorously denying the existence of any
Spanish treaty, the Duchy of Tuscany was formally presented to the Duke of Parma—except that
a considerable number of French troops still encum-
bered its territory—and the First Consul's brother,
Lucien Bonaparte, was sent to Madrid.

He was not pleased, upon his arrival, to find the
Prince of the Peace installed once more in authority as Superintendent General of Spain. It had finally occurred to Don Carlos IV that Napoleon was
a troublesome friend and that his eagerness to
place an army on Spanish soil, under pretext of an
approaching conflict between Spain and Portugal,
might contain elements of concealed peril to his
kingdom. And so the Prince Godoy was called
back, and in June, true to his title, made a peace with
Portugal, for the consent to which on the part of
Lucien Bonaparte he gave the latter "as much
more" as he had for the consummation of the Tuscany transfer—which was, in Lucien's bland report
to his brother, "twenty good pictures" for his gal-
lery and "diamonds to the value of one hundred
thousand crowns."

Napoleon was furious; at Lucien who had let
the Portuguese pretext slip through his fingers; at
the Prince Godoy who had not only saved Spain,
but now, in July, refused to ratify the cession of
Louisiana, on the grounds that the Duke of Parma
was King of Tuscany merely in name. But Napoleon was too busy at the time to bother with Spain.

There was the black, Toussaint—the "gilded African" as he called him—to be punished; and in October, an army under General Leclerc was on its way to Santo Domingo. It took them until May 1, 1802; and then only by the darkest treachery was Toussaint captured, and carried back to France to die wretchedly in a Swiss mountain dungeon. Napoleon was free once more to attend to the Prince Godoy, and on October 15, 1802, the order ceding Louisiana to France was finally signed. The Prince kept the Floridas, and obtained from Mr. de Talleyrand a promise that the Province would be returned to Spain in the event of the Duke of Parma losing any considerable portion of his domain —as a result of which Louisiana could never be "alienated" by France. This was distinctly understood.

2

Mr. Jefferson hardly knew what was happening. Some eight months after the signing of the Treaty of San Ildefonso he was still writing to the Governor of the Mississippi Territory, in July, 1801, that "with respect to Spain, our disposition is sincerely amicable and even affectionate. We consider her possession of the adjacent country as most favorable to our interests and should see with an extreme pain any other nation substituted for them." A statement which may, or may not, have pleased Kentucky and Tennessee.

The fact was, Mr. Jefferson was becoming very apprehensive of France; and by November, 1801, the whole Louisiana affair was known at Washington. The Santo Domingo incident provided a respite, but

early in 1802 Mr. Jefferson was really alarmed.
Napoleon was coming, at any time now. "It has,"
Colonel Burr wrote Mr. Alston in February, "for
some months past been asserted that Spain has ceded
Louisiana and the Floridas to France"—the Floridas were not included in the cession, but it was so
believed in America—"and it may . . . be assumed as a fact. How do you account for the
apathy of the public on this subject? To me the
arrangement appears to be pregnant with evil to
the United States. I wish you to think of it, and
endeavour to excite attention to it through the
newspapers."

In his own inimitable manner, Mr. Jefferson began
to whirl upon his whirligig chair. The moment that
Napoleon took possession of Louisiana, he sent
word to him, "from that moment we must marry
ourselves to the British fleet and nation." Napoleon was not impressed. For Mr. de Talleyrand, Mr.
Livingston was instructed to inform him, Mr. Jefferson entertained "the most friendly dispositions";
he must forget the quarrel during Mr. Adams's
administration, which had been merely the "artifice
of a party willing to sacrifice him to the consolidation of their power. This nation had done him justice by dismissing them." Mr. de Talleyrand was
not even amused.

And in October, they heard at Washington the
news that the Spanish Intendant at New Orleans
had closed the Mississippi again, and forbidden the
American merchandise depots. And still more
loud, they heard the roar that arose from Kentucky
and Tennessee for immediate war on Spain. The

MARQUIS DE CASA YRUJO

Marquis de Casa Yrujo—he was a Marquis now—
assured Mr. Madison that the Intendant had acted
without orders, and as soon as he found out, the
Prince Godoy ordered the river opened; but Congress, led by John Randolph, had asked for the
"papers" in the case. "This circumstance," Mr.
Pichon, the French Minister, notified his government
in December, "will be decisive for Mr. Jefferson.
If he acts feebly, he is lost among his partisans;
it will be then the time for Mr. Burr to show himself with advantage." Mr. Jefferson sent some
papers, and the House determined to rely "with perfect confidence on the vigilance and wisdom of the
Executive."

The time had come, Mr. Jefferson told Mr. Monroe, when "something sensible, therefore, has become
necessary," and prepared to send him to France.
As for the free navigation of the Mississippi, if the
United States, Mr. Jefferson declaimed to the
British Minister, were "obliged at last to resort to
force, they would throw away the scabbard." Just
like that.

3

And so, in March, 1803, Mr. Monroe went to
France, with instructions authorizing him and Mr.
Livingston to negotiate with Napoleon for the purchase of New Orleans and West Florida—still that
misapprehension concerning the status of the Floridas. They could pay two million dollars. "Peace
is our passion," Mr. Jefferson explained, "and wrong
might drive us from it. We prefer trying every
other just principle, right and safety before we would

recur to war." He was extraordinarily like Mr. Woodrow Wilson in that respect, and some others. . . .

Mr. Monroe arrived at Paris on April 12, and before they knew it, he and Mr. Livingston were haggling with Mr. de Talleyrand and Minister Marbois of the Treasury—not for New Orleans, but for the whole of Louisiana. The First Consul had suddenly made up his mind to sell the Province —in spite of Mr. de Talleyrand who saw his colonial empire vanishing, and in spite of Lucien and Joseph Bonaparte who came to expostulate with their brother while he was in his bath, and got themselves splashed for their pains. The First Consul had decided to sell, for one reason—and they were many and intricate—in order to annoy the Prince Godoy. Everyone was in a great state over the affair, but finally, on May 2, 1803, it was settled. America would pay sixty million francs for Louisiana, and twenty million more representing the American damage claims against France—fifteen million dollars in all.

And, as Mr. Henry Adams points out, the sale was invalid; since, if the territory belonged to France, the consent of the Chambers was necessary, and, in any case, the Spanish treaty forbade the "alienation" by France of Louisiana under any circumstances. Indeed, at Madrid, the news was received with consternation. The Prince Godoy was infuriated. . . .

4

At home, in America, people were no less astonished. Mr. Jefferson had offered a bid of two mil-

lion dollars for New Orleans and West Florida; he
found himself faced with the whole of Louisiana and
a bill for fifteen million.

Fifteen million dollars, the Federalists cried—
why, fifteen million dollars stacked up dollar on
dollar would make a pile three miles high; there were
not that many dollars in the country; it would take
eight hundred and sixty-six waggons—fifteen million
dollars! And as for Louisiana, what was it, this
territory? A place full of wild animals, and gigantic
Indians, and bear trappers; an enormous wilderness of no use whatever. Not at all, the Republicans
replied. There were tremendous prairies covered
with buffalo, and mountains of salt. Mr. Jefferson
himself said so. "One extraordinary fact relative to
salt must not be omitted," he reported to Congress.
"There exists about one thousand miles up the
Missouri . . . a salt mountain! The existence of
such a mountain might well be questioned, were it
not for the testimony of several respectable and enterprising traders . . . who have exhibited several
bushels of the salt to the curiosity of the people of
St. Louis. . . . This mountain is said to be 180
miles long and 45 in width, composed of solid rock
salt, without any trees or even shrubs on it."

Mountains of salt! Lakes of whisky, too, and valleys of hasty pudding, the Federalists laughed, and
began to sing—

> "Jefferson lately of Bonaparte bought,
> To pickle his fame, a mountain of salt!"

But aside from all that, the purchase was uncon-
stitutional. The Constitution did not permit the

Executive to acquire territory, and the treaty making power did not include the right to take new States into the Union. There was a great fuss over it, and for a while Mr. Jefferson wanted to submit a Constitutional amendment; but they got around it, finally, by having the Senate ratify the proceedings without any regard for the provisions of the Constitution, and Mr. Jefferson was even authorized to appoint officers without any reference to the Senate. From beginning to end, in France and in America, the entire transaction was illegal. But the country, on the whole, was pleased, and the Southwest was delighted.

In the meantime, Mr. Laussat, the French Prefect, had arrived at New Orleans, followed, later, by the Marquis de Casa Calvo from Havana. On November 30, 1803—while from the balcony of the Cabildo the Marquis proclaimed the sovereignty of Spain at an end—Mr. Laussat received from Governor Manuel de Salcedo the keys of the town. For twenty days the Creole city rejoiced in the restoration of its old nationality; and then, on December 20, Mr. Laussat transferred his keys to Governor Claiborne and General Wilkinson, while people wept in the Place d'Armes at the final passing of the banner of France. Slowly, at the masthead, the American flag unfurled.

5

Louisiana was American, but what about West Florida? If Mr. Jefferson experienced any passion comparable to his passion for peace, it was that which he entertained—and the country with him—for the

possession of West Florida. But West Florida was
not included in the sale of Louisiana by France to
America, since it had not been included in the original cession by Spain to France. Mr. Livingston, in
Paris, had tried to make out otherwise, basing his
arguments on ingenious assumptions—and anyway,
he wrote to Mr. Madison, "the moment is so favorable for taking possession of that country that I
hope it has not been neglected, even though a little
force should be necessary to effect it."

But it had been neglected, just as the securing of
a definition of the actual eastern boundaries of
Louisiana, as understood by France, had been neglected by Mr. Livingston and Mr. Monroe. But
still Mr. Jefferson insisted on having West Florida;
in fact, he calmly claimed West Florida, and gave
his signature to John Randolph's Mobile Act, in
February, 1804, in which the House proclaimed
that "all the navigable waters, rivers, creeks, bays
and inlets lying within the United States, which
empty into the Gulf of Mexico east of the river
Mississippi, shall be annexed to the Mississippi
District." And this could only mean that West
Florida was a part of the United States, since otherwise they did not own any navigable waters, rivers,
creeks, bays and inlets lying within their borders
and emptying into the Gulf of Mexico east of the
river Mississippi.

It is not necessary in these pages to discuss the
long months of intricate and fruitless negotiations
which followed; the quarrels with the Marquis Yrujo,
who kept pointing out to Mr. Madison that, far
from acquiring West Florida, the United States had

not even legally purchased Louisiana; the weary days spent at Paris and at Madrid by Mr. Livingston, and Mr. Pinckney, and Mr. Monroe, in the effort to put into practice the curious theories of Mr. Jefferson's opportunist diplomacy. Spain would combat the Florida claims, he had written to Mr. Breckenridge, in August, 1803, "and if as soon as she is at war [with England] we push them strongly with one hand, holding out a price with the other, we shall certainly obtain the Floridas, and all in good time." That was the plan—to "push" the claims, since he had the effrontery to call them claims, to threaten war, he who was so passionately pacifist; and at the same time to offer money for something which the Prince Godoy did not wish to sell.

Of all the Presidents, Mr. Henry Adams observes, none used his arbitrary diplomatic powers with more freedom and secrecy than Mr. Jefferson—"his ideas of presidential authority in foreign affairs were little short of royal." Once again, a similarity to Mr. Woodrow Wilson presents itself irresistibly. And Mr. Thornton, lately British Minister, was perhaps not far wrong when he told his Foreign Office that "the cession of Louisiana, notwithstanding that the circumstances under which it was made ought to convince the vainest of men that he was not the sole agent in the transaction, has elevated the President beyond imagination in his own opinion."

And the situation had not changed essentially when, in March, 1805, Mr. Jefferson was declaring to Mr. Bowdoin that as for Spain, "we want nothing of hers."

6

The thing went on.

For a while, during the summer of 1805, Mr. Jefferson's diplomacy envisaged an alliance with England. "The first wish of every Englishman's heart," he assured Mr. Madison in August, "is to see us once more fighting by their sides against France; nor could the King or his Ministers do an act so popular as to enter into an alliance with us. . . . I think it possible that for such a provisional treaty" —whatever a provisional treaty might be—"they would give us their general guaranty of Louisiana and the Floridas. At any rate we might try them."

Someone must always be induced to play monkey to Mr. Jefferson's cat. Mr. Madison and Mr. Gallatin thought very little of all this, but on the other hand *something* must be done; Mr. Monroe at Madrid, and now Mr. Armstrong at Paris, kept telling the President that some degree of firmness was necessary in his policy if he expected to accomplish anything with such personages as Mr. de Talleyrand and the Prince Godoy; and Mr. Jefferson was all for that, too. It would "correct the dangerous error that we are a people whom no injuries can provoke to war." Europe must realize that some day Mr. Jefferson would throw away that scabbard. That was in September. But in October, Mr. Jefferson heard that a European coalition had been formed against Napoleon, and "this," he gleefully informed Mr. Madison, "gives us our great desideratum, time. In truth, it places us quite at our ease."

With all Europe going to war—and with hostile

acts against America by the Spaniards a constant
occurrence on land and sea—there would have
been an excellent opportunity and justification for
the occupation of Texas, over which there was
also argument with Spain, and for the seizure of
the Floridas, and an end to the business; but Mr.
Jefferson allowed the opportunity to pass, and
turned again to the negotiations which he had been
conducting through France. And in November,
Mr. de Talleyrand actually had a proposal to submit. In return for certain considerations, France
would force Spain to sell the Floridas for two million dollars, and in the meantime let Mr. Jefferson
be very warlike. And so, in his December message
to Congress, the President advised that body that
"with Spain our negotiations . . . have not had
a satisfactory issue. . . . Propositions for adjust-
ing amicably the boundaries of Louisiana have not
been acceded to. . . . Inroads have been recently
made into the territories of Orleans and the Mississippi, our citizens have been seized and their property plundered in the very parts of the former
which have been actually delivered us by Spain.
. . . I have therefore found it necessary at length
to give orders to our troops on that frontier to be
made in readiness . . . and to repel by arms any
similar aggressions in future."

It was a war message. Mr. Jefferson had sent
a war message! The country rang with it, the
whole Atlantic seaboard took it for a virtual declaration, the Southwest was overjoyed. At last, America was going to fight Spain. Perhaps the Marquis
Yrujo was not so tremendously impressed; or Brit-

ish Mr. Merry; or French Mr. Turreau who was soon to write Mr. de Talleyrand that "Mr. Jefferson lacks the first of the qualities which make a statesman; he has little energy, and still less of that audacity which is indispensable in a place so eminent. . . . The slightest event makes him lose his balance, and he does not even know how to disguise the impression he receives." But the nation believed Mr. Jefferson and was delighted.

In Congress, however, there were other matters on the floor. For Mr. Jefferson had not sent one message, but *two*—the first, the published, warlike, "ostensible" one; and the second, the secret, peaceful, "real" one, the one explaining Mr. de Talleyrand's proposal. Mr. Jefferson had perhaps never done anything quite so clever—in his estimation. The United States were to buy the Floridas—war, good heavens no—and Mr. Jefferson, it seemed, must have two million dollars for France. Yes; for while the money was to be offered to Spain, it was to be offered through France, and it was understood that France would keep the money. John Randolph thought the whole proposition outrageous, but after a week's secret debate the House voted the necessary two million for "extraordinary expenses in foreign relations," the Senate, with many expressions of disgust, approved this "extraordinary" fund, and in March, 1806, Mr. Armstrong was authorized to make formal offer to France for the Floridas and Texas.

Nothing came of it, of course. Spain did not sell the Floridas that time—or at any time during Mr. Jefferson's administration—and Mr. Jefferson did

not make war. The "ostensible" message was a
falsehood, a hoax on the American nation. It
should have been taken with those mountains of
salt which Mr. Jefferson had discovered in Louisiana.
But many people trusted in its contents, and gov-
erned their actions accordingly—and among these,
to his ruin, the late Vice President of the United
States. . . .

CHAPTER III

DOWNSTREAM

I

ALREADY in 1804, that summer after the duel, Colonel Burr had realized that within a year he must contrive some occupation for himself, some employment for his energies, some recuperative enterprise for his fortunes. A place to go, something to do, and some money to do it with. In the North, in New York, in New England, he was ruined; in Washington there would be no place for him after inauguration day of 1805; there was no attraction, at his age, in the prospect of a laboriously reconstructed law practice in any of the cities of the Atlantic seaboard. There remained the Southwest, the Territories, that valley of the Mississippi and the new Louisiana; regions to explore, lands to settle, new states to be formed, maybe, numberless opportunities to be grasped. He was popular out there—the West had never cared for Alexander Hamilton—he had many friends there, Senator Smith of Ohio, and Senator Brown of Kentucky, and General Wilkinson, and General Andrew Jack-

son. It was in the West that he would find political
rehabilitation—unless, as seemed more than likely,
there should be war with Spain, in which case
Colonel Burr, a veteran of Quebec, would know
what to do. In fact, there was an old project of his
—a project dating back to the days before Alexander Hamilton and General Miranda even—which
might at last come to belated fruition.

But first, he must find money, and that must be
done in the East. In Philadelphia, during his sojourn there in July and August of 1804, Colonel
Burr looked around him, and allowed the gaze of
speculation to rest upon His Excellency Anthony
Merry, who was then but lately come upon the
American scene as Minister from Great Britain.
It had not been a comfortable coming to the distressing wilderness of Washington, nor had the
republican simplicity of Mr. Jefferson's social deportment, with its genial lack of regard for precedence,
increased the charm of residence in the Federal City
to Mr. Merry, or to his tall, tempestuous lady.
Along with the whole of Washington society, the
Vice President had witnessed the progress of the
diplomatic feud—into which the Marquis Yrujo
had not been slow to inject his personality—engen-
dered during the winter of 1803 by the failure of
the President to conduct Mrs. Merry to a place at
his table upon the occasion of her first appearance
at a White House dinner, to which, with bland indifference to accepted neutral procedure in the case
of two countries at war, he had also invited the
Minister from France. Mrs. Merry had been very
angry, so that in January Mr. Jefferson was writing

that "she has already disturbed our harmony extremely"; indeed, she was "a virago, and in the short course of a few weeks has established a degree of dislike among all classes which one would have thought impossible in so short a time . . . If [she] perseveres she must eat her soup at home."

But in the meantime, Mr. Jefferson himself had established a degree of dislike on the part of Mr. Merry fully as considerable as that of his wife's unpopularity. Mr. Merry disliked Mr. Jefferson, he disliked Washington, he disliked America. Aside from that, he was an extremely worthy, earnest gentleman who took himself and American affairs quite seriously—so that he listened with enthusiastic interest to certain proposals which the Vice President made to him on August 6, 1804. "I have just received an offer from Mr. Burr," he told his Foreign Office, "to lend his assistance to his Majesty's government in any manner in which they may think fit to employ him, particularly in endeavouring to effect a separation of the western part of the United States . . . in its whole extent."

There was nothing extraordinary about this, of course. A few months before, almost every Federalist Senator in Washington had been to see Mr. Merry to enlist his efforts on behalf of New England separation, in which venture they were naturally expecting "support and assistance" from England; if Mr. Merry knew anything at all about America, he knew that the idea of separation as a solution of domestic disputes was considered perfectly normal and logical, even by Mr. Jefferson himself, the guardian, ostensibly, of the Constitution. If the obligations of membership in the Union became too irksome, if the Federal policy ran counter to local interests—leave the Union. The West had been talking of it for years.

Colonel Burr's plan was being taken to England by a certain Colonel Charles Williamson, and it was only necessary for Mr. Merry to add that "if after what is generally known of the profligacy of Mr.· Burr's character, his Majesty's ministers should think proper to listen to his offer, his present situation in this country, where he is now cast off as much by the democratic as by the Federal party, and where he still preserves connections with some people of influence, added to his great ambition and spirit of revenge against the present Administration, may possibly induce him to exert the talents and activity which he possesses with fidelity to his employers."

In spite of his poor opinion of Colonel Burr, Mr. Merry thought so well of the scheme—whereby, in return for her assistance, England was to profit commercially—that he failed to see that he was being sold a "Mississippi bubble."

2

Colonel Burr went south that summer, all the way to St. Augustine in Florida, and in the winter he was back at Washington for his final session in the Senate. And in December, three Creole gentlement from New Orleans—Mr. Sauvé, Mr. Derbigny and Mr. d'Estrehan—arrived at the capital to lay certain grievances before the Government. It was not just that the people of the Territory disliked

American ways, and resented American judicial interference with long established Spanish precedents, and loathed their American Governor Claiborne; it was that the treaty had not been fulfilled. It had been promised the inhabitants of Louisiana that they would be incorporated in the Union, and admitted to the rights of American citizenship as soon as possible, but now a year had passed and they were no better than conquered subjects. Congress took note of these complaints, and on March 2, 1805, graciously conferred upon Louisiana the privilege of electing a General Assembly and certain other concessions.

The three Creole deputies were very angry. They expressed their dissatisfaction "very publicly," Mr. Merry reported to his government; they would seek redress elsewhere, they said; and it was their opinion, "after witnessing the proceedings of Congress," that the Union was extremely unstable, and that the connection with it into which they had been "forced" was most regrettable. So these aggrieved gentlemen talked quite openly to anyone who cared to listen, and among others to the Vice President, to whom they had been introduced by General Wilkinson who was then waiting for his commission as Governor of Upper Louisiana. Separation—separation—the word filled the air. . . .

And now on that same March 2, the Vice President left the Senate chamber for the last time. What was he going to do? Congressman Matthew Lyon, of Kentucky—the Vermont victim of the old Sedition Act had moved lately to the West—thought that he should establish a residence in Tennessee and have himself elected to Congress. Mr. Lyon suggested this to General Wilkinson who "clapped his hands" saying it was "a heavenly thought," rang the bell, "ordered his boots" and went off to tell "the little counsellor." The Colonel made an appointment with Mr. Lyon, who was kept waiting for a long time because his host was engaged with a numerous company, including the General and Senator Dayton; when "the little counsellor" finally came he said that "the meeting was about some land concern, in the western country," as for the election to Congress, he "did not seem to be so much enamoured with the project." Still, it was something to think about, more especially as the Colonel was planning a journey to the Ohio.

But first, there was that business of Mr. Merry's to which no answer had been received. On March 21, Colonel Burr was at Philadelphia; and on March 29 Mr. Merry was writing to Lord Harrowby that "Mr. Burr (with whom I know that the deputies became very intimate during their residence here) has mentioned to me that the inhabitants of Louisiana seem determined to render themselves independent of the United States, and that the execution of their design is only delayed by the difficulty of obtaining . . . assurance of protection and assistance from some Foreign power, and of concerting . . . their independence with that of the inhabitants of the western parts of the United States. . . . It is clear that Mr. Burr . . . means to endeavour to be the instrument of effecting such a connection." All that was necessary was a British squadron at the mouth of the Mississippi, and

JONATHAN DAYTON

a loan of half a million dollars. And Mr. Merry had only to add that "if strict confidence could be placed in him," Colonel Burr possessed, more than anyone else, "all the talents, energy, intrepidity and firmness which are required for such an enterprise."

Mr. Merry was all breathless about it, but a complete suffocation would have overtaken him had he for a moment understood the real objective of the late Vice President's venture, and the use to which the British treasury's gold was actually destined. At no time does it seem to have occurred to Mr. Merry that he was being gloriously bamboozled. As for the Colonel, he wrote to Theodosia that "in ten or twelve days I shall be on my way westward . . . as the objects of this journey, not mere curiosity, or *pour passer le temps*, may lead me to Orleans, and perhaps farther, I contemplate the tour with gaiety and cheerfulness." And perhaps farther—Mexico, then? At all events, he procured a passport from the Marquis Yrujo. Aside from that, "I have such a levee about me of visitors, from distant parts, that it is with difficulty I can find an hour, day or night, to write a letter, or attend to private concerns"; and "I have not been a day without some one, two, or more [visitors]. They stay generally two or three days with me, and I am privileged to take them with me wherever I dine."

The Colonel was *very* busy. . . .

3

There were, at the time, probably not more than two other men in the East who knew what it was all about—General Wilkinson and Jonathan Dayton.

The General one has already seen in various aspects, some of the most significant of which entirely unknown, unfortunately, to Colonel Burr; an old friend of Canadian days, with whom, for the last four or five years, the Colonel had been in quite close cipher correspondence—for his old Princeton habit of secrecy and mystery had not diminished. They had lost sight of one another for a while after the Revolution, until the General had come to New York, in 1799, to confer with General Hamilton— on which occasion, General Wilkinson having enquired whether his superior officer had any objections to his calling on Colonel Burr, Mr. Hamilton had replied "Little Burr?   Oh no, we have always been opposed in politics but always on good terms." Since then, they had talked much together on the subject of the Spanish possessions, and accumulated considerable topographical material concerning those regions.   Jonathan Dayton was another good friend; a veteran, too, of the Quebec expedition, married to the sister of Colonel Burr's boyhood chum, Matthias Ogden who had died in 1791.   Mr. Dayton had graduated from Princeton, he came of a fine New Jersey family, he had served with distinction in the war, and prominently in Federalist politics, and he had recently closed his career in the United States Senate.

And the purpose which filled their minds was simply the invasion of Mexico. In the event, and perhaps without it, of war between America and Spain, an eventuality which became day by day more imminent. A rousing of the West, which would not require to be called twice to such an adventure; a stirring up of Louisiana, which asked for nothing better than the "liberation" of the neighboring empire; and then, with New Orleans as a base, a descent on the one hand upon the Floridas which must be made American, and upon the other a march into the treasure filled land of Montezuma. A driving out of the hated Spaniard, and for the adventurers wealth, glory and dominion. A fig for Mr. Merry and the western separation—if the idea ever seriously occupied the thoughts of the conspirators it was soon abandoned for a far greater vision. What they wanted was Mr. Merry's English gold, with which to reach the silver mines of Mexico, with which to carve out a domain of their own. And if justification is needed for this unlovely intrigue with Mr. Merry—and for the similar one which followed with the Marquis Yrujo—it must be found in the sordid character of contemporary diplomacy, and in the willingness of those two Ministers themselves to dip their fingers into such concoctions. And if, in the wake of Mexican conquest, Louisiana, or any other State, chose to detach itself from the Union, what of it? "If they see their interests in separation, why should we take sides with our Atlantic rather than our Mississippi descendants?" Mr. Jefferson had asked, in 1803. "God bless them both, and keep them in union, if it be for their good, but separate them, if it be better." Once and for all, it must be understood that in 1805 secession pure and simple was not a crime.

And it was not a castle in Spain, it was not a

vision without very solid foundations. Louisiana
was talking of it night and day. "So popular is an
enterprize on that country [Mexico] in this," Mr.
Jefferson was to write, in 1807, in one of his illumi-
nating communications to Mr. Bowdoin at Madrid,
"that we had only to be still, and [Burr] could have
had followers enough to have been in the city of
Mexico in 6. weeks. . . . We ask"—then, in 1807
—"but one month to be in . . . the city of Mexico." *That we had only to be still*, Mr. Jefferson
wrote. It will perhaps be necessary in subsequent
pages to ask why Mr. Jefferson was still so long. . . .

Mexico. It was there that Colonel Burr was
going. To strike a blow at the enemy, Spain, to
make himself master of that fabulous territory, of
"the lands beyond," that was what he was going
to do. What General Wilkinson may have thought
he was going to do is another matter. . . .

4

Colonel Burr left Philadelphia on horseback, in
the company of Mr. and Mrs. Gabriel Shaw, on
April 10, 1805, for Pittsburgh, where he arrived on
April 29. On May 2 they were all floating down
the Ohio, aboard the boat which the Colonel had
ordered in advance—"properly speaking a floating
house," he wrote Theodosia, "sixty by fourteen feet,
containing dining room, kitchen with fireplace, and
two bedrooms; roofed from stem to stern; steps to
go up, and a walk on top the whole length; glass
windows, etc. This edifice cost one hundred and
thirty-three dollars, and how it can be made for that
sum passes my comprehension."

Soon after leaving Pittsburgh they overtook Matthew Lyon in his barge, and the two boats were lashed together. They stopped at "the town of Wieling, sometimes erroneously spelled Wheeling," where there were some eighty houses and "several well dressed women," and on May 5 they were at Marietta, being taken to see the Indian mounds. A little while later they came floating down to the mouth of the Little Kanawha, and to an attractive wooded island, called Blennerhassett's, the owner of which had been introduced to Colonel Burr at Marietta by Doctor David Wallace.

Harman Blennerhassett had come to America, in 1796, from Ireland where he had owned valuable properties and enjoyed the advantages of fortune and good family. These he had sacrificed to seek shelter in America because, it was said, of his friendship for certain Irish patriots who had been executed for treason, and whose cause he had too ardently espoused. Actually, he had left Ireland and gone to the American wilderness because his wife, Margaret Agnew, daughter of the Lieutenant Governor of the Isle of Man, was his own niece. He was perhaps a man of forty in 1805, an eccentric, improvident person, a musician, an astronomer, a chemist and once a lawyer, a dabbler, and a fatuous windbag.

"Who is Blennerhassett?" Mr. William Wirt was to declaim at a later date, for judicial purposes of his own. "A native of Ireland, a man of letters, who fled from the storms of his own country to find quiet in ours. His history shows that war is not the natural element of his mind. If it had been, he never would have exchanged Ireland for America."

Seeking "quiet and solitude in the bosom of our
western states," he had carried with him "taste,
and science, and wealth. . . . Possessing himself
of a beautiful island in the Ohio, he rears upon it a
palace, and decorates it with every romantic em-
bellishment of fancy. A shrubbery that Shenstone
might have envied blooms around him. Music that
might have charmed Calypso and her nymphs is
his. An extensive library spreads its treasures
before him. A philosophical apparatus offers to
him all the secrets and mysteries of nature. Peace,
tranquillity and innocence shed their mingled delights around him. And to crown the enchantment
of the scene, a wife who is said to be lovely even
beyond her sex . . . had blessed him with her
love, and made him the father of several children."
A man whose soul, according to another contemporary biographer, was "accustomed to toil in the
depths of science and to repose beneath the bowers
of literature, whose ear [was] formed to the harmony
of sound, and whose touch and breath daily awaken
it from a variety of melodious instruments." On
the other hand, in the opinion of Dudley Woodbridge
who was for a while his partner in business, he had
"every kind of sense but common sense."

At all events, Mr. Blennerhassett had purchased
a part of this island in the Ohio, and erected upon it,
at a cost of some forty thousand dollars, barns and
stables, and a two story mansion with curving wings,
facing a fan-shaped lawn set in the midst of beautiful trees and shrubberies. Just the sort of place
to attract the attention of the late owner of Richmond Hill, had it not already been the talk of that

DON FRANCISCO DE MIRANDA

From Justin Winsor, "Narrative and Critical History of America."

countryside for magnificence and elegance. Colonel
Burr went ashore with Mrs. Shaw, and while they
were strolling through the grounds word came from
the house inviting them to supper. They spent the
evening there pleasantly, talking of this and that—
trees probably—with Mr. and Mrs. Blennerhassett. . . .

5

The boats floated on. At Cincinnati, Senator John
Smith and Mr. Dayton were there to greet the
Colonel, and these gentlemen talked over some
business matters concerning the proposed construction of a canal around the Falls of the Ohio, on the
Indiana side; a proposal which met with the approval of the Legislature of the Territory of Indiana,
which in August passed an Act to incorporate the
Indiana Canal Company, with a capital of one
million, and naming as directors George Rogers
Clark, Jonathan Dayton, Aaron Burr, John Brown,
Benjamin Hovey, Davis Floyd and several others.
Naturally, since it was a water company, there was
a clause in the charter authorizing the founding
of a bank. "Those people cared nothing about
the canal," Joseph Daveiss was soon to insist, in his
View of the President's Conduct. "Canal was only
for color and pretext—it was a bank they wanted."
At any rate, Colonel Burr was finding things to do.

At Louisville, he left his boat, and rode through
Kentucky; to Frankfort, where he stayed with
Senator Brown and met General John Adair, per-
haps the foremost Kentuckian of his day, and to
Lexington. The Colonel talked with everybody,

about war with Spain and a possible expedition to
Mexico, while everywhere along the route people
turned out to cheer the man who had shot Alexander
Hamilton. And on May 29, he was at Nashville,
the guest of that long, cadaverous, duelling Andrew
Jackson in his blockhouse at the Hermitage, to
spend five days reviewing "the most magnificent
parades that had ever been made at that place," and
attending banquets and festivities at which everybody "seemed to be contending for the honour of
having best treated or served Colonel Burr." And of
course he talked with his host, about war with Spain
and a possible expedition to Mexico.

Early in June he was on his way again, in a boat
of General Jackson's down the Cumberland to rejoin
his own, and at Fort Massac he found General
Wilkinson who had followed him down the river
from Pittsburgh. For four days they talked, about
war with Spain and a possible expedition to Mexico—
or, as the General put it, "a peep at the unknown
lands beyond me." And the General gave his
friend a letter of introduction to Daniel Clark, one
of the most important merchants of New Orleans—
"if the persecutions of a great and honorable man
can give title to generous attentions, he has claim
on all your civilities"—and another to the Marquis
de Casa Calvo, the Spanish boundary commissioner,
recommending "my eminent friend, Colonel Burr,
a man of a million qualities." And in a private
letter which the Colonel was asked to carry, General Wilkinson advised the Marquis to "serve this
gentleman, he is my friend. . . . Your great family interests will promote the view of Colonel Burr

and the great interest of your country will be served by following his advice. . . . Do as I advise you and you will soon send to the devil that boastful idiot W. C. C. Claiborne." The separation of Louisiana was evidently to be dangled before the eyes of the Marquis in order to blind them to Mexico.

On June 24, General Wilkinson ordered Lieutenant Pike to explore the headwaters of the Arkansas, which was another way of telling him to find a road to Santa Fé; the General himself then went north, dropping obscure remarks to his subordinates about a "distant situation," full of danger, requiring enterprise, but if successful, "full of fortune and glory;" the Colonel, in a fine barge fitted with colored sails and manned by ten soldiers and a sergeant, had gone on down the river. On June 17, he was at Natchez, being royally entertained by the planters, and talking to them about war with Spain and a possible expedition to Mexico. Everywhere he went he was greeted with hopeful acclaim as the leader the West was in need of, and everywhere he talked about war with Spain and a possible expedition to Mexico. Not a syllable concerning separation does he seem to have uttered. And on June 25, he was at New Orleans.

6

The Creoles were delighted to see the ex-Vice President who had been so kind to their deputies at Washington; the Creoles were still chafing and straining at the American leash, and making disparaging remarks about Governor Claiborne; the Americans in New Orleans were consumed with a

desire to invade Mexico. Indeed, for the purpose
of securing information concerning that neighboring
country, there had existed for some time in the city
a society known as the Mexican Association, con-
sisting of perhaps three hundred adventurous souls
whose hope it was to carry the banner of freedom to
the Spanish Viceroy's doorstep, and on the roster
of which were to be found the names of John Wat-
kins, Mayor of the city, and of James Workman,
Judge of the County Court. That the name of
Aaron Burr might be added to it was their earnest
wish, but the Colonel did not join societies. He was
not enrolled in the Cincinnati, he had not joined
the Tammany Society, he did not become a member of the Mexican Association. But just as the
Martlings had taken their orders from Richmond
Hill, so now the New Orleans club looked to him
for guidance. And the members of the Mexican
Association had some interesting things to tell
him. . . .

He had a splendid time in New Orleans for about
three weeks; his letters of introduction brought
him in contact with all classes of society; he met
d'Estrehans, Borés and Marignys; bishops took
him to visit Ursuline convents; John Prevost was
still Federal Judge; his old friend Edward Livingston was just married to beautiful Louise d'Avezac,
and making his home on Chartres Street, in the Fau-
bourg, the center of all elegant and literary life;
they gave him private dinners and balls, public
banquets and receptions—and in the quiet of the
early night he sat on the balustered balconies of
ancient mansions, talking in their own language to

French grandees, about war with Spain and a possible expedition to Mexico—and a possible separation of Louisiana? Perhaps; why not. . . .

And then the Colonel was off again, late in July,
with three hundred dollars advanced to him by Daniel Clark, and a string of horses for the overland
journey of some four hundred miles through the
wilderness to Nashville. And again, everywhere
along the route, he was acclaimed and fêted. "The
invasion of Mexico was in every heart, on every
tongue," Mr. Beveridge records. "All that was
yet lacking to make it certain was war between Spain
and the United States, and every Western or Southern man believed that war was at hand." On August
6, he was at Nashville, once more the object of a
most enthusiastic welcome, and for ten days or so
he stayed at the Hermitage telling General Jackson
the news from the South. Then on through Kentucky, where he met a young lawyer called Henry
Clay; to St. Louis, on September 12, where General
Wilkinson was a little discouraged because his officers did not seem to be taking so readily to the
Mexican idea. But he gave the Colonel a letter to
General Harrison in Indiana, who turned out to be
a fine fellow, and "fit for other things," although he
was not able to do anything for his visitor with regard
to a seat in Congress—any more than Matthew
Lyon in other localities—and as to the "subject"
which filled their minds, "we have gone round about
it," the Colonel wrote General Wilkinson, "and there
is every evidence of good will, in which I have entire belief. There is probably some secret embarrassment of which you and I are ignorant."

And late in October, Colonel Burr was once more in Marietta—the Blennerhassetts were away from home when he passed the island—visiting Jonathan Meigs, the son of an old Quebec comrade, and a Territorial Judge of Upper Louisiana. And at his house the traveler met General Edward Tupper, a gentleman who owned a store and shipyard in Marietta, with whom, no doubt, he discussed the matter of barge construction—in the event of war with Spain and a possible expedition to Mexico. The same General Tupper who may, or may not, have had seven or eight muskets pointed at him in fun at Blennerhassett's Island, on a certain December evening in 1806.

Finally, at Pittsburgh in November, Colonel Burr turned his horse to the eastward.

7

And down the river, at Natchez, a certain Stephen Minor—another American gentleman on the payroll of Spain—had started a rumor which was following the Colonel up the Valley, and which preceded him by several months in the East. Colonel Burr was hatching a revolution, Colonel Burr was preparing a separation of the Western States. Mr. Merry, who was expecting just that, was extremely worried. "He or some of his agents have either been indiscreet . . . or have been betrayed by some person," he wrote to Lord Mulgrave, in August, "for the object of his journey has now begun to be noticed in the public prints."

The newspapers were at it, aroused to bitter controversy by Mr. Minor's terrible Spanish revela-

tions; for somewhere, somehow—could it possibly
have been through Number Thirteen already—the
Spaniards had evidently smelled the Mexican rat.
"How long will it be," the Lexington *Gazette* wanted
to know, "before we shall hear of Colonel Burr being
at the head of a revolutionary party on the Western waters? Is it a fact that Colonel Burr has
formed a plan to engage the adventurous and enterprising young men from the Atlantic States to Louisiana? Is it one of the inducements that an immediate convention will be called from the States bordering on the Ohio and Mississippi to form a separate
government. . . . How soon will the forts and
magazines and all the military posts at New Orleans
and on the Mississippi be in the hands of Colonel
Burr's revolutionary party? How soon will Colonel
Burr engage in the reduction of Mexico by granting
liberty to its inhabitants, and seizing on its treasures, aided by British ships and forces?"

No wonder Mr. Merry was disturbed. . . .

And Daniel Clark at New Orleans was disturbed
too. "Many absurd and wild reports," he informed
General Wilkinson, on September 7, "are circulated
here, and have reached the ears of the officers of
the late Spanish government, respecting our ex
vice president. You are spoken of as his right hand
man; and even I am now supposed to be of consequence enough to combine with generals and vice
presidents. . . . I believe that Minor, of Natchez,
has a great part in this business, in order to make
himself of importance—he is in the pay of Spain.
. . . Perhaps finding Minor in his way, [Mr. Burr]
was endeavoring to extract something from him;

he has amused himself at the blockhead's expense, and then Minor has retailed the news to his employers. . . . The tale is a horrid one . . . Kentucky, Tennessee, the state of Ohio, with part of Georgia and Carolina, are to be bribed with the plunder of the Spanish countries west of us, to separate from the union: this is but a part of the business. Heavens, what wonderful doings there will be in those days! But how the devil I have been lugged into the conspiracy . . . is to me incomprehensible. . . . Amuse Mr. Burr with an account of it. But let not these . . . almost imperial doings prevent you from attending to my land business [in Illinois]. Recollect that you great men, if you intend to become kings and emperors, must have us little men for vassals. . . . Think of this . . . that I may have . . . wherewith to buy a decent court dress, when presented at your levee. I hope you will not have Kentucky men for your masters of ceremonies."

Mr. Clark was annoyed, because his business affairs often took him to Mexico, and he felt "cursedly hurt at the rumors, and might, in consequence of Spanish jealousy, get into a hobble I could not easily get out of." And Mr. Clark probably knew a great deal concerning Colonel Burr's real intentions, and those of the Mexican Association—and yet this is not the letter of a desperate conspirator, caught in a black treachery against his country. And the Colonel was not especially impressed, when he received a copy of the letter. "I love the society of that person [Minor], but surely," he wrote back, "I could never be guilty of the folly of confiding to one of his levity anything which I wished not to be repeated. Pray do not disturb yourself with such nonsense."

Precisely—nonsense, all the revolutionary part of it. Except at the hands of Number Thirteen Wilkinson, there was never produced against Colonel Burr any evidence that he had ever mentioned the subject even, during his Mississippi journey. Colonel Burr was not disturbed by what the papers were saying. And what is perhaps more interesting, the Government was not disturbed. Could it have been, then, that certain important personages in the Government saw no cause for alarm because they were perfectly aware of what the Colonel was actually planning?

CHAPTER IV

ENVOYS AND GENERALS

I

COLONEL BURR had found everything that he
needed in the Southwest, except money. That must
still come from the East. Kentucky, and Tennessee,
and Louisiana would march and fight, but they
could not pay for it all. Upon his return to Washington, in November, 1805, the Colonel went at
once to Mr. Merry—and still there was no answer.
Colonel Burr was extremely disappointed, and Mr.
Merry wrote at great length to Lord Mulgrave.
Everything was in readiness; the Creoles were prepared to rise in March or April; General Wilkinson,
General Adair, General Jackson were all committed
—Colonel Burr was not afraid to tell Mr. Merry
anything—all that was needed was a British squadron to cruise off the mouth of the Mississippi on April
10, and "to continue there until the commanding
officer should receive information from him or from
Mr. Daniel Clark of the country having declared
itself independent." Just two or three ships of the
line and some frigates, and one hundred and ten
thousand pounds.

The negotiations with Mr. Merry dragged along until June, 1806, when that credulous envoy suddenly learned from his government that a request for recall which he had never made had been graciously granted by the King—in other words, the British Foreign Office was tired of Mr. Merry's melodrama. But long before that, probably in November, 1805, already, the Colonel had made up his mind that no funds would be forthcoming from England. He looked around him again, therefore, and allowed his gaze to rest upon the last individual one would have thought he would presume to approach.

Don Carlos Martinez de Yrujo had been created Marquis de Casa Yrujo in 1802. He was an obstinate, impetuous and rather vain little person with reddish hair; enormously wealthy, endlessly touchy, extremely intelligent and vastly attractive. The husband of Sally McKean, of Philadelphia, he was almost as much an American as a Spaniard; he liked America, he understood it and enjoyed it; he was tremendously popular at Philadelphia, and at Washington when he condescended to appear there; he was on intimate terms at the President's House. If he lost his temper from time to time, and thought nothing of haranguing the country through the newspapers, he served his King with energetic loyalty; he went about his business with dignity and shrewdness; he never forgot the respect due to his official person, however much he might indulge his democratic tendencies in private intercourse; he was the only Minister of the first rank in America, and consequently the leading figure in the diplomatic corps; he contributed to American society

the brilliant qualities of his elegant and felicitous
personality; he was a very great gentleman. It was
to him, to the Minister Plenipotentiary from Spain,
that Colonel Burr now turned.

2

First, it was Mr. Dayton who came, in December,
to the Marquis Yrujo, with a request for money in
return for certain secrets which he was prepared to
betray. Colonel Burr was conniving with Mr. Merry
for the purpose of launching an expedition against
Mexico and the Floridas. The secret was known to
only three persons, and the Marquis was now one
of them. But the Marquis did not give Mr. Dayton
any money, nor did he believe the Mexican part of
the story, since he had seen clear through Mr. Dayton and found Colonel Burr behind the ex-Senator;
and the Colonel would naturally not be sending Mr.
Dayton to him with information involving an attack
on Spanish territory. So it seemed to the Marquis
Yrujo, and not long after, Mr. Dayton admitted
that Colonel Burr had failed to interest England in
a project of western separation, and that he was
now ready to sell his services to Spain.

But still the Marquis was not carried away with
enthusiasm, and late in the month Mr. Dayton had
a much more exciting story to tell him. Colonel
Burr had a new plan, and "for one who does not
know the country," the Marquis wrote to Madrid,
"this plan would appear almost insane . . . but I
confess . . . it seems to me easy to execute, although it will irritate the Atlantic States. . . . It
is beyond question that there exists in this coun-

try an infinite number of adventurers, without property, full of ambition and ready to unite at once under the standard of a revolution which promises to better their lot. Equally certain is it that Burr and his friends, without discovering their true object, have succeeded in getting the good will of these men, and inspiring the greatest confidence among them in favor of Burr."

And the plan was to fill Washington with men in disguise, and when the Colonel gave the signal, to seize the President, the Vice President and the substitute President of the Senate, the public moneys and the arsenal. If Washington could not be held, Colonel Burr would take the ships in commission at the Navy Yard, burn the rest, and sail to New Orleans to establish the independence of Louisiana and the West.] None of the Spanish possessions were to be molested. It was as idiotic a goblin tale as was ever told a naughty child—and the fantastic purpose of it was presumably to distract the Marquis Yrujo's attention from Mexico—but the Marquis believed it. He was very angry at Mr. Jefferson for his recent public "war message" against Spain, he was having a spirited quarrel with Mr. Madison, and he evidently thought that in America anything was now possible.

At all events, the Marquis was quite impressed, and in May, 1806, he was advising his government that "the communications I have had with [Burr] confirm me in the idea, not only of the probability, but even of the facility of his success, under certain circumstances. To insure it, some pecuniary aid on our part and on that of France is wanted," but the

French Minister at Washington must not be told, because the conspirators "lack confidence in him." Some "very respectable persons" from Louisiana, Kentucky and Tennessee were soon to visit Spain, but the Marquis had not "compromised myself in any manner." The Marquis did, however, think that the King of Spain might do well to support the enterprise. But the Spanish Foreign Minister thought differently, and instructed his envoy at Washington to contribute no money whatever.

Colonel Burr's efforts to raise funds had again failed, although in June he was still trying to scare the Marquis into it by a pretended renewal of the English scheme for an attack on the Spanish dominions. . . .

3

But in the meantime a certain General William Eaton—the conspiracy was peopled with Generals—had overheard the *canard* about the seizure of Washington prepared for the Marquis Yrujo's consumption, and was regaling certain Congressmen with a recital of its more dreadful aspects. He had, so he said, heard it direct from Colonel Burr, in his lodgings at the home of Sergeant at Arms Wheaton, and on the facile tongue of General Eaton it became a matter of turning Congress "neck and heels" out of doors, "assassinating" the President, seizing the Treasury and the Navy, and establishing the Colonel as "protector of an energetic government." And there were to be a division of the Union and a Mexican empire. To which the Congressmen replied that "they believed Colonel Burr capable of anything and agreed that the fellow ought to be hanged, but thought his projects too chimerical . . . to give the subject the merit of serious consideration."

General Eaton was subsequently to do a considerable amount of important testifying, and—quite aside from the fact that Colonel Burr was ordinarily the most reticent of men, although it was true that he enjoyed mystifying people—one would be more inclined to place credence in the General's veracity were it not for the further fact that he was rapidly, at the time, becoming a notorious drunkard, and that while his most startling revelations were being made he had had pending for many months before Congress a claim seeking the reimbursement of various expenditures incurred by him while Navy Agent to the Barbary States.   He was not a General in any case, having assumed the rank in 1805, while in command of a mixed detachment of Americans, Greeks and Arabs whom he had led from Egypt across the desert in the attempt to place Hamet Bashaw upon the throne of Tripoli, during the American-Tripolitan war. In other words, he was the Hero of Derne—a town on the African coast which he had succeeded in capturing—in whose honor Boston had just named one of her streets; a disgruntled hero for many quite legitimate reasons—he had suffered much from Mr. Jefferson's changes of mind—and a much impoverished one.

And now, in January, 1806, General Eaton insisted that Colonel Burr had told him all manner of astonishing things—perhaps he had; it is very difficult to determine just what the Colonel did say to anyone during the spinning of the web of mystery

with which he surrounded himself during these
months—and in March, the General went to see
Mr. Jefferson. Colonel Burr, he warned the President, was a dangerous man; so dangerous that it
would be a good thing to send him abroad as Minister to some foreign country; for if he were not
"in some way disposed of we should within eighteen
months have an insurrection if not a revolution on
the waters of the Mississippi." And if Mr. Jefferson doubted Colonel Burr's integrity, so did General Eaton, but he believed that the Colonel's
"pride of ambition had so predominated over his
other passions, that when placed on an eminence
and put on his honor, a respect to himself would
secure his fidelity"—perhaps the truest words which
the Hero of Derne ever uttered.

But Mr. Jefferson was not alarmed, not at all
alarmed. He had "no apprehensions" whatever.
General Eaton was not able to instill in the President's mind any realization of the imminent peril
overhanging the country—a circumstance which
renders all the more remarkable General Eaton's
failure to say anything at all to Mr. Jefferson about
the proposed seizure of Washington and his own
assassination. The General was telling Congressmen all about it, but it was not until much later—
when all danger of their occurrence had passed—
that he found it convenient to apprise the President
of the catastrophes which had threatened him. . . .

4

Mr. Jefferson was not alarmed in March, 1806;
he had not been alarmed during the summer of 1805,

nor at any time during the intervening months. The
newspapers were full of accusations against Colonel
Burr, people were writing to the President from the
West warning him of pernicious plots, but Mr. Jefferson was not alarmed. A letter from Judge Easton
of St. Louis to a member of the Senate, denouncing
General Wilkinson, was burned, and the judge told
to stop meddling with high officials. Mr. Jefferson
was not alarmed.

The French Minister thought it curious, and
wrote to Mr. de Talleyrand that it seemed to him
"the government does not penetrate Burr's views,
and that the difficult circumstances in which it
finds itself . . . force it to dissimulate." And
the Marquis Yrujo could not understand the administration's indifference. "I know," he informed
Madrid on December 5, 1805, "that the President,
although penetrating and detesting as well as fearing [Burr], and for this reason, not only invites him
to his table, but only about five days ago had a
secret conference with him which lasted more than
two hours, and in which I am confident there was
as little good faith on the one side as there was on
the other."

Only about five days ago, the Marquis stated on
December 5; that would have been on November
30, approximately; and on November 30, Mr. Jefferson was preparing his "war message" against
Spain for Congress, he was looking for any means of
threatening Spain and forcing the Floridas out of
her—while at the same time intending to purchase
them through France, a circumstance which remained secret until mid-February at the earliest.

And on November 30, Mr. Jefferson was having a
secret conference with Colonel Burr which lasted
more than two hours. What were they conferring
about, what did Colonel Burr suggest to Mr. Jefferson, what did Mr. Jefferson hint to Colonel Burr?
Was Mexico mentioned, did the verbal assurance
of a tacit understanding pass between them? These
questions have never been, they can probably never
be answered. To some people—to Commodore
Truxtun who despised Mr. Jefferson—Colonel Burr
said that the President was not involved in his
Mexican venture; to a far greater number of persons the Colonel always maintained that Mr. Jefferson was conversant with his scheme and that the
administration viewed it with complaisance. It
was so understood by the Mexican Association.
Certain it is that for some fifteen months the Government did not lift a finger against Colonel Burr.
Mr. Jefferson was not alarmed. . . .

He seems, indeed, if one may read with any certainty between the lines of the contemporary record,
to have at this time—in December and January
—encouraged another expedition against Spain.
For in November, 1805, who should make his appearance at New York but that ever devoted apostle of
South American liberty, Mr. Hamilton's old friend,
General Francisco de Miranda. An American war
with Spain was looked upon as a certainty; General
Miranda was full of his old idea for an attack on
the Spanish South American possessions; New York
received him as a hero; and, while Colonel Burr was
not inclined to favor an enterprise which might interfere with his own, Mr. Dayton, and John Swart-

JAMES WILKINSON

After the Painting by C. W. Peale.

wout, the United States Marshal, and John Adams's son-in-law, Colonel William Smith, Surveyor of the Port, all offered their enthusiastic support. A vessel, the *Leander*, was chartered from Samuel Ogden, and Colonel Smith undertook the furnishing of supplies and the enlistment of men, the latter, frequently, under false pretences. The affair was a matter of common knowledge, the officers of Government could not have remained entirely in ignorance of it, and in December General Miranda was at Washington, conferring with Mr. Madison and picking his teeth—it was his "constant habit"—at Mr. Jefferson's dinner table.

And what did they talk about? Mr. Madison said afterwards that the General had outlined his plan and that he, Madison, had told him that the United States could not countenance it. The General, on the other hand, wrote to Colonel Smith and informed him that Mr. Madison was prepared, at least, to look the other way; and upon his return to New York, the South American leader referred openly to the American Government's connivance. "We are encouraged in our belief that our Government has given its implied sanction to this expedition," one of the adventurers recorded. And on January 22, 1806, General Miranda wrote to Mr. Madison, taking formal leave of him before he sailed. The General did not doubt that the important matters which he had communicated to the Secretary of State would be kept "in the deepest secret until the final result of this delicate affair." He had acted "on that supposition, conforming myself in everything to the intentions of the Government,"

which he hoped he had "seized and observed with
exactitude and discretion." And Mr. Madison filed
the letter with an endorsement to the effect that the
important matters in question merely referred to
General Miranda's previous negotiations with England. But did they?

On February 2, the *Leander* sailed, unmolested,
to her South American destination; carrying with
her General Miranda, Colonel Smith's son—"a
number of Americans, some of them gentlemen,"
one of them wrote, "though mostly, I believe, of
crooked fortunes"—and the other members of that
filibustering expedition for which according to Henry
Ingersoll, it had not been "so easy to engage any to
enlist as soldiers. Great circumspection was necessary not only to prevent public alarm but to allay
any suspicion which might arise in the breasts
of those who were engaged. In this transaction I
cannot but admire the cunning and skill of Miranda
or his agents, as well as reprobate the falsehood and
duplicity resorted to." Mr. Ingersoll was languish-
ing in a Spanish prison when he wrote his disgruntled journal, but it was true that some of his
comrades had been engaged "to enlist as soldiers to
go to New Orleans to serve as guard to the United
States Mail." But the *Leander* was not bound for
New Orleans. . . .

5

The Miranda expedition was to bear an extraordinary resemblance to Colonel Burr's so-called conspiracy. Each was in effect, although the details
varied, a filibustering adventure organized on Amer-

ican soil against a technically friendly nation; each was reported to have enjoyed the private support of the Government; each resulted in a trial involving the testimony of administration officials; and each was betrayed by a traitor, necessitating, perhaps, a hasty repudiation by the Executive.

In the case of General Miranda, it was Mr. Dayton—that eager vendor of secrets—who came, in December, to the Marquis Yrujo with the news. Whether he came of his own accord, or whether he came under instructions from Colonel Burr, is a question which must be asked. "Colonel Burr will not treat with Miranda whom he considers imprudent," Mr. Dayton told the Marquis. Did the Colonel consider General Miranda an interloper, did the Colonel see in a betrayal of his movements an opportunity of securing money from the Marquis Yrujo—Mr. Dayton was actually given three thousand dollars for his information—these questions have not been answered. At all events, Mr. Dayton revealed to the Marquis all the details of the *Leander's* voyage, and reported to him that Mr. Madison had told General Miranda that his official approval was out of the question, "but that if private citizens . . . chose to advance their funds for the undertaking . . . the Government would shut its eyes to their conduct, provided that Miranda took his measures in such a way as not to compromise the Government." And if there should be war with Spain, "this undertaking would prove to be a diversion favorable to the views of the American Government."

One seems to see Mr. Jefferson saying exactly the

same thing to Colonel Burr about his expedition to Mexico. As for General Miranda, someone was lying—and the benefit of the doubt has inevitably always been granted to the American Secretary of State. The Marquis Yrujo, for his part, sent the necessary warnings to the Spanish authorities; the *Leander*, with the assistance of the British Admiral Cochrane, landed her men near Caracas where they achieved a temporary success; but the withdrawal of British help, owing to a rumored peace, forced the Miranda party to flight.

But the Marquis Yrujo did not content himself, naturally, with a mere notifying of his own people. He was already, in January, quarreling with Mr. Madison over the President's "war message," concerning which the Marquis had expressed himself very vigorously in the newspapers, so that Mr. Madison had informed him that his presence at Washington was dissatisfactory to Mr. Jefferson. To which the Marquis had replied that he would remain in Washington, "this city four miles square," as long as it suited the interests of his King or his own convenience, and that "the Envoy Extraordinary and Minister Plenipotentiary of his Catholic Majesty in the United States received no orders except from his sovereign." And the Marquis Yrujo further hinted to Mr. Madison that he, at all events, was not in Washington to "hatch plots"—which, in view of the Marquis's dealings with Colonel Burr was not exactly true, but most annoying to Mr. Madison, especially when General Miranda's farewell letter reached him.

And now, in February, after the sailing of the

Leander, the Marquis did not lose an instant in protesting against the American breach of neutrality—
through General Turreau, the French Minister,
since the Marquis had retired to Philadelphia immediately after the confession by Congress that he was
absolutely within his rights in remaining at Washington as long as he pleased! And General Turreau
reported that Mr. Madison "was in a state of extraordinary prostration. . . . It was with an effort
that he broke silence." The Marquis Yrujo had put
him in the wrong twice in succession. But Mr. Madison did manage to explain that the President was
moving against the culprits in New York. As for
Mr. Jefferson, "although [Miranda's] measures were
many days in preparation at New York," he was
still writing in 1809, "we never had the least inti-
mation or suspicion of his engaging men in his enterprise until he was gone." Anything to the contrary
was "impudent falsehoods and calumnies."

And so Colonel Smith was removed from office,
and he and Mr. Ogden were indicted for breach of
the neutrality laws, after testifying voluntarily
to their activities—which was all perfectly proper,
unless it was true that the administration had winked
at their participation. And this was what the
defendants claimed at once—they were tried sep-
arately, but both procedures and defences were iden-
tical—and issued memorials to Congress, which were
tabled, and subpoenas to the Vice President, the
Secretary of State, the Secretary of the Treasury,
the Secretary of War, the Secretary of the Navy,
the Postmaster General, the Spanish Minister,
Senator Bradley of Vermont, Rufus King and the

President's son-in-law, John W. Eppes. Colonel
Smith filed an affidavit stating that with Mr. Madison's testimony he would prove that the expedition
"was begun, prepared and set forth with the knowledge and approbation of the President . . . and
. . . of the Secretary of State of the United
States."

But, Mr. Jefferson ordered the subpoenas to be
ignored, on the grounds that attendance in court
would interfere with the performance of official
duties—a decision strikingly prophetic of his conduct at the time of the trial of Colonel Burr—and
the Secretary of State did not appear to explain his
dealings with General Miranda, which was perhaps
very fortunate for the Secretary of State. But the
lawyers for the accused were not slow to take advantage of his absence. "We did expect," Mr. Colden
informed the court, "to show you by the most conclusive evidence that the acts of the defendant which
are now . . . charged upon him, were done with
the sanction and approbation of the President of the
United States. . . . Had our affairs with Spain
taken the course that was expected when Miranda
was at Washington, this would have been called a
glorious and generous enterprise; and the executive
officers of our country would have challenged the
approbation and applause of the world for having
given it their sanction and encouragement."

And Mr. Hoffman had something to say. "The
President . . . countenancing the offence for which
Colonel Smith was indicted—the President . . .
precipitately removing Colonel Smith from office
. . . the President . . . ordering the prosecu-

tion . . . the President . . . interdicting the attendance of witnesses essential to the justification of the defendant. In vain do we seek, in judicial records, for a parallel to such conduct"—but he was to be furnished one not many months later, in the treason suit against Colonel Burr at Richmond. "Did the President . . . and the Secretary of State approve of and countenance this expedition . . . the man who can doubt it, after hearing this trial, must be obstinate indeed in prejudice . . . Colonel Smith . . . was willing . . . to assist an enterprise which, had it succeeded, would have drawn down the blessings of a rescued nation, and the plaudits of an admiring world. He facilitated it under the express knowledge, unequivocal countenance, and implied authority of Government."

The thing was a matter of considerable public scandal and indignation, and seemed to corroborate John Randolph's recent opinion that Mr. Jefferson and men like him were "whimsicals" who "advocated the leading measures of their party until they were nearly ripe for execution, when they hung back, condemned the step after it was taken, and on most occasions affected a glorious neutrality." And Colonel Smith and Mr. Ogden were acquitted; inevitably in any case, since United States Marshal Swartwout had taken pains to summon "a panel of jurors the greater part of which were of the bitterest Federalists"—a precaution which, in connection with his earlier championing of the "Aristides" pamphlet, eventually lost him his post.

So the Miranda fiasco passed into oblivion; but there would appear to have been concerned in it cer-

tain official states of mind such as caused Andrew
Jackson to tell his friend Judge Overton—while riding
with him to his duel with Mr. Dickinson, in May,
1806—that Colonel Burr would never succeed in his
scheme "with Jefferson in the presidency," because
the Federalists would assail the venture "tooth and
toenail," and then Mr. Jefferson would "run like a
cotton tail rabbit."

CHAPTER V

THE PROMOTER

1

THROUGHOUT the winter of 1805 and 1806 Colonel Burr spent his whole time in the effort to raise men and funds for his western enterprise—in various places, from many different people and in an infinity of ways. One has seen his financial intrigues with Mr. Merry and the Marquis Yrujo; among his personal friends he was no less active and persistent. Matthew Davis, Marinus Willett, the Swartwouts, the Van Nesses, the Edwards relatives, they were all solicited and persuaded to contribute. Commodores Decatur and Truxtun were invited to join the expedition; Charles Biddle was consulted; in the South, during a brief visit to Theodosia in February, Joseph Alston was induced to subscribe.

In the case of Mr. Alston, as in that of most of the private sources which the Colonel approached, the plea for money was made on the basis of western land speculation. Colonel Burr was planning to establish a colony on the great Bastrop Grant—a million acre tract on the Washita River in Louisiana, ceded by the Spaniards to the Baron Bastrop, and now in great part owned by Colonel Charles Lynch, of Lexington, from whom Colonel Burr expected to purchase some four hundred thousand acres. And :f the Mexican expedition was always in his mind—and an expenditure on it of any moneys which he might collect always an accepted intention—the Colonel was quite sincere also about the Bastrop project.

As Charles Biddle heard the plan, "he would have collected a number of military men round him near the lines"—the Bastrop Grant was not far from Natchitoches—"formed a barrier between us and the Spaniards which would have prevented their ever disturbing us." The colony was to be a volunteer American garrison, developing the land until an opportunity offered to advance against Mexico. Mr. Biddle told the Colonel that such a plan "would probably involve us in a war with Spain, and I would therefore have nothing to do with it." This was in the early summer of 1806, when the administration's pacific character was more clearly understood. But Colonel Burr said "whether we invaded the country or not, we should have a war with Spain," and when Mr. Biddle "mentioned Miranda's expedition as one that should never have been countenanced by any person in this country, he said Miranda was a fool, totally unqualified for such an expedition." But whatever he decided to do, the Colonel assured his friend that "he would not do anything that could injure the country."

2

Already in December, Colonel Burr had guessed that Mr. Jefferson would not attack Spain of his

THOMAS TRUXTUN

own accord. "About the last of October," he wrote General Wilkinson on December 12, "our cabinet was seriously disposed for war . . . but more recent accounts of the increasing and alarming aggressions . . . of the British, and some courteous words from the French, have banished every such intention. . . . The utmost now intended is that sort of marine piracy which we had with the French under the former administration."

But still, there was a chance. Spanish aggressions on the border were increasing; invasions of American territory were occurring; the Spaniards had already occupied the Bayou Pierre and Nana posts, from which their retirement was to be demanded and obtained in February; on both sides of the Sabine warlike preparations were going forward; General Wilkinson could, at any time he chose, precipitate a conflict. Colonel Burr did not entirely despair of his war; he was writing to Generals Tupper and Jackson for information concerning the likelihood of organizing regiments in their districts; the Mexican expedition was by no means abandoned, the "auspices" were favorable, he assured General Wilkinson, "and it is believed that Wilkinson will give audience to a delegation composed of Adair and Dayton in February;" and in the meantime, the Bastrop colony was something to think about, an excellent substitute enterprise if war should be much postponed. Or an excellent blind for the other affair!

At no time does the Colonel, or the Mexican Association, seem to have openly advocated an invasion of Mexico without a preliminary state of war between the two countries. At no time does he seem to have

contemplated anything very different from what the
Texans were to do some thirty years later, and Mr.
Fremont another ten years or so after that. "There,
you see?" he was to exclaim long afterwards, when
the Texas news reached New York. "I was right! I
was only thirty years too soon! What was treason
thirty years ago, is patriotism now!" Those pathetic
words, spoken by a very wretched old man, are
perhaps worthy of respectful attention.

3

As for the methods Colonel Burr employed to
enlist his men and to obtain the fifty thousand odd
dollars which he finally accumulated—he was a
promoter, the first great American promoter. He
saw his vision—as tremendous a vision as has ever
dazzled the imagination of any of his many suc-
cessors in this country of continuous promotion—
and he went out to sell his shares in glory and adventure, with a bonus in Bastrop lands. Not a bad in-
vestment, on the whole. And he talked the promoter's language. To the prudent he talked Bastrop and
agriculture; to the eager he talked war; to the
young, honor; and to the old, honors. To each man
what would most appeal to him. And sometimes,
unfortunately, he talked sheer nonsense; from love
of mystery, or because his hearer was a numb-head
whom it amused him to bewilder, or because he was
himself not immune to delusion, and to the vanity
of fabulous imaginings. Because, as Andrew Jackson summed him up, because he was too sanguine,
because he relied too much on what people said and
did not sufficiently watch what they were doing,

because he was "as far from a fool as I ever saw, and yet . . . as easily fooled as any man I ever knew."

And sometimes it was not necessary to talk very long. To Mr. Blennerhassett, for instance. Much was to be made later by Mr. Wirt of the "seduction" of that gentleman from his island paradise. "In the midst of all this peace, this innocent simplicity and this tranquillity, this feast of the mind, this pure banquet of the heart, the destroyer comes; he comes to change this paradise into a hell. . . . A stranger presents himself. . . . The conquest was not difficult. Innocence is ever simple and credulous. . . . [Colonel Burr] winding himself into the open and unpracticed heart of the unfortunate Blennerhassett found but little difficulty in changing the native character of that heart. . . . In a short time the whole man is changed. . . . No more he enjoys the tranquil scene; it has become flat and insipid to his taste. His books are abandoned. His retort and crucible are thrown aside. His shrubbery blooms and breathes its fragrance upon the air in vain; he likes it not. His ear no longer drinks the rich melody of music; it longs for the trumpet's clangor and the cannon's roar. Even the prattle of his babes . . . no longer affects him; and the angel smile of his wife, which hitherto touched his bosom with ecstasy so unspeakable, is now unseen and unfelt. . . . His imagination has been dazzled by visions of diadems, of stars and garters and titles of nobility."

According to Mr. Wirt, Colonel Burr had done all that. Actually, he had written to Mr. Blennerhas-

sett in December, 1805, expressing regret at not having seen him on his return from New Orleans, and,
with a few flattering phrases, suggesting that a man
of Mr. Blennerhassett's talents might better employ his time and fortune than in vegetation upon a
western island. To which Mr. Blennerhassett, who
had seen the Colonel twice for a few hours in company, eagerly replied that he was hoping to sell or
lease his property—so much for the island paradise
—and that he would be only too pleased to associate himself with Colonel Burr in any enterprise
whatever—"I should be honored in being associated
with you in any contemplated enterprise you would
permit me to participate in"—he had no idea, at
the time, what the Colonel was planning; but he
was ready to do anything which might serve to
ameliorate his fortunes, for when all was said and
done the great lord of the manor did not possess,
aside from his land and house, much more than
fifteen thousand dollars. And as for the clangor of
trumpets, "not presuming to know or guess at
the intercourse, if any, subsisting between you
and the present government," Mr. Blennerhassett
explained, "but viewing the probability of a rupture with Spain . . . I am disposed, in the confidential spirit of this letter, to offer you my friends'
and my own services to [cooperate] in any contemplated measures in which you may embark."

Mr. Blennerhassett even offered to serve as the
Colonel's lawyer. Anything. Pleased and honored,
tickled to death. And the Colonel solemnly answered
that "your talents and acquirements seemed to
have destined you for something more than vegetable

life, and since the first hour of our acquaintance I
have considered your seclusion as a fraud to society."
He did have a speculation in mind, but as it would
not be "commenced before December or January
[of 1806 and 1807] if ever," he preferred to wait to
tell him about it until he saw him in person.

So that Mr. Blennerhassett can scarcely be said
to have been seduced with lures of diadems, stars
and garters. In December, 1805, when he offered
his services so unconditionally to Colonel Burr, he
was fully aware of all the rumors concerning the
latter's activities; he was simply reacting to his
own ambitions, or possibly to those of his wife.
And perhaps the Colonel thought that Mr. Blennerhassett was wealthier than he was. . . .

4

The winter was passing, and the money was coming in slowly, and there was no war. For a while
Colonel Burr seemed discouraged, and ready to
abandon his projects; for in March, 1806, he went
a second time to Mr. Jefferson to ask him for some
employment. He said, Mr. Jefferson recorded,
that "he had supported the administration, and that
he could do me much harm; he wished, however, to
be on different ground . . . if I should have anything to propose to him." But Mr. Jefferson told
him that "the public had withdrawn their confidence
from him . . . that as to any harm he could do
me . . . I feared no injury which man could do
me." Colonel Burr took his leave of the President
a few days later, and the probabilities are that the
two men never saw each other again.

It is a curious thing that in that same month General Eaton was advising Mr. Jefferson to send Colonel Burr abroad because he was a dangerous man. General Eaton did not tell Mr. Jefferson about the Washington conspiracy, nor did he give him any details of the Colonel's western projects, and now a reason for this reticence suggests itself. General Eaton himself explained to Gideon Granger several months later that he had not done so because "the answer he received to the idea of giving Burr employment in a foreign country induced him to believe the President considered him as acting with a design to aid Col. Burr." And was not this perhaps the exact truth? Was not General Eaton acting as an emissary of Colonel Burr, and was he not told the story—if he was ever told it—of the Washington conspiracy for the purpose of frightening Mr. Jefferson? One can not hope to answer those questions—one can only remark on the coincidence of these threats and warnings addressed to the President by both the Colonel and the General, and leading up to a request—or a hint—that Colonel Burr be given some mission. . . .

And now something must be done about General Wilkinson. "The execution of our project," Colonel Burr wrote him in April, "is postponed till December: want of water in Ohio"—that was to say, money in Philadelphia—"rendered movement impracticable: other reasons rendered delay expedient. The association is enlarged, and comprises all that Wilkinson could wish. Confidence limited to a few. Though this delay is irksome, it will enable us to move with more certainty and dignity. Burr will be throughout the United States this summer. Administration is damned with Randolph aids. . . ."

May and June went by. The Spanish depredations on the border were continuing; troops were being sent to the Sabine; if General Wilkinson only held firm, if he provoked the Spaniards, the long desired war would come at last, the war which the "conspirators" must have. The General must be aroused, and for this purpose Mr. Dayton informed him in July that "it is now well ascertained that you are to be displaced in next session. Jefferson will affect to yield reluctantly to the public sentiment, but yield he will. Prepare yourself, therefore, for it. You know the rest. You are not a man to despair, or even despond, especially when such prospects offer in another quarter. Are you ready? Are your numerous associates ready? Wealth and glory! Louisiana and Mexico! I shall have time to receive a letter from you before I set out for Ohio."

Perhaps if the General could be made to believe that his command was in danger, he would seek to preserve it by means of victorious military action. So much depended on General Wilkinson! So much more than they ever for a moment realized. Without him they were ruined; with him they were to be betrayed—indeed, they were already, to all intents, betrayed; ever since the General had learned of the death of Prime Minister Pitt in London, and understood that no help could be expected from England. From that day forth—it was in the spring of 1806 that he heard the news—General Wilkinson's rôle in Colonel Burr's concerns was that of Judas. . . .

5

The Colonel was winding up his affairs, and
spending as much time as possible with Theodosia
and her little boy, who were summering in Pennsylvania. In June he was at Falsington, receiving the
visit of his relative Paul Prevost whom he took to
call on the exiled General Moreau at Morrisville, before making an excursion by boat up to New Hope
with Theodosia to see Mr. Prevost's own family.
In July, Theodosia had gone to Bedford; Colonel
Burr was at Philadelphia, expecting to follow her
in a few days; and he was writing to Mr. Blennerhassett, on July 24, thanking him for the invitation
extended to Mrs. Alston to stop at the island if
she should come West. She was "charmed with
your hospitality and friendly overture," the Colonel
told the Blennerhassetts, "and wished much to
avail herself of it," but it could not be until October,
at the period of his own return there from Kentucky.

And in the meantime, just to keep him in good
humor and make him think that the Mexican project was at its ripest, Colonel Burr wrote to General Wilkinson, on July 29. Two copies were made
of the communication, one of which was given, to
be carried overland, to young Samuel Swartwout
and Peter Ogden, the son of Matthias Ogden and
Jonathan Dayton's nephew, and the second of
which, to be taken to New Orleans by water, was
entrusted to Doctor Justus Erich Bollmann, whom
it had originally been the Colonel's intention to send
to England to continue the financial negotiations.
Doctor Bollmann was famous in America as the

HARMAN BLENNERHASSETT

author of the attempted rescue from prison of the
Marquis de Lafayette, for which enterprise he had
been banished from Austria; he was perhaps thirty-
five years old, a great admirer of Colonel Burr, and
one of the few prominent members of the conspiracy
who did not call himself General.

The letter was in the number and symbol cipher
in use between Colonel Burr and General Wilkinson,
and what its actual contents may have been will
never be known, since the General altered parts of
it to suit his own purposes. That the references in
his official version, for instance, to Commodore
Truxtun and Joseph Alston appeared in the original was flatly denied afterwards by Samuel Swartwout who helped to code the copy which he carried.
That the first sentence of the letter—"Your letter
postmarked thirteenth May is received"—was at
first omitted by General Wilkinson from his trans-
lation was subsequently admitted by him. However, not very many months later, Colonel Burr was
to learn that he had sent the following fatally compromising document to General Wilkinson—

"You letter postmarked thirteenth May is received. At length I have obtained funds, and have
actually commenced. The Eastern detachments,
from different points and under different pretences,
will rendezvous on the Ohio first of November.
Everything internal and external favors our views.
Naval protection of England is secured. Truxtun
is going to Jamaica to arrange with the admiral on
that station. It will meet us at the Mississippi.
England, a navy of the United States, are ready to
join, and final orders are given to my friends and

followers. It will be a host of choice spirits. Wilkinson shall be second to Burr only; Wilkinson shall dictate the rank and promotion of his officers.

"Burr will proceed westward first August, never to return. With him goes his daughter; her husband will follow in October, with a corps of worthies. Send forthwith an intelligent and confidential friend with whom Burr may confer; he shall return immediately with further interesting details; this is essential to concert and harmony of movement. Send a list of all persons known to Wilkinson, west of the mountains who could be useful, with a note delineating their characters. By your messenger send me four or five commissions of your officers, which you can borrow under any pretence you please; they shall be returned faithfully. Already are orders given to the contractor to forward six months' provisions to points Wilkinson may name; this shall not be used until the last moment, and then under proper injunctions.

"Our object, my dear friend, is brought to a point so long desired. Burr guarantees the result with his life and honor, with the lives and honor and the fortunes of hundreds, the best blood of our country. Burr's plan of operation is to move down rapidly from the Falls, on the fifteenth of November, with the first five hundred or a thousand men, in light boats now constructing for that purpose; to be at Natchez between the fifth and fifteenth of December, there to meet you; there to determine whether it will be expedient in the first instance to seize on or pass by Baton Rouge. On receipt of this send Burr an answer. Draw on Burr for all expenses, etc.

The people of the country to which we are going are prepared to receive us; their agents, now with Burr, say that if we will protect their religion, and will not subject them to a foreign Power, that in three weeks all will be settled.

"The gods invite us to glory and fortune; it remains to be seen whether we deserve the boon. The bearer of this goes express to you. He is a man of inviolable honor and perfect discretion, formed to execute rather than project, capable of relating facts with fidelity, and incapable of relating them otherwise; he is thoroughly informed of the plans and intentions of Burr, and will disclose to you as far as you require, and no further. He has imbibed a reverence for your character, and may be embarrassed in your presence; put him at ease, and he will satisfy you."

To Doctor Bollmann's copy was added the postscript "Doctor Bollman, equally confidential, better informed on the subject and more enlightened, will hand this duplicate."

And so, in August, 1806, Colonel Burr rode westward, "never to return."

PART VII

The Filibuster

1806–1807

"The gods invite us to glory and fortune; it remains to be seen whether we deserve the boon."

AARON BURR.

CHAPTER I

BOATS FOR BASTROP

I

LATE in August, accompanied by his secretary, Charles Willie, and a French officer named Julien De Pestre, Colonel Burr was on the Ohio. He seemed extremely "taciturn," and was travelling "incognito." At Pittsburgh, several young men were enrolled, including Morgan Neville, a son of the Chief Justice of Pennsylvania; and a visit was made to Colonel George Morgan.

The Morgans, father and sons, had been previously engaged in certain questionable land transactions, claims concerning which on their part were at the time pending before Congress—a circumstance which may or may not have influenced their subsequent behavior. At all events, after his departure, it occurred to the Morgans that Colonel Burr's conversation had been of an alarming and mysterious nature —he probably had talked grandiosely, as seems to have been his habit when haranguing mediocre persons—and Colonel Morgan reported certain misgivings aroused in his mind to three gentlemen of

Pittsburgh, who thereupon wrote to Mr. Madison expressing their patriotic fears, and explaining that "much more was to be concluded from the manner in which things were said, and hints given, than from the words used." And Colonel Morgan himself wrote to the President; one of several correspondences addressed during this period to Mr. Jefferson, and in which he does not appear to have found cause for any precautionary action. . . .

Meanwhile, the Colonel was at Wheeling, then at Marietta, where he reviewed the militia with his friend, Jonathan Meigs, and obtained a few more recruits; and some boats were ordered to be built on the Muskingum by the firm of Woodbridge and Company, of which Mr. Blennerhassett was a partner. And then they were at Belpré, spending the night with Mr. Blennerhassett. And now, at last, Mr. Blennerhassett was told about the Colonel's plans, about the expedition to Mexico in the event of war with Spain, and about the Bastrop colony. And Mr. Blennerhassett was tremendously impressed—to him also, no doubt, the Colonel had talked grandiosely— Mr. Blennerhassett became tremendously occupied, tremendously zealous at recruiting and purchasing, and probably tremendously and fatuously indiscreet. And over the name of "Querist," Mr. Blennerhassett proceeded to write some articles for the *Ohio Gazette* in which he advocated a separation of the Western States from the Union. A stupid thing for Mr. Blennerhassett to have done, just at that moment. . . .

The Colonel went on to Cincinnati, where he stayed with Senator John Smith and conferred with Mr. Dayton; to Lexington, where more recruits were en-

gaged—adventurous youngsters, most of them, with
no thought of wrongdoing—and finally, on September 6, to Nashville, where they gave him another
splendid banquet, while Andrew Jackson took orders
for boats to be constructed by his general merchandise concern, and talked enthusiastically about war,
and even called his militia to arms and offered their
services to the Federal Government—so confident
were they in Tennessee that hostilities were inevitable.

2

And in October, Colonel Burr was back at Lexington; at Blennerhassett's Island, which was all in a
pother of preparation, Mr. Blennerhassett packed up
his portmanteaux to join him, bringing with him the
Alstons who had been visiting Mrs. Blennerhassett,
and enchanting that good lady whose lot it seldom
was to entertain such prominent guests—the wealthy
Mr. Alston of South Carolina, the celebrated Mrs.
Alston of New York and Charleston, the fascinating
little "Gampy," grandson of the ex-Vice President;
at Pittsburgh, young Comfort Tyler of Syracuse
was enlisting colonists; at Jeffersonville, Davis
Floyd of Indiana was similarly employed; boats were
building on the Muskingum and Cumberland; stores
of pork, corn meal, flour, ammunition and tools were
accumulating for the Bastrop venture—they must all
have been very busy, very hopeful, very happy.

And late in the month, Colonel Burr deposited five
thousand dollars with Colonel Lynch and acquired
from him the rights to four hundred thousand Bastrop
acres. "I have bought of Col. Lynch 400 M. acres

of the tract called Bastrop's lying on the Washita,"
he wrote a Mr. Latrobe on October 26. "The excel-
lence of the soil and climate are established to my
satisfaction by the report of impartial persons. I
shall send on forty or fifty men this autumn to clear
and build cabins. These men are to be paid in land
and to be found for one year in provisions. It is my
intention to go there with several of my friends next
winter. If you should incline to partake and to join
us, I will give you 10000 acres. I want your Society.
I want your advice in the establishment about to be
made. In short you have become necessary to my
settlement. As the winter is your leisure I reason, if
you should incline to go and view the country, you
may do it at my expense. I shall pass through
Pittsburgh on my way to Ph^a about the last of
Novr—would it be possible that I could meet you
there?"

Forty or fifty men to Bastrop's, there was the extent of the Colonel's "expedition"—some sixty
actually started—and in October the Colonel was not
even planning to go with them. So much for the
thousands who were to rendezvous on the Ohio from
various eastern points, and whom the Colonel was to
join, "never to return."

And of course they were in high spirits, and they
talked among themselves at Lexington; about how
they would found an empire in Mexico some day,
and Colonel Burr would be Emperor Aaron I, and
Theodosia Chief Lady of the Court, and Mr. Alston
Head of the Nobility, and "Gampy" Heir Apparent,
and Mr. Blennerhassett—oh, Mr. Blennerhassett
would be Minister to England at least. One seems to

see them there laughing and winking at each other, and telling Mr. Blennerhassett all these wonderful things; and some of them were true, and Mr. Blennerhassett believed them all, and repeated them afterwards to his wife, and to his gardener, and to anyone who cared to listen. A perfect fool, Mr. Blennerhassett. And they talked about money, and some arrangement was made whereby Mr. Blennerhassett advanced funds, borrowing on his property with the understanding that Mr. Alston would give his own "vast estates and other property" as security for the repayment of the loan—for the rich son-in-law had had a series of crop failures which prevented him from contributing any immediate cash.

Along in November, the Alstons went home, and Colonel De Pestre was sent east with reports and messages. . . .

3

And now someone had talked too much—quite possibly the Colonel himself, for he never seemed able to remember that unintelligent persons usually take everything literally—and trouble was brewing.

For one thing, "Regulus" in the *Western Spy* had been answering the separation articles by "Querist," and the good citizens of Wood County, Virginia, had held a mass meeting, in October, presided over by Colonel Phelps, at which the preparations then going forward at Blennerhassett's Island had been condemned as suspicious, and resolutions passed enrolling volunteers for the purpose of marching to the island and destroying the supplies known to be gathered there. Their intention was, however, communicated

by Colonel Phelps to Mrs. Blennerhassett, and a messenger despatched to warn her husband. Mr.
Blennerhassett came home for a while, followed
shortly after by Colonel Burr, and the alarm in Wood
County was finally stilled.

And in Kentucky there was more trouble; for
Humphrey Marshall and Joseph Hamilton Daveiss
were printing rumors of rebellion in the West, and
reviving all the old Kentucky secession intrigues and
accusing Colonel Burr of attempting to establish an
independent government of the Western States,
Louisiana and Florida—all this in the columns of the
Frankfort *Western World*, edited by that same John
Wood whose "history" had once been suppressed by
the Colonel. And Humphrey Marshall had been a
Federalist Senator; and Joseph Hamilton Daveiss
was District Attorney for Kentucky, the brother-in-
law of Chief Justice Marshall, a determined Federalist as well, and so devoted an admirer of Alexander
Hamilton that he had assumed his name. A blind
enemy, consequently, of Colonel Burr, who had
"murdered" his idol.

These gentlemen were convinced that the Colonel
was hatching a disruption of the Union, and Mr.
Daveiss had already been corresponding with Mr.
Jefferson and Mr. Madison on the subject. "This
plot is laid wider than you imagine," he had told
the President. "Mention the subject to no man from
the Western country, however high in office he may
be. Some of them are deeply tainted with this
treason." And to the Secretary of State he had
written that "it is somewhat like Cataline's conspiracy, as it respects its leader and his adherents

. . . men without fortune or expectation, save from some revolution." And they had discussed it, finally, in the Cabinet and almost decided to take vigorous action, but there was "not one word . . . of any movements by Colonel Burr" in reports received by him from persons on the spot, Mr. Jefferson recorded on October 22. "This total silence of the officers of the Government, of the members of Congress, of the newspapers, proves he is committing no overt act against law." Still, John Graham of the State Department should be sent out "with confidential authority to inquire into Burr's movements, put the Governors, etc., on their guard, to provide for his arrest if necessary, and to take on himself the government of [Upper] Louisiana." Mr. Jefferson might perhaps better have sent Mr. Graham to explain to Colonel Burr that what had been sauce for the Miranda gander was not to be sauce for his goose. . . .

But in Kentucky the *Western World* continued its revelations; Mrs. Blennerhassett sent word to her husband at Lexington that he had better stay away from the island for a while; Senator Smith wrote to Colonel Burr and asked him for the truth, to which the Colonel replied that as for separation he was "totally ignorant of it," and had "never harbored or expressed any such intention to anyone"—for the Foreign Ministers at Washington did not count; and at Frankfort—for one reason, to embarrass the Republican President who did not seem inclined to take any steps of his own—Mr. Daveiss, on November 5, appeared before Judge Innis and moved for a compulsory process requiring the presence of Colonel Burr and various witnesses to answer a charge of "treasonable practices"; the District Attorney's affidavit stating that "Aaron Burr . . . for several months past, hath been, and is now engaged in preparing and setting on foot, and in providing and preparing the means, for a military expedition and enterprise within this district for the purpose of descending the Ohio and Mississippi therewith, and making war upon the subjects of the King of Spain, who are in a state of peace with the people of these United States."

And the District Attorney had "information on which I can rely, that all the Western territories are the next object of the scheme—and finally all the region of the Ohio is calculated as falling into the vortex of the new proposed revolution . . . certainly any progress in [the scheme] might cost our country . . . at the least great public agitation . . . I am determined to use every effort in my power as an officer and as a man to prevent and defeat it."

The Court promptly denied the motion.

4

But as soon as the news reached him at Wilson's Tavern, at Lexington, Colonel Burr went to Frankfort and demanded an investigation. A grand jury was summoned, and the hearing postponed until November 12 to permit Mr. Daveiss to collect his witnesses. And on November 12 Colonel Burr was in court with his lawyer, Mr. Clay of Kentucky, but Mr. Daveiss could not produce any witnesses, and the Colonel was discharged before a cheering crowd to which he addressed a few graceful words.

But Mr. Daveiss had not done; on November 25 he again demanded the Colonel's arrest, and this time

Mr. Clay thought that he had better have a written denial from his client. "I have no design," Colonel Burr replied, on December 1, "to promote a dissolution of the Union . . . I have no design . . . to disturb the tranquility of the United States. . . . I do not own a musket or a bayonet, nor any single piece of military stores. . . . My views have been fully explained to and approved by several of the principal officers of Government, and, I believe, are well understood by the administration and seen by them with complacency. They are such as every man of honour and every good citizen must approve. Considering the high station you now fill in our national councils"—Mr. Clay had just been elected United States Senator—"I have thought these explanations proper . . . to satisfy you that you have not espoused the cause of a man 'in any way unfriendly to the laws, the government or the interests of his country.'"

And to General Tupper the Colonel wrote that "I had a very great desire to interest you in the extensive speculation in which I am engaged. . . . I am authorized in saying that it is the wish of Government that American settlers should go to the country west of the Mississippi in the Orleans Territory. Indeed a man high in office and in the confidence of the President told me that I should render a very great service to the public and afford pleasure to the administration, if I should take ten thousand men to that country—(I wish it was in my power)— Notwithstanding all this, I am told that the utmost alarm has been excited in your neighborhood on account of preparations which I am making for about 100 or 150 settlers. The rumors of my building Gun Boats, Ships etc., have been fabricated by a few designing men . . . and I am surprised to hear that some well disposed and intelligent men have become the Dupes."

And to General Harrison he wrote that "it may not be unsatisfactory to you to be informed that I have no wish or design to attempt a separation of the Union . . . that I never meditated the introduction of any foreign power or influence into the United States . . . in fine, that I have no project or views hostile to the interest, or tranquility, or union of the United States, or prejudicial to its government; and I pledge you my honour for the truth of this declaration."

And on December 2, in court, for the second time Mr. Daveiss had no witnesses, and asked for a further adjournment so that General Adair might be attached. The motion was denied. The next day, Mr. Daveiss asked that he be permitted to appear before the Grand Jury to explain such evidence as he had. Mr. Clay opposed, and the motion was denied. Whereupon the Grand Jury refused to find an indictment, and, on the contrary, sent in a written statement completely exonerating Colonel Burr. The accused was once more discharged in a tumult of cheers, and while the Federalists of Frankfort were drinking "Damnation to all conspiracies!" at the Washington Inn, at Taylor's Tavern a grand ball was being tendered the Colonel. He had, the Frankfort *Palladium* remarked, "throughout this business conducted himself with the calmness, moderation and firmness which have characterized him through life.

ERICH BOLLMANN

From the C. F. Pidgin Collection.

He evinced an earnest desire for a full and speedy
investigation . . . he excited the strongest sensa-
tion of respect and friendship in the breast of every
impartial person present."

5

The Colonel went back to Lexington—he had already made trips to Cincinnati and Chillicothe—and
on December 14, he was at Nashville with General
Adair, knocking at General Jackson's door. .But the
General was away, and Mrs. Jackson, ordinarily so
hospitable—such a cheerful, friendly "Aunt Rachel"
—seemed very hostile all of a sudden, and Colonel
Burr went back to the tavern at Clover Bottom,
where General Jackson's store was located. Mrs.
Jackson had evidently not been satisfied by the
Colonel's written explanation of his purposes to her
husband, early in November, at which time the
General had thought it necessary to order the militia
put in readiness, and to warn the Governors of Tennessee and Louisiana. But when the General returned to the Hermitage later on in December, he
called immediately on Colonel Burr with Judge Overton, and finally declared himself perfectly satisfied.
And if Mr. Clay and many others were eventually to
change their minds, General Jackson never did, and
from that day forth believed implicitly in Colonel
Burr's innocence of any treacherous intentions, although he was not convinced of the practicability of
the Mexican scheme.

The Colonel was free again to complete his arrangements. Mr. Blennerhassett was at the island—at
least Colonel Burr imagined that he was at the island

—preparing to start with his Muskingum flotilla; there were some boats to be finished and stores to be supplied by General Jackson; everything was moving forward satisfactorily. "If there should be a war between the United States and Spain," Colonel Burr wrote Senator Smith, "I shall head a corps of volunteers and be the first to march into the Mexican provinces. If peace should be proffered, which I do not expect, I shall settle my Washita lands, and make society as pleasant as possible. . . . I have been persecuted, shamefully persecuted."

But he did not know that a gentleman called John Graham had arrived in Ohio. . . .

6

In all these letters, in all these declarations and assurances—one must try to record the apparent underlying facts—Colonel Burr was probably making out the best case for himself. Ostensibly, he was preparing a colonizing expedition to the Bastrop lands—actually, there can be no doubt that Mexico was his principal objective; Mexico, the whole Spanish dominion in North America judging by his maps, involving a naval expedition to Vera Cruz. That this invasion of Spanish territory must be contingent upon an American war with Spain was always his professed proviso, and that of his friends in the New Orleans Mexican Association—that it would not have taken place in time, war or no war, is not so certain. It was understood differently in many enlisting centers! The Colonel always maintained that the Government approved of his plans; in his recruiting he made use of a letter from the Secretary of War which Mr. Jefferson afterwards pronounced a forgery; the fact remains that Colonel Burr had had several conferences in Washington with government officials, and that, in any case, the evident connivance of the administration with the Miranda adventure was enough to justify the assumption that its attitude would be no less accommodating in the matter of Mexico.

The Mexican project of 1806 was perhaps the most magnificent enterprise ever conceived upon the American continent—with the exception, possibly, of Citizen Genêt's, which had also included Canada within its scope. It had existed in the minds of many men long before Colonel Burr turned to it. It looked to a complete overrunning of the Spanish dominions; it implied land and sea operations of the first importance, only the very preliminaries of which ever made themselves manifest; it numbered among its supporters some—and it may be more than will ever be realized—of the most prominent persons in the country; it is likely that had the signal been given, regiment upon regiment of enlisted volunteers would have come marching from the western and southern territories, and let the Government catch the hindmost if it chose to be particular about states of war; in Mexico itself there were agents at work upon a popular cooperation with the "liberators." In all this, there was nothing treacherous to the United States. A breach of its neutrality, perhaps, but what was good for Miranda must surely be good for Burr.

As for a separation of the Western States, and even of Louisiana, Colonel Burr always denied it. "I would as soon have thought of taking possession of the moon, and informing my friends that I intended to divide it among them," he exclaimed, three months before his death. It is certain that he did not advocate it as a part of his program. It seems equally certain, when one attempts to examine his private conception of his undertaking, that he did not consider unlikely the occurrence of such an event as a result of the Spanish invasion. Separation—the word had no terrors in his time; voluntary, deliberate separation; and this the Colonel undoubtedly foresaw and contemplated as an inevitable feature of his scheme. What he does not appear to have contemplated or intended was an enforced separation, a coercion of the territories, a conflict by force of arms with the United States over the allegiance of the regions concerned. If the Mississippi Valley States decided to throw in their lot with him in a great western "empire," all well and good, and Mr. Jefferson himself would have been obliged, in his own written words, to say "God bless them!" It was not Colonel Burr's purpose to incite them to rebellion if, indeed, the term can be used in connection with so loose a bond as was that holding together the Union in his day.

As he stands at the moment of beginning his last journey down the "Great Long River," one feels it necessary, to the best of one's understanding, to remark briefly upon these matters. On another later page one will be obliged to remark upon them again in the light of a different aspect. In December, 1806, and in January, 1807, one is to see him and his associates perform the acts for which they were placed on trial for their lives. With all due regard for his

possible intentions—and in these it is difficult to
find the proof of any premeditated treason—one is
bound to remember that the case of the Federal
Government against Aaron Burr could only be
founded on misdemeanors actually committed by
him, not on misdemeanors which he may, in his own
mind, have proposed to commit. He was to be arrested for being in process of conducting an expedition
against Spain; he was to be tried for having levied
war against the United States. These were to be
the Federal Government's chief accusations against
him; these are the crimes the execution of which one
must observe. . . .

CHAPTER II

TREASON IN THE WEST

I

COLONEL DE PESTRE had arrived at Philadelphia in December, 1806, to tell the Marquis Yrujo a number of interesting things. Various detachments from the East were on the point of embarking for Charleston, where Mr. Alston was to take command; a number of officers, including John Swartwout and Colonel Smith of New York, were preparing to leave for their posts; the western conspiracy was in full swing; and, since it had been necessary to make some ostensible excuse for it, the Marquis might hear that Colonel Burr was intending to attack Mexico, but he must not believe "such rumors."

There had been a time when the Marquis might have been taken in by these fairy tales, but not any longer. In November, already, he had been sending his government details of the expedition. Five hundred men, he was informed, were being gathered on the upper Ohio by Colonel Burr "under pretext of establishing them on a great land purchase he is supposed to have made." There was talk of western independence, but the real purpose was a descent to

100

New Orleans and an attack on the Spanish possessions. "It is indubitable," the Marquis had decided,
"that Colonel Burr and his subordinates are carrying
out their plan. . . . It seems to me to be his intention to profit by the hostile appearance on the
Sabine to arm his friends preliminary to the rupture
with Spain." And the Marquis had warned all his
people in the Floridas and in Mexico—although they
must have been advised, "through the confidential
channel of No. 13 . . . who is one of the conspirators"—and as for Governor Folch of West Florida,
the Marquis was convinced that through his "connection with General Wilkinson he must be perfectly
informed of the state of things and of Burr's intentions."

The Marquis did not realize that General Wilkinson's contract as a pensioner of Spain had come to
an end, but it was quite true that Governor Folch
was prepared for the worst. He was going to be
attacked, and so were they, he notified his colleagues
in Mexico, and as he understood it the Government
of the United States was behind the expedition.
This point of view was prevalent among the Spanish
officials. "In February or March," Governor Folch
wrote, "ten thousand Kentuckians, three thousand
regular troops, eight or ten thousand militia from
Louisiana who will be forced to go, will march for
Mexico. They will raise a corps of five thousand
blacks. . . . This will make an army of from
twenty-eight to thirty thousand men. . . . Congress will act only in the defensive, but if once these
troops are united they will march toward Mexico with
great proclamations."

And so, when Colonel De Pestre came to the
Spanish Minister, he found, as he afterwards confessed to Mr. Blennerhassett, that the Marquis had
"pierced the cobweb tissue of Burr's intrigues with
him at a single glance." In fact, the Marquis Yrujo
laughed at him. Moreover, the Marquis sent a spy
of his own—one José Vidal, lately arrived from Cadiz
—out to the Ohio to watch every gesture of the
Colonel's. . . .

2

And down in the Southwest, General Wilkinson had
been busy with his own affairs.

As far as the conspirators could tell, during the
summer of 1806, the General was all eagerness for
the Mexican venture. They were on the high road
to Mexico, he had written Charles Biddle; "the time
long looked for by many and wished for by more
has now arrived for subverting the Spanish Government in Mexico," he informed General Adair, in
September. "Be ready and join me; we will want
little more than light armed troops. . . . More
will be done by marching than by fighting. . . .
We cannot fail of success. Your military talents are
requisite." And to Senator Smith he sent the assurance that he would "surely push [the Spaniards] over
the Sabine. . . . You must speedily send me a
force to support our pretensions . . . 5000 mounted
infantry . . . may suffice to carry us forward as far
as Grand River, there we shall require 5000 more to
conduct us to Mount El Rey . . . after which from
20 to 30,000 will be necessary to carry our conquests
to California and the Isthmus of Darien. I write in

haste, freely and confidentially, being ever your friend."

Yes indeed—and the letters were presumably written to induce them to commit themselves, at least, so the General explained them afterwards.
. . .

And now everything depended on General Wilkinson. For in July, the Spaniards had again crossed the Sabine, and occupied the post at Bayou Pierre; in August, Colonel Herrera had marched in with reinforcements; Acting Governor Cowles Meade, of the Mississippi Territory, had called out the militia; and Governor Claiborne of Louisiana was wondering why General Wilkinson, who was away somewhere, had countermanded the earlier War Department orders which had stated that the enemy must be kept on the further side of the Sabine. "It seems to me that there is wrong somewhere!" he observed to Mr. Meade. Still, the massing of troops went on at Natchitoches, and finally, on September 22, General Wilkinson arrived, after an incomprehensibly leisurely journey of two weeks from Natchez, where— although he was looking for "fame and honour," and hoping for a chance at the Spaniards—he had written to the Secretary of War that he would "drain the cup of conciliation to maintain the peace of our country." But scarcely anyone, and least of all his associates up the river, wanted him to do that. "We are happy to learn," the *Orleans Gazette* announced, "that the Government has at length issued positive orders to repel the aggressions of our enemies by force. . . . If the enemy be forced to recross the Sabine he must be driven still farther. . . . Gal-

lant Louisianians! Now is the time to distinguish
yourselves."

And now, if ever, was the time for General Wilkinson to distinguish himself. But something had happened to General Wilkinson; in England, Mr. Pitt
was dead; at Natchez, Mr. Minor knew too much;
in Kentucky and on the Ohio the outlook was not so
very brilliant; for one reason and another, General
Wilkinson had decided to turn his coat. Procrasti-
nate, keep things sufficiently embroiled on the border
so as to encourage Colonel Burr to start down the
river—that was General Wilkinson's plan, and then—
then General Wilkinson would see which way his
cats were jumping. . . .

And so General Wilkinson began to negotiate
with General Cordero, the Spanish commander at
Nacogdoches. The Spanish troops must be removed
across the Sabine. General Cordero was not of that
opinion. General Wilkinson settled himself down
to argue about it, when suddenly, of his own accord,
on September 27, Colonel Herrera evacuated Bayou
Pierre and withdrew across the disputed river. The
casus belli had decamped. General Wilkinson was
very much surprised, but now his mind was made up.
There must be no war with Spain—he would see to
that—and his share in Colonel Burr's expedition
must be disavowed. General Wilkinson's cats had
jumped.

To begin with, he notified General Cordero that
he would immediately occupy the east bank of the
Sabine, but merely "as signifying the pretensions of
the United States." Just to pass the time, for he
had no intention of doing so, General Cordero replied

that he would oppose such a move. The days of
General Wilkinson's immediate advance passed, and
on October 8 he was still at Natchitoches. And on
the evening of that day a young gentleman called
Swartwout arrived at the camp, with letters for the
General.

3

Samuel Swartwout and Peter Ogden, carrying
Colonel Burr's cipher letter of July 29 to-General
Wilkinson, had missed the latter at St. Louis, and
had followed him south; on horseback to Kaskaskias,
and thence by boat to Natchez; young Ogden himself
continuing direct to New Orleans, while his compan-
ion proceeded to the American headquarters. There
Mr. Swartwout had no trouble in persuading Colonel
Cushing that he had come to volunteer, and obtained
an interview with the commander.

General Wilkinson was more than gracious to his
visitor and kept him at the camp for some ten days,
during which—according to the General—he secured
from the young man all manner of incriminating information concerning Colonel Burr's plans, with
especial regard to New Orleans, all of which Samuel
Swartwout afterwards vigorously denied. At all
events, a few days after Mr. Swartwout's departure—
General Wilkinson let him go for the time being—
Lieutenant Thomas Smith was sent, on October 22,
to Washington with dispatches for the President, not,
however, including a copy of Colonel Burr's cipher.

But there was enough, without that, if it was
anonymous. Everything that young Swartwout
had, or had not said, and a great deal that no one

had said.   There was treason afoot, treason in the
West.   In what terms General Wilkinson saw fit to
make these belated revelations to Mr. Jefferson will
shortly appear.   To Colonel Cushing, and to Colonel
Burling, and to various officers, he had already con-
fided the contents of Colonel Burr's letter.   To
Colonel Freeman, in command at New Orleans, he
wrote ordering palisade fortifications to be constructed, and stating cryptically that "under my
present views and impressions, I have not the least
doubt we shall soon be engaged in hostilities, and
therefore every preparation for defense should be
made which our humble means will enable."   General Wilkinson had committed the only treasonable
act which occurred within the borders of the United
States during the year 1806—an act of treason against
Colonel Burr, against Jonathan Dayton, against his
old friends, his old comrades in arms, his associates
in a venture in which he had been irrevocably
concerned.

The Marquis Yrujo knew how to describe it when
it was made known to him.   "Wilkinson is entirely
devoted to us," he advised Madrid.   "He enjoys a
considerable pension from the King. . . .   He
anticipated . . . the failure of an expedition of
this nature.   Doubtless he foresaw from the first
that the improbability of success . . . would leave
him like the dog in the fable"—without his pension
and without his American salary.   But by his betrayal of Colonel Burr "he assures his pension; and
will allege his conduct on this occasion as an extraordinary service, either for getting it increased or for
some generous compensation.   On the other hand,

WILLIAM EATON

this proceeding secures his distinguished rank in the
military service of the United States. . . . In such
an alternative he has acted as was to be expected;
that is, he has sacrificed Burr in order to obtain, on
the ruins of Burr's reputation, the advantages I have
pointed out."

There is, in some ways, no more revolting a figure
in history than that of General James Wilkinson. . . .

4

And how devoted he was to Spain, when such devotion could be made to coincide with his own interests, was shortly to become apparent, although the
significance of the affair was not at the time fully
understood, since it was kept a secret matter of state
by the administration.

For several weeks General Wilkinson had been
blaring about marching to the Sabine, and finally he
did so, in superb battle array through a region from
which he knew that the last enemy patrol had long
since departed. And on October 29, through Colonel
Burling, he proposed to General Cordero the terms
of an agreement whereby the Spaniards were to re-
tire to Nacogdoches *and the Americans to Natchitoches*. General Cordero rejected the proposal, but
Colonel Herrera immediately accepted it, and on
November 5, the famous Neutral Ground Treaty was
signed. General Wilkinson began to trumpet his
triumph; he had "complied with my orders in pro-
claiming the jurisdiction of the United States here";
the army had accomplished the objects of its expedition; the Spaniards were no more to cross the Sabine.
What General Wilkinson did not point out was that

neither were the Americans to cross the Arroyo
Hondo; that the jurisdiction of the United States
over the Sabine was not established at all, since it
had been made neutral ground; and that all the long
standing American boundary and Texas claims were
vitiated by his brilliant achievement. And at the
trial of Colonel Burr, both General Wilkinson and Mr.
Jefferson knew better than to "divulge" the contents
of this pact which the Spaniards considered a victory
of no mean quality.

But now General Wilkinson was free to play the
saviour of his country. Having marched his army
to the Sabine, he marched it back again, and sent it
to New Orleans under Colonel Cushing. "I perceive
the plot thickens," he wrote that officer, on November
7. "Yet all but those concerned sleep profoundly.
My God! What a situation has our country reached.
Let us save it if we can . . . if I mistake not, we
shall have an insurrection of blacks as well as whites
to combat. . . . Hurry, hurry after me, and, if
necessary, let us be buried together in the ruins of
the place we shall defend." Colonel Burr's "declaration," it seemed, was to be made in Kentucky and
Tennessee on the fifteenth! And to Colonel Freeman
he wrote: "Let your measures [for defense] be taken
as if by order from the secretary of war; but profess
utter ignorance of motives. Manifest no hurry or
emotion, for you are surrounded by secret agents,
yet use every exertion in your power. . . . I shall
be with you by the twentieth instant; in the meantime, be you as silent as the grave."

And on November 12, at Natchez, it occurred to
him that it might be time to advise Governor Clai-

borne that "you are surrounded by dangers of which
you dream not, and the destruction of the American
government is seriously menaced. The storm will
probably burst in New Orleans, where I shall meet it
and triumph or perish. . . . You have spies on
every movement . . . and our safety and success
depends vitally on the concealment of our intentions.
I therefore make this communication, in the most
solemn confidence, and in the name of our common
country, that you do not breathe nor even hint it to
the most intimate friend of your bosom. . . . Within six days . . . the President will be fully apprised
of the plot which implicates thousands; and among
them some of your particular friends, as well as my
own."

The General was slaying his thousands—with a
pen, grown suddenly much mightier than his reluc-
tant sword. . . .

5

Lieutenant Smith, with his dispatches for the
Government, reached the President's House on November 25. There were two documents awaiting
Mr. Jefferson's immediate and panic stricken attention; one, an official War Department communication
dated October 20, and the other a private letter to
the Executive, written by General Wilkinson on
October 21.

In the first, Mr. Jefferson read that "The following
information appears to rest on such broad and explicit
grounds as to exclude all doubts of its authenticity:
A numerous and powerful association, extending from
New York through the Western States, to the terri-

tory bordering on the Mississippi, has been formed,
with the design to levy and rendezvous eight or ten
thousand men in New Orleans, at a very near period,
and from thence, with the cooperation of a naval
armament, to carry an expedition against Vera Cruz.

"Agents from Mexico, who were in Philadelphia in
the beginning of August, are engaged in this enterprise; these persons have given assurances that the
landing of the proposed expedition will be seconded
by so general an insurrection as to insure the sub-
version of the present government, and silence all
opposition in three or four weeks. A body of the
associates is to descend the Alleghaney river, and the
first general rendezvous will be held near the Rapids
of the Ohio, on or before the 20th of next month, from
whence this corps is to proceed in light boats, with
the utmost possible velocity, for the city of New Orleans, under the expectation of being joined in their
route by auxilliaries from the State of Tennessee and
other quarters.

"It is unknown under what authority this enterprise has been projected, from whence the means of
its support are derived, or what may be the intention
of its leaders in relation to the territory of Orleans.
But it is believed that the maritime cooperation will
depend on a British squadron from the West Indies,
under ostensible command of American masters.
Active influential characters have been engaged in
these transactions for six or eight months past; and
their preparations are reported to be in such a state
of maturity that it is expected the van will reach
New Orleans in December, where the necessary
organization and equipments are to be completed

with promptitude, and it is proposed that the expedition should sail for Vera Cruz about the first of February.

"This information has recently reached the reporter through several channels so direct and confidential, that he cannot doubt the facts set forth: and, therefore, he considers it his duty to make this representation to the executive by a courier extraordinary, to whom he has furnished five hundred dollars; being persuaded, should it prove unfounded, his precaution will be justified, and that otherwise his vigilance will be applauded."

But the General did not consider it his duty to mention Colonel Burr's name; it was unknown "under what authority this enterprise has been projected," although Colonel Cushing, for one, had been told immediately. In his confidential letter General Wilkinson unburdened himself further.

"Whatever may be the general impropriety," he informed Mr. Jefferson, "I persuade myself that on a subject irrelative to my official obligations, I shall be excused for addressing you directly and confidentially; but I have another and a more cogent reason for deviating, in this instance, from the ordinary course of my correspondence. It is possible the momentous occasion of this letter, and the vital importance attached to it, may have excited solicitudes to beguile my understanding and delude my judgment; and in such case I trust the integrity of the intention will secure me to your confidence, and that this letter, with the communication it covers, may find their graves in your breast.

"For although my information appears too direct

and circumstantial to be fictitious, yet the magnitude
of the enterprise, the desperation of the plan, and the
stupendous consequences with which it seems pregnant, stagger my belief, and excite doubts of the
reality, against the conviction of my senses; and it is
for this reason I shall forbear to commit names, because it is my desire to avoid a great public calamity,
and not to mar a salutary design or to injure any
one undesignedly." Then the General *did* know who
was concerned; and if the enterprise was so stagger-
ing, why not simply have enclosed a copy of Colonel
Burr's cipher?

"I have never in my whole life found myself under
such circumstances of perplexity and embarrassment
as at present; for I am not only uninformed of the
prime mover"—the General was not only lying, he
was contradicting himself, with that clumsiness which
must inevitably accompany falsehood—"and ultimate objects of this daring enterprise, but ignorant
of the foundation on which it rests, of the means by
which it is to be supported, and whether any immediate or collateral protection, internal or external,
is expected. Among other allurements proposed to
me, I am informed you connive at the combination,
and that our country will justify it; but when I
examine my orders of the 6th May, I am obliged to
discredit it—these imputations.

"But should this association be formed in opposition to the laws, and in defiance of government"—
the General did not seem certain of that—"then I
have no doubt that the revolt of this territory will be
made an auxilliary step to the main design of attacking Mexico, to give it a new master in the place of the

promised liberty. Should the fact be ascertained by me, I believe I should hazard my discretion, make the best compromise I could with [Spain] in my power"—this was paving the way for the Neutral Ground Treaty—"and throw myself with my little band into New Orleans, to be ready to defend that capital against usurpation and violence. It is true the works of the place have mouldered to ruin, yet I think they may, by extraordinary exertions, in a few weeks, be rendered defensible against an undisciplined rabble acting in a bad cause. But sir, with my instructions before me, and without knowledge of the design, principle or support, of the corps of associates expected from the Ohio, I dare not turn my back on the Spaniards, now in my front, and abandon this scene of disaffection to the certain evils which, without some strong measure of prevention, may possibly accrue in New Orleans."

The General did not know whether any immediate or collateral protection, *internal* or external, could be expected for the expedition; he did not know whether it was formed in "defiance of government"; he was very careful to point this out. If one had never believed in the administration's connivance with the Mexican expedition, certain portions of the General's letter would lead one to do so. And that was not all. There was a postscript; the General was subsequently to deny its authenticity, but there was a postscript. "N. B. Should Spain be disposed to war seriously with us, might not some plan be adopted to correct the delirium of the associates and by a suitable appeal to their patriotism to engage them in the service of their country? I merely offer the suggestion as a possible expedient to prevent the horrors of a civil contest, and I do believe that with competent authority I could accomplish the object." As Mr. McCaleb remarks, "truly a wonderful spectacle, a body of traitors metamorphosed into patriots!" If this postscript meant anything, was it not a hint to Mr. Jefferson to declare himself as favoring the expedition—in which case all of General Wilkinson's cats would have jumped back again. . . .

6

Mr. Jefferson took the hint; at all events, he declared himself. The Cabinet was immediately summoned and "came to the following determinations . . . that orders go . . . to Pittsburg . . . to be vigilant in order to discover whether there are any preparations making, or boats, or arms . . . providing by any persons against whom there is reasonable ground to suspect that they have in contemplation a military enterprise against any of the territories of Spain . . . to stop all bodies of armed men who may be assembled to descend the Ohio under circumstances . . . so different from those of common emigrants as to induce a reasonable suspicion that they are part of a combination of persons believed to have such an enterprise in view; to have them bound to the observance of the peace . . . or put in a course of legal prosecution, according to the strength of the evidence . . . Marietta . . . the collector to proceed to seize the gunboats building in that neighborhood"—what gunboats?—"and suspected to be destined for this enterprise . . . Governor Tiffin to furnish a guard of militia sufficient

for the detention of the boats. . . . General Jackson . . . to furnish any aid of militia which may
be necessary. . . .

"Louisville . . . same tenor as to the officer at
Pittsburg. Massac . . . same tenor, and particularly to stop armed vessels suspected on good grounds
to be proceeding on this enterprise. . . . Chickasaw Bluffs . . . same orders. . . . Fort Adams,
ditto; New Orleans, General Wilkinson to direct the
stations of the armed vessels, and if the arrangements
with the Spaniards will permit him to withdraw, let
him dispose of his force as he thinks best to prevent
any such expedition, or any attempt on New Orleans.
. . . He is also to arrest persons coming to his
camp and proposing a concurrence in any such
enterprise. . . ."

The next day, further orders were sent to Marietta
that two hundred militia be posted along the river
to prevent the passage of "gunboats"; and on November 27, the Secretary of War instructed General
Wilkinson to "use every exertion in your power to
frustrate and effectually prevent any enterprise which
has for its object, directly or indirectly, any hostile
act on any part of the territories of the United States,
or on any territories of the King of Spain."

There must have been two reasons for so whole-
hearted an acceptance of General Wilkinson's most
unconvincing reports. Whether or not certain government officials had been disposed to shut their eyes
to a proposed expedition to Mexico, now that the
news was definitely out, and the country grown in-
creasingly uneasy with rumors, the administration
did not intend to be caught in another Miranda affair;

and the administration no longer desired hostilities of
any sort with Spain; so that already on November 8
the Cabinet had agreed to notify General Wilkinson
that "the great probability of an amicable and early
settlement of our differences with Spain at Paris has
rendered the Executive extremely desirous of avoiding hostilities. He has therefore determined to
assume the Sabine as the temporary line; and that
the Spaniards shall not hold any fort save Bayou
Pierre beyond the Sabine." The Executive was
prepared to grant the Spaniards Bayou Pierre, and
in case war had already begun, "hostilities shall be
suspended," and if "any Spanish posts east of the
Mississippi have been taken, they will be surrendered." If hostilities had not begun, "Wilkinson
must remain on the defensive, and in no event cross
the Sabine."

Mr. Jefferson did not want hostilities of any kind
with Spain, because he was alarmed now at what
might be the French answer—how grateful to him,
then, must have been the news of the Neutral Ground
Treaty—and Mr. Madison did not want the Marquis Yrujo in his office again with another filibustering enterprise to put under his nose. To Mr. Madison, Colonel Burr's expedition was dangerous; to
Mr. Jefferson, whatever might have been his previous
attitude, it was become inconvenient. General
Wilkinson's letters had arrived at a most opportune
time. As General Jackson had foretold, Mr. Jefferson was ready to "run like a cotton tail rabbit."

And on November 27—while Mr. Merry was remarking that "it is astonishing that the Government
here should have remained so long in ignorance of the

intended design"—Mr. Jefferson issued a public proclamation setting forth that "whereas information has been received that sundry persons . . . are conspiring and confederating together to begin . . . a military expedition or enterprise against the dominions of Spain . . . I have therefore thought proper to issue this, my proclamation, warning and enjoining all faithful citizens who have been led without due knowledge or consideration to participate in the said unlawful enterprise to withdraw from the same without delay;" and also enjoining all citizens, and all civil and military authorities, to be vigilant, to seize all boats and supplies, to give information, and to apprehend the guilty.

The "sundry persons" were not named, but the country did not need to be told where to look. . . .

CHAPTER III

MARTIAL LAW

I

GENERAL WILKINSON was getting more and more excited.

On October 21, he had again written to the President, referring to certain accusations against him in the *Western World*, to say that "I have at times been fearful your confidence might be shaken by the boldness of the vile calumnies leveled at me; but the reflection that I have not only enjoyed but merited the confidence of General Washington . . . and that the honest but wrong-headed President Adams approved my conduct . . . combined with the consciousness that the wealth and power of the wide world could not for a moment divert my course from the path of honor, dissipated my apprehensions and determined me not to descend to the task of refuting by . . . testimony and authentic documents every imputation alleged against me, from the most frivolous to the most sane." Aside from that, "pardon . . . the honest pride which impels me to bare my bosom to you. My ultimate views are limited to the acquisition of an honorable fame. I have ever condemned the sordid interests of the world, and estimated property by its immediate utility only—and it is the highest ambition of my soul on a proper occasion, to spend my last breath in the cause of my country. A frail character, but a just one. To you I owe more than I will express, lest I should be suspected of adulation, which I detest."

And on November 12, from the home of Stephen Minor at Natchez, the General wrote again to the President. "Many circumstances," he informed him, "have intervened since my last, confirmatory of the information previously received, and demonstrative of a deep, dark and wicked conspiracy. My doubts have ceased, and it is my opinion that naught but an immediate peace in Europe can prevent an explosion which may desolate these settlements, inflict a great wound upon our republican policies, involve us in a foreign conflict, and shake the government to its very foundations." There.

"This is indeed a deep, dark and widespread conspiracy, embracing the young and the old, the democrat and the federalist, the native and the foreigner, the patriot of '76 and the exotic of yesterday, the opulent and the needy, the ins and the outs; and I fear it will receive strong support in New Orleans, from a quarter little suspected, from whence I have been recently addressed by a Gallo-American." He was referring to Doctor Bollmann, who had arrived at New Orleans and sent on his copy of Colonel Burr's cipher letter. "By masking my purposes and flattering his hopes I expect to discover the extent and leading characters of the combination in that

city, and, till this is effected, I shall carry an equivo-
cal exterior to every person who may see me. . . .
Nothing shall be omitted which can be accomplished
by indefatigable industry, incessant vigilance and
hardy courage, and I gasconade not when I tell you
that in such a cause I shall glory to give my life to
the service of my country; for I verily believe such
an event to be probable. . . ."

And now: "To give effect to my military arrangements, it is absolutely indispensable New Orleans
and its environs should be placed under martial law;
for without this the disaffected can neither be apprehended nor banished; private property can neither be
appropriated nor occupied for public purposes . . .
and my every disposition will of course be hourly
and daily exposed to my adversaries. To effect this
necessary measure I must look to your influence and
authority. To insure the triumph of government
over its enemies, I am obliged to resort to political
finesse and military stratagem . . . and therefore
my own bosom, were it possible, should be the sole
repository of my determinations . . . for were my
intentions exposed, there are more than three desperate enthusiasts in New Orleans who would seek my
life, and although I may be able to smile at danger in
open conflict, I will confess I dread the stroke of the
assassin, because it cannot confer an honorable
death."

Mr. Isaac Briggs, "with whose good sense and
integrity I have been long acquainted," was to carry
these interesting written communications, "with
certain oral communications which I dare not letter,
because nothing less than an overt act will, in my

judgment, warrant the official commitment of names, and none such has as yet been committed, within my knowledge." But unofficially General Wilkinson did not hesitate, now, to mention Colonel Burr, Jonathan Dayton, Commodore Truxtun, and various other gentlemen. He did not, however, transmit to the President a copy of Colonel Burr's cipher letter. Mr. Briggs presented himself at the President's House on New Year's Day, 1807, and assured Mr. Jefferson that the General was "sound in this business."

In spite of which Mr. Jefferson was obliged to point out to General Wilkinson, on January 3, that "the very man"—Truxtun—"whom they represented to you as gone to Jamaica . . . has never been from home, and has regularly communicated to me everything which has passed between Burr and him. No such proposition was ever hazarded to him." But no matter. "Go on . . . with your works for the defense of New Orleans," and "I beseech you to take the most special care of the two letters which [Briggs] mentioned to me, the one in cipher, the other from [Dayton], and to send them to me by the first conveyance you can trust."

2

And just to show to what extent General Wilkinson "condemned the sordid interests of the world," and how great a share of his solicitude was enjoyed by "the cause of my country," a few days later, under the public pretext of purchasing mules, he sent Walter Burling to Mexico, with a passport stating that "Whereas, Aaron Burr . . . is preparing to carry on an expedition into the territory of his Catholic

Majesty . . . I have thought proper . . . to exonerate my government from a suspicion of participating in this design, to authorize the bearer . . . to pass all guards . . . of the United States and to proceed to the City of Mexico for the purpose of handing to the viceroy a detailed report of said Burr's plans and designs."

And Mr. Minor also gave him a passport, in which "I, Stephen Minor, captain in the royal armies and actually in the territory of Natchez by his Majesty's orders, solicit the commanders . . . of the Internal Provinces of the Kingdom of Mexico to pass Walter Burling to the City of Mexico on business of the royal service. . . ." The Spanish officials rendered him every assistance, and late in January Mr. Burling rode into the capital, whereupon the nature of his business became immediately apparent to the Viceroy.

In General Wilkinson's letter, the Viceroy advised his government, "he lays great stress on the measures which he has taken at the risk of his life, fame and fortune in order to save . . . this kingdom from the attacks of the insurgents. . . . He finally comes to what I had anticipated"—the Spaniards knew their Number Thirteen—"the question of payment for his services. He asks for $85000 in one sum, and $26000 in another. But, not content with this, he says he considers it just and equitable to be reimbursed for those sums he has been obliged to spend in order to sustain the cause of good government, order and humanity.

"Understanding the desires of the General I destroyed his letter . . . in the presence of his aide . . . whose conversation with me did not forward the demands of his General, nor add anything to the information I had of the intentions of Colonel Burr. In my answer to the General I gave him to understand that the revolutionists had not caused me any alarm . . . I informed him that I could not pay the sums of money asked . . . and that I had arranged for the hasty return of his aide. In conclusion I thanked him for his martial zeal, and insinuated that I wished him happiness in the pursuit of his righteous intentions. . . ."

No comment can possibly add to the disgust and contempt for General James Wilkinson which distinguish the Spanish Viceroy's account of this pretty transaction. Mr. Burling returned emptyhanded, and, on the grounds that he had secured a report of conditions in Mexico, Mr. Jefferson was persuaded to pay his expenses! And on November 25 the saviour of his country flung himself into New Orleans.

3

The Creole city was in a fearful state.

Peter Ogden and Erich Bollmann had arrived, the latter on September 27, with news which they imparted to whom it might concern—to Judge Prevost, no doubt, and to Daniel Clark, and to Edward Livingston. The town was filled with rumors. The whole Territory was filled with rumors; all the Spanish dominions were filled with rumors. "It is believed that [Burr's] band of adventurers will destroy whatever appears before it," a Spaniard was writing early in November to Mexico, "and that the public banks [of New Orleans] will be robbed. . . . It is

rumored that Colonel Burr had been obliged to fly
from the interior of the United States." It was
rumored that "Colonel Burr . . . has placed himself at the head of 20,000 men . . . and it is further
stated that the members of Congress from Kentucky,
Tennessee and Carolina have withdrawn from Congress." No one knew what to believe, and those who
knew best of all said nothing. "There is in this
city," Governor Claiborne exclaimed in October, "a
degree of apathy . . . which mortifies and aston-
ishes me." The Governor was thinking of the situation on the Spanish border, but his remark was applicable to the subsequent attitude of his Creoles who
so disliked him, and whom he so slightly understood.

Some of the Americans in New Orleans, however,
were not to remain so reticent. Judge Workman of
the Mexican Association, for instance, took occasion,
a few weeks later, to enlighten Colonel Freeman concerning the innocent character of the Association's
aims. The Judge had come to see General Wilkinson's second in command on a court martial matter,
and proceeded to make certain revelations of considerable interest which Colonel Freeman recorded,
on December 30, in a signed statement now in the
possession of the New York Historical Society.

"In the course of conversation," the Colonel stated,
"Judge Workman informed me that he had been one
of the persons who had long contemplated a plan to
emancipate Mexico from the Spanish Government;
that this plan was to raise an army at the expense of
the adventurers, under the auspices of the United
States; that the first objects would be to take Baton
Rouge and Mobile and then to march into the Span-

ish provinces west of the Mississippi; if they should succeed there, to erect an independent government under the protection of the United States. That Colo. Burr had nothing whatever, as far as he knew, to do in this project. He was mentioned as a proper person to command, and General Wilkinson was also named as a fit person to be put at the head of the enterprise; that secrecy was enjoined to the associates lest the scheme should become known to the Spaniards, but not for any purposes whatever injurious to the interests of the United States. That this plan was contemplated at the time it was supposed the United States would inevitably be involved in a war with Spain; when De Miranda's expedition was believed to have been sanctioned by the General Government. But so soon as this was disavowed all conversation whatever in relation to the proposed conquest of Mexico ceased."

The Judge allowed Colonel Freeman to "communicate to General Wilkinson the substance of the foregoing statement"—although most of it cannot have been news to him—and in the evening "the Judge made me another visit. . . . I repeated to him what I had related to General Wilkinson in the morning; he assented to the correctness of my statement. We then conversed freely upon the subject of erecting an independent government in Mexico. The Judge premised that the whole plan and its execution was to have depended on the approbation and concurrence of the United States; without these nothing was to have been undertaken." How obstinately convinced of that the "conspirators" always seemed to be!

Judge Workman then "observed that the emancipation of the Spanish provinces had been for many years his favorite object. That he had when he was a British subject proposed it to that Government; that he had applied himself particularly to acquire . . . such geographical information as would be required and be useful in case his plan should be adopted. . . . He declared upon his honor, a separation of the Union was never mentioned or even, he believed, contemplated by any person then associated with him. Colo. Burr was mentioned, as were General Wilkinson and General Dayton as fit to be placed at the head of the expedition."

As for the expedition, "the plan proposed, was that such force should march as to give the adventurers reasonable hopes that they would beat the Viceroy of Mexico in the field. This force was estimated at twenty thousand men. . . . Two million of dollars would have been required. . . . It was expected that merchants and men of property in every part of the United States would contribute. . . . That the march to Mexico might be performed in forty days from Natchitoches. If the Viceroy should be beaten the whole country would submit and with proper management might be separated forever from Spain. . . . It was understood that the military chief would of course be placed at the head of government whatever might have been its form. . . . It was to have been a government of laws in which the rights of all the citizens were to be respected. . . . In its foreign relations, it was to be placed in the situation of Portugal to England . . . as respected its connection with the United States—alliances of

commerce and defence were to have been entered
into with the United States and the parent country
was also to have been regarded as the protectrix of
the new government.

"The Judge repeated frequently that all these
things were to be done under the presumption that
the United States must inevitably go to war with
Spain, and that not a motion was to be made without
the approbation of the General Government. That
no scheme whatever to dissever the Union. formed
any part of the plan. That since the Government
had expressed their disapprobation of De Miranda's
expedition, all thoughts of the conquest of Mexico
had been given up and abandoned. He however expressed his opinion that the United States would at
some future day find it for their interest to carry
into operation an expedition upon similar principles."

The question inevitably arises whether, after all,
it was not simply jealousy of Colonel Burr which
caused General Wilkinson to betray him. The first
Emperor of Mexico was to have been Aaron I, not
James the Inimitable; or perhaps Judge Workman
was himself simply exercising that prudence which
at the time so inspired the more prominent citizens
of New Orleans. . . .

As for Daniel Clark, who perhaps knew better than
all of them what Colonel Burr really hoped to do, he
took immediate steps to safeguard his future from his
past, whatever the eventual emergency. That gentleman had just been chosen by the Legislature to repre-
sent them in Congress, and was on the point of
departure when Doctor Bollmann arrived. He called
together a number of his Creole friends, who later

testified to that effect, and "informed them of the
. . . intentions imputed to Colonel Burr, which were
then almost the sole topic of conversation, and which,
from the reports daily arriving from Kentucky, had
caused serious alarm; and he advised them all to exert their influence . . . to support the Government
of the United States and to rally round the Governor.
. . . And Mr. Clark strongly recommended to . . .
members of the Legislature . . . not to attend any
call or meeting of either House in case Colonel Burr
should gain possession of the city." After which
sage advice Mr. Clark departed for Washington,
leaving behind him material for the most irreproachable affidavits should they become necessary—but
not a word of all this reached the Governor; not a
word of warning did Mr. Clark, or anyone else,
whisper in the Governor's ear. New Orleans held
its breath, and waited—those who knew, for whatever it was that they expected; those who did not
know, for whatever it was that they feared. . . .

And in the midst of all this mystery, with threatened war on his borders for which his militia showed
little enthusiasm, and the most alarming conjectures
floating down the River—one must remember that
the whole Mississippi Valley was seething with
curiosity over Colonel Burr's supposed movements
during the fall of 1806—Governor Claiborne wan-
dered hither and yon, hopelessly alone, utterly in the
dark. An earnest, well meaning gentleman whom
his people had never tolerated, of "estimable private
qualities." as Commissioner Laussat saw him, but
with "little capacity and much awkwardness," and
"extremely beneath his place." So that it was with

dismay and a perfect bewilderment that he received
General Wilkinson's Natchez communication of November 12, informing him that he was "surrounded
by dangers of which you dream not;" followed not
long after by that letter which General Jackson had
been moved to send him at the time of his suspicion
of Colonel Burr, advising him that "treachery has
become the order of the day . . . defend your city
as well against internal enemies as external. . . .
Be upon the alert! Keep a watchful eye on our
General and beware of an attack as well from your
own country as Spain! I fear there is something
rotten in the state of Denmark. . . . Beware of
the month of December!"

Beware of the month of December! Keep a watchful eye on our General! And here it was December,
and here was our General himself. . . .

4

Into New Orleans he came, "a flighty, rattle-
headed fellow," according to Mr. Laussat who had
known him in 1804,"often drunk, who has committed
a hundred impertinent follies." And nothing happened. The mountain had given forth a great noise,
and not even a mouse had appeared. His arrival
"excited great attention," he afterwards stated;
work was continued on the fortifications; the General
interviewed Erich Bollmann; Edward Livingston
interviewed the General, and—according to the
latter—asked him for what post he was destined in
Mexico; the Mayor interviewed the General, and—
according to the latter—advised him that if Burr
came down not a man would join him, Wilkinson; the

General assured Governor Claiborne that the safety
of the Territory was seriously menaced; but nothing
happened. Almost the Governor may have been
prepared to believe what Cowles Meade had suggested in November, that "General Wilkinson is the
soul of the conspiracy. . . . Is New Orleans invaded? Is it threatened . . . General Wilkinson
is concentrating the whole military force of the
United States at New Orleans. . . . What is all
this for? Is it to act for you or against you?"

But on December 6, the General finally told the
Governor what it was for. "The dangers," he notified him, "which impend over this city . . . from
an unauthorized and formidable association must be
successfully opposed at this point, or the fair fabric
of our independence . . . will be prostrated, and
the Goddess of Liberty will take her flight from this
globe forever. . . . Extraordinary measures must
be resorted to and the ordinary form of civil institu-
tions must for a short period yield to the strong arm
of military law. . . . I most earnestly entreat
you to proclaim martial law over the city," otherwise
"the defects of my force may expose me to be over-
whelmed by numbers, and the cause and place will
be lost." And the militia would be of no use for
"you could not . . . withstand the desperation
and superiority of numbers . . . and the brigands
. . . might resort to the dreadful expedient of exciting a revolt of the negroes."

And the next day he wrote again. "Proclaim
martial law. . . . I must entreat you to act with
decision. . . . Our measures must be taken with
promptitude . . . for I apprehend Burr with re-

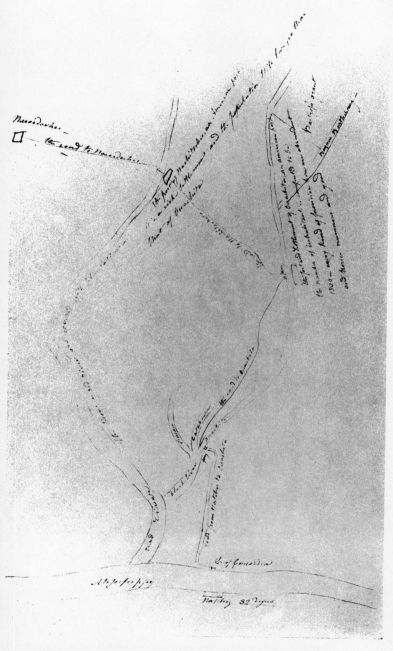

FACSIMILE OF AARON BURR'S SKETCH MAP OF THE BASTROP GRANT

Original in the possession of the New York Public Library.

bellious bands may soon be at hand." Always these
brigands, these rebellious bands, these overwhelming
thousands descending upon the devoted city—just
as later, at Washington, Mr. Jefferson had shouted
treason and had to keep on shouting it, so at New
Orleans, General Wilkinson had bellowed rebellion
and had to keep on bellowing it. And to play his
melodrama properly, he must have martial law.
But Governor Claiborne would not give him martial
law. The Legislature was not in session, and pre-
paratory to martial law, he told Cowles Meade,
"the suspension of the writ of *habeas corpus* would
be necessary." He would summon the militia, but
"as to martial law, I shall not proclaim it."

So matters stood on December 9, when the members of the Chamber of Commerce were finally summoned to Government House to be told what all the
uproar was about. With Mr. Lanusse presiding,
Governor Claiborne explained the emergency, whereupon General Wilkinson outlined the "base plot"
in which the desperate conspirators had tried to involve him, but without success—and there he was to
defend the city against the onslaught of unnumbered
rebels and to sacrifice himself, if needs be, in the
cause of patriotism and duty. It was all going to be
very dreadful unless they took the most stringent
measures to assist him; and if he had not told them
before, it was because the hero was afraid of being
assassinated. The merchants were mildly impressed,
and voted an embargo on shipping, so that sailors
might be free to enlist in the navy.

"I am here," the General wrote to Daniel Clark
the next day, to defend "our darling city and poor

devoted Louisiana" against "revolution and pillage
by a hand I have loved." But he must have martial
law. "For heaven's sake take decisive measures to
raise the sailors required," he urged the Governor on
December 12; but Governor Claiborne replied that
"many good disposed citizens do not appear to think
the danger considerable, and there are others who
. . . endeavor to turn our preparations into ridicule;"
the people were beginning to laugh at General Wilkinson, and on December 15 he was bellowing again.

"Having put my life and character in opposition
to the flagitious enterprise," he informed his col-
league, "of one of the ablest men of our country,
supported by a crowd of co-equals, ceremony would
be unseasonable and punctillio unprofitable. . . .
Pardon the honest candor which circumstances require and my situation demands, when I observe
that with the most upright . . . intention you
suffer yourself to be unduly biased by the solicita-
tions of the timid, the capricious or the wicked. . . .
What will our alertness import, without force and
energy to support it? And can we be prepared without means? Shall our reverence for our civil insti-
tutions produce their annihilation, or shall we lose
the house because we will not break the windows?"

5

But General Wilkinson had already started in to
break the windows, and the reign of terror had begun.
Mr. Swartwout and Mr. Ogden had been arrested, at
Fort Adams on December 12; Doctor Bollmann in the
city, on December 14. They had all three been
placed aboard the bomb ketch *Ætna*, in close con-

finement, deprived of their papers and belongings—
the General had Mr. Swartwout's watch—and denied
legal representation. Writs of *habeas corpus* issued
by the Superior Court, on December 16, found Mr.
Ogden alone aboard, the other two prisoners having
already been transferred to a war vessel bound for
Baltimore, consigned to the President of the United
States.

Mr. Ogden was released by Judge Workman on
December 17. He "now struts at large," General
Wilkinson complained to Mr. Jefferson. But not for
long. As for Erich Bollmann, the General notified
the Court that he "had arrested Bollmann, as I shall
arrest, without respect to class or station, all those
against whom I have positive proof of being accom-
plices in the machinations against the state." And
in support of the absent prisoners' treason, General
Wilkinson submitted Colonel Burr's cipher letter of
July 29, which he had not yet sent to Mr. Jefferson—
he did so soon after—and which now found its way
into the newspapers. And inside of twenty-four
hours Mr. Ogden was rearrested and imprisoned, together with the friend who had sworn out his writ,
a certain James Alexander who in a few days was
shipped to Baltimore with hardly more than the
clothes on his back.

New Orleans was in a perfect panic. It was plain
that the General had set aside all civil authority
and proposed to make arrests right and left. Writs
for Mr. Alexander and Mr. Ogden drew from him the
reply that his explanation in the case of Erich Bollmann was sufficient. A motion by Edward Livingston, on December 26, to attach the General brought

forth the statement "that the body of the said Peter
V. Ogden is not in his power, possession or custody."
The Governor, in the face of repeated appeals, re-
fused to give the judges any assistance, and Judge
Workman adjourned his court and resigned. Gen-
eral Wilkinson then had the Judge arrested, and held
for trial at Natchez, but a United States District
Judge finally released him.

Martial law hung over the city; no one dared
breathe, no one dared move; who was to be the next
victim of General Wilkinson's military patrols?
General Adair! That gentleman arrived—on private
business, so he declared—at noon on January 14,
and sat down to dinner at Madame Nourage's boarding house, after making his presence known to Judge
Prevost and Governor Claiborne. At four o'clock
in the afternoon, while he was still at dinner, one
hundred and fifty soldiers surrounded the house—a
lesser number would perhaps have been uncompli-
mentary—and General Adair was "violently dragged
from the table, paraded through the streets," placed
on a schooner and taken to a swamp twenty-five miles
below the city, and finally shipped in his turn, with
Peter Ogden, to Baltimore. The trouble with John
Adair—aside from the letters which General Wilkinson had previously written to him—was that he had
presumed to laugh at the danger threatening New
Orleans, since he had left Colonel Burr at Nashville
late in December with exactly two boats!

6

General Wilkinson was dictator of New Orleans;
he had arrested Bollmann, Swartwout, Ogden, Alex-

ander, Workman, Adair, and one or two minor individuals; there were in the city any number of people equally "implicated" whom he might have arrested at any moment—but General Wilkinson did not arrest them. He did not arrest any of the influential Creoles, he did not arrest the Mayor, he did not arrest Edward Livingston. On the contrary, he made it plain that they had nothing to fear from him; he wrote insinuatingly reassuring letters to Daniel Clark in which he disparaged Governor Claiborne and promised never to expose Mr. Clark's friends "unless compelled by self defense;" and throughout this period he remained in detailed correspondence with the Spanish Governor of West Florida. One really begins to wonder what was going on in General Wilkinson's mind. New Orleans was his; what did he think he might do with it?

The weeks passed. General Wilkinson was still rendering Colonel Burr's cipher "to my satisfaction;" Mr. Jefferson wrote approving the General's arrests; Cowles Meade kept warning Governor Claiborne to "be on your guard against the wily general . . . consider him a traitor and act as if certain thereof;" New Orleans began to yawn a little at its saviour's fits and starts of alarm. "From the best information we can collect," the *Orleans Gazette* decided, "the object of Colonel Burr is . . . an attack upon Mexico and not, as has been alleged, the parricidal attempt to dismember the Union."

Messages and proclamations passed back and forth; General Wilkinson made a great to-do of gathering "papers" and "evidence" with his secret police; the Governor made up his mind that Colonel Burr was not coming—nor did he ever come—and that the Louisianians were loyal in any case; and in March the Legislature was finally remarking, concerning the recent military outburst, that "though nothing can justify, yet circumstances of extreme danger . . . might excuse some of these violent measures. But here no foreign enemy or open domestic foe was then, or has yet been proved to have been within any perilous distance of this city, or that treason lurked within our walls." And that "the acts of high-handed military power" to which they had been exposed were "acts too notorious to be denied, too illegal to be justified, too wanton to be excused."

But to the perpetrator of them, to the inimitable General James Wilkinson, there came no punishment. . . .

CHAPTER IV

HABEAS CORPUS

I

THE President's proclamation of November 27, 1806, made very little stir in Washington, after the first surprise. Indeed, in his message to Congress, on December 1, Mr. Jefferson said very little about the conspiracy. It was an attempt "to carry on a military expedition against the territories of Spain," and the information concerning it was "chiefly in the form of letters, often containing . . . a mixture of rumors, conjectures and suspicions." The proclamation, he explained, was an act of good faith towards Spain. Not a word about treason.

But in his own mind the President was worried; he did not know what might be happening in the West; he was writing to the Secretary of the Navy concerning the measures to be taken should it become necessary to recapture New Orleans! Still, he had confidence in the Western States, he pretended to have confidence in Louisiana, and publicly, officially, he did nothing. He had moved to prevent *an expedition to Mexico;* the necessity for any further genuine concern does not appear to have impressed him. December passed, and the world was full of rumors. "The news from the West is by no means agreeable," Senator Mitchill told his wife. "Burr is gone to Nash ville with postnotes from the Bank of Kentucky to the amount of $20,000 and is changing them away for boats and provisions." Burr would "go down the river and give us trouble," Samuel Smith feared. "And yet not one step taken except the proclamation." The state of things, John Randolph wrote Mr. Monroe, was "unexampled." As for Senator Plumer, he was "both amused and perplexed," and he must have "plenary evidence" before he believed "one hundredth part of the absurd and foolish things" ascribed to Burr. And anyway, Mr. Jefferson had informed him "that he knew of no evidence sufficient to convict [Burr] of either high crimes or misdemeanors." And John Adams thought that Burr "must be an Idiot or a Lunatick" if he had planned such a project as was imputed to him.

In fact, no one knew what to think. "There cannot now remain any doubts of Burr's seditious and treasonable designs," Senator Plumer had decided in January, in spite of his former opinion. "I have no doubt but that the Marquis de Yrujo was duped by Burr. The Marquis had no doubt induced the Spanish commander to march his troops to the Sabine . . . and thereby draw our feeble army from New Orleans." But in February Senator Plumer had changed his mind again, and was writing that "it is now very apparent Wilkinson himself has created much of the alarm, and has greatly exaggerated the force and importance of Burr. I think Burr's object was the Mexican provinces—not a separation of the Union."

But finally John Randolph could not stand it any longer, and on January 16, 1807, he moved that the President be asked for the "papers" in the matter of Aaron Burr. At that, the resolution was purely a political one, offered for the purpose of embarrassing the President and precipitating war with Spain. Mr. Jefferson understood that, and that he must now make up his own mind in the matter of Aaron Burr. Either General Wilkinson or Colonel Burr must be discredited. And so, in a special message on January 22, Mr. Jefferson sent to Congress a not altogether candid version of his acquaintance with the affair; he submitted the documents from General Wilkinson —including the cipher letter received at last—he set forth his belief not only in a proposed invasion of Mexico but also in a project to dismember the Union; he explained that his General had been obliged to make certain extraordinary arrests at New Orleans; he announced the inevitable failure of the rebellion as a result of his proclamation; and he permitted himself to state that, although in the "voluminous mass" of information there was little legal evidence, Colonel Burr's "guilt is placed beyond question"—a statement which must have startled Senator Plumer, and which drew from John Adams the rebuke that "if [Burr's] guilt is as clear as the Noon day Sun, the first Magistrate ought not to have pronounced it so before a Jury had tried him."

But Mr. Jefferson had done so little before that he was now prepared to do anything. Congress was

making enquiries, and the "cotton tail rabbit" was
running. . . .

2

The country nearly went into hysterics. Colonel
Burr had committed treason; he had tried to seize
New Orleans; he had wanted to revolutionize the
West; the President had said so. What could be
expected of a man who had been with Arnold, who
had served under Conway, who had taken sides with
Lee. Noble President Jefferson! Brave General
Wilkinson! Treacherous Colonel Burr! Let him be
hanged! Colonel Burr was already tried and con-
demned. His "guilt" was "placed beyond question."

In Congress, some of them were not so sure.
General Wilkinson "is not an accurate and correct
man," Senator Plumer remembered. That cipher
letter of the Colonel's! "I am confident the letter
is not accurately stated—it sounds more like Wilkinson's letter than Burr's . . . if Wilkinson's communications are correct, Burr either discovers want
of talent . . . or a mania, a phrenzy, has seized
his mind." Still, something must be done, and, to
begin with, the Senate passed and sent down to the
House a bill whereby, when "any person or persons
. . . charged on oath with treason . . . endan-
gering the peace . . . or neutrality of the United
States, have been or shall be arrested . . . by
virtue of any warrant or authority of the President
. . . or from any person acting under [his] direction
or authority . . . the privilege of the writ of
habeas corpus shall be, and the same hereby is suspended, for and during the term of three months."

An obvious attempt to fortify General Wilkinson,
introduced by Mr. Giles, the President's representative in the Senate.

In the presence of this astonishing document, the
House immediately voted, with only three dissenting
voices, that "the message and bill received from the
Senate ought not to be kept secret, and that the doors
be now opened." The bill was doomed. Mr. Eppes
of Virginia, the President's son-in-law, moved that
the bill be rejected. Mr. Burwell of Virginia attacked the bill. Why suspend the writ of *habeas
corpus* when in his message the President had stated
that New Orleans was not in serious danger? Mr.
Elliott of Vermont attacked the bill. "Is this a
crisis of such awful moment?" he enquired. "Is it
necessary . . . to constitute a dictatorship . . .
to create one great Dictator and a multitude . . .
of petty despots. . . . Is this one of those great
crises that require a suspension, a temporary prostration of the Constitution itself? Does the stately
super-structure of our Republic thus tremble to its
centre and totter towards its fall?" Mr. Elliott
thought not, and quoted from the presidential message to support his conviction. "Shall we," Mr.
Eppes asked, "suspend the chartered rights of the
community for the suppression of a few desperadoes,
of a small banditti?" Certainly not.

Mr. Varnum of Massachusetts thought differently.
This insurrection was "the most aggravating of all
insurrections of which history gives an account."
Mr. Sloan of New Jersey agreed with him, but he
would vote against the bill. Mr. Smilie of Virginia
doubted whether a single law of the United States

had been broken.   Mr. Randolph of Virginia hit the
nail on the head.   He considered the bill "an oblique
attempt to cover a certain departure from an established law. . . .   I will never agree in this side way
to cover up such a violation by a proceeding highly
dangerous to the liberty of the country, or to agree
that this invaluable privilege shall be suspended because it has been already violated."   The Senate bill
was rejected, by a vote of one hundred and thirteen
to nineteen.

And that was not all.   On February 7, Mr. Broom
of Delaware resolved that "it is expedient to make
further provision for securing the privilege of the
writ of *habeas corpus* to persons in custody under or
by color of the authority of the United States."   It
was perfectly clear what was happening.   General
Wilkinson, and through him the President who supported his acts, were being attacked, by the Federalists and by the "Quid" faction of the Republican
party, led by John Randolph.   While the country
was echoing Mr. Jefferson's shout of treason, the
House was answering *Habeas Corpus!*   Mr. Randolph did not hesitate to accuse the General of twofold treachery, to the Constitution and to Colonel
Burr.   Mr. Broom—when the debate opened on February 17—referred to the abuses "committed by a
military officer at the head of the Army . . . in full
view of the highest authorities of the Union."   For
his part, he wished to live "under a government of
laws, and not of men."   Mr. Alston of North Carolina remarked that the proposed legislation would
have the result that "if any person shall even see
treason committed . . . or Aaron Burr marching

THE BLENNERHASSETT MANSION

at the head of the marine corps, he shall not dare to arrest them." For four days they talked, and at the end the motion was tabled by a vote of only sixty to fifty-eight.

Mr. Jefferson's great treason affair was not starting so well. . . .

3

But there was more trouble in store for him.

The prisoners, Swartwout and Bollmann, had arrived at Baltimore, and had been transferred to Washington on January 22. On January 26, the Attorney General applied for and obtained from Judge Cranch a warrant for their arrest on the charge of treason. The prisoners at once applied to the Supreme Court for a writ of *habeas corpus*, which was issued on February 13. On February 16, consequently, their attorneys moved for their discharge. In the meantime, Mr. Alexander had been landed at Baltimore, where, on February 6, he was discharged for lack of any evidence against him. On February 17, General Adair and Peter Ogden were landed at Baltimore, where, on February 18, they were discharged because "there was no proof of any nature whatsoever against them"—as a result of which General Adair sued General Wilkinson for damages, and finally recovered twenty-five hundred dollars which a benevolent Congress ultimately reimbursed. It was of the utmost importance to the administration, therefore, that a conviction be secured in the case of Swartwout and Bollmann.

They were charged specifically with "treason in levying war against the United States," evidence in support of which was submitted in the form of General Wilkinson's documents, and an affidavit of General Eaton's, relating all his allegations of the previous year against Colonel Burr—the allegations which he had hitherto concealed from the President. Now there was something very curious about this affidavit. General Eaton, it will be remembered, had had certain long standing financial claims pending before Congress, which that body had shown no disposition to honor. Three days prior to the swearing out of the General's affidavit, however, his claims had been referred to a Committee of the House; one month later a bill authorizing their settlement was passed without debate—"by surprise," as it seemed to John Randolph—and one week later General Eaton was paid ten thousand dollars. A profitable six weeks for General Eaton. And in Senator Plumer's opinion, General Eaton's mind was "so irregular, wild and confused . . . that I think every man who converses with him or in his hearing is in danger of being misrepresented by him. . . . The more distant the time, the more distant from Burr, and the louder public opinion is expressed agt. Burr—the fuller and stronger are the declarations of Eaton against the accused."

For three days arguments for and against the discharge of the prisoners were heard, and on February 21, Chief Justice Marshall delivered his opinion. To conspire to levy war, and actually to levy war were two distinct offences, he pointed out. "The first must be brought into operation by the assemblage of men for a purpose treasonable in itself," although they need not actually appear in arms against the country. "If a body of men be actually assembled for the purpose of effecting by force a treasonable purpose, all those who perform any part, however minute or however remote from the scene of action, and who are actually leagued in the general conspiracy are to be considered as traitors." An interpretation which was to cause the Chief Justice infinite embarrassment a few months later at Richmond. "But there must be an actual assembling of men for the treasonable purpose to constitute a levying of war."

The prisoners, charged with levying war, were therefore discharged. General Eaton's affidavit did not apply to them at all. In Colonel Burr's letter to General Wilkinson there was "no expression . . . which would justify a suspicion that any Territory of the United States was the object of the expedition;" there was not in the letter, "so far as that letter is laid before the Court, one syllable which has a necessary or a natural reference to an enterprise against any territory of the United States." As for what Mr. Swartwout was supposed to have told the General, the worst threatened at New Orleans was robbery. And if "those whose duty it is to protect the nation . . . shall suppose those who have been charged with treason to be proper objects for punishment, they will, when possessed of less exceptionable testimony, and when able to say at what place the offence has been committed, institute fresh proceedings against them."

Senator Giles, for his part, was all for removing criminal cases from the jurisdiction of the Supreme Court! At all events, the administration's case

against Swartwout and Bollmann had failed. All
five of General Wilkinson's prisoners had been released. The Chief Justice of the United States, as
opposed to the Chief Magistrate, could not discover
that any act of treason had been committed. . . .

4

In the West, before ever the President's proclamation was issued, John Graham had been discovering
"that no serious impressions have been made unfriendly to the Union." From Pittsburgh—where a
certain José Vidal was preparing a boat for himself,
his wife and his children—Mr. Graham went down
to Marietta, and interviewed Mr. Blennerhassett.
He also visited General Neville, some people called
Henderson who were unfriendly to the Blennerhassetts, and the Morgans. From Chillicothe, on
November 28, he wrote to Mr. Madison that "at
this place they seem to know nothing of the plans of
Colonel Burr and I am rather induced to think that he
has no one at work for him here . . . for all is quiet."

But to Governor Tiffin of Ohio Mr. Graham had
told a different story. Mr. Blennerhassett had been
perfectly frank about the expedition to Bastrop's;
boats were building on the Muskingum; the Hender-
sons and the Morgans had contributed their versions;
and on December 2, Governor Tiffin was informing
the Legislature that he had it "from a gentleman of
great respectability, clothed by the United States
with a public character," that an expedition was
preparing on the Ohio for the purpose of seizing New
Orleans, and "finally to force or draw the people of
the western country to secede from the Union."

And on December 2, the President's proclamation was at Pittsburgh, and on its way to Marietta where it was distributed on December 12. On December 6, the Ohio Legislature passed an "Act to Prevent certain Acts hostile to the Peace and Tranquility of the United States;" the militia was called out, and posted along the river where it became the nightly sport of countless practical jokers; and on December 10, fifteen boats in various stages of completion, and two hundred barrels of provisions were seized on the Muskingum. As for Mr. Graham, he had gone on his leisurely way to Kentucky, in search of other Legislatures.

The militia was watching the river; that of Wood County which had already received the proclamation was watching Blennerhassett's Island from both banks, but still boats passed down the river. Mr. Vidal went floating by with his children on his sightseeing tour; and Comfort Tyler and Israel Smith came down with four boats and thirty-two colonists—settlers, Mr. Tyler called them—and stopped at the island. Mr. Blennerhassett was very much alarmed; he was expecting to be arrested; it was known that the Wood County militia were planning to invade the island; the whole place, on the evening of December 10, was in a turmoil of confused preparation and hasty departure. Fires were burning, lanterns waved back and forth, there was a carrying of stores and supplies, some of the men had pistols and fowling pieces. Being for the most part youthful, adventurous colonists, some of them were no doubt armed to the teeth; just as in 1848 whole companies of young men were to go parading across the continent, brist-

ling with weapons, without for that reason being suspected of any nefarious design against the commonwealth.

In the midst of it all, at about eleven o'clock in the
evening, General Tupper arrived to collect some
money owing to him by Mr. Blennerhassett and tried
to persuade him, and Mr. Tyler, to remain at the
island and face whatever civil prosecution might en-
sue. But Mr. Blennerhassett was afraid of the
militia, and did not wish to fall into the hands of
"such an ignorant enraged multitude." General
Tupper saw "two pair of pistols, a coarse sword or
cutlass, and . . . some of the persons wore dirks."
No guns were levelled at him, "nor any incivility
offered to him." After a while they all went down
to the river—the men, the General, a Mr. and Mrs.
McCastle who were there, and Mr. and Mrs. Blennerhassett. At the bottom of the bank there was a
"footway" of "rails" to the boats, and since it was
a very dark, rainy night and uncertain walking, Mrs.
Blennerhassett stopped at the footway to take leave
of her husband. General Tupper stood near her,
watching the people go aboard the boats by the light
of lanterns placed at that point, and he could not
detect "any warlike appearance in the assemblage."
To Mr. Blennerhassett he remarked that he hoped
he had "no idea of making any resistance in case
attempts shall be made to arrest you." No, Mr.
Blennerhassett replied, "certainly not . . . we shall
surrender ourselves to the civil authority whenever it
shall present itself; our object is both lawful and
honorable as respects the United States;" and Mr.
Tyler added that "if we were disposed to defend

ourselves, we are not in a situation to do it, having
but three or four or five guns, some pistols and dirks
on board;" however, they would defend themselves
as best they could against unauthorized attempts to
molest them. Mrs. Blennerhassett then said good-
bye to her husband, and returned with General
Tupper and Mr. and Mrs. McCastle to the house.
The next morning, December 11, the boats were gone.

So much for Mr. Wirt's subsequent portrayal of
the distracted Mrs. Blennerhassett—he did not mention Mrs. McCastle—"shivering at midnight, on the
winter banks of the Ohio and mingling her tears with
the torrents, that froze as they fell." The description of Mr. Blennerhassett's departure from the
island, with his boats and his men, as testified to by
Edward Tupper—a Brigadier General in the war of
1812 and a member of the Ohio Legislature in 1813—
is perhaps worth all the affidavits gathered from
gardeners, and boatmen, and such miscellaneous
gentry with regard to the incidents which occurred on
that evening. And the scene is one to be remembered, for it was on that night, and on that spot,
according to the Federal Government's charge, that
war was levied by Mr. Blennerhassett, on behalf of
Colonel Burr, against the United States. . . .

5

On the morning of December 11, Mrs. Blennerhassett went to Marietta to take possession of the
family boat in which she proposed to follow her husband. Soon after her departure, Colonel Phelps
landed on the island, and finding the Blennerhassett
estate deserted, set out with a part of his force over-

land to intercept the flotilla at the mouth of the Great
Kanawha. The sturdy volunteers of Wood County
having, however, succeeded in drinking themselves
to sleep, the Tyler boats slipped by unnoticed during
the night; on December 16 they joined Davis Floyd
at the Falls; and two days later they were at the
mouth of the Cumberland, waiting for Colonel Burr.

Meanwhile, a boatload of young Bastrop colonists
from Pittsburgh—fourteen youths led by Morgan
Neville—had been captured by the militia near the
mouth of the Little Kanawha, and taken to the island.
In the face of their protests, two justices of the peace
were summoned, and a trial begun which soon turned
into a comedy, during the course of which the soldiery
broke into the cellar. Upon her return from Marietta—at which place she had learned of the seizure
of the Muskingum boats—Mrs. Blennerhassett found
her house a wreck, curtains, pictures and mirrors
having been torn down and mutilated, bullets fired
into the walls and ceilings, everything trampled and
smashed. In the grounds, her shrubberies were destroyed, arbors had been pulled apart, and fences
and trellises ripped up to build fires. Here, at least,
an act of war had been committed, upon a defenceless
home, by a band of drunken stalwarts summoned to
defend their country against rebellion.

Colonel Phelps made such mortified apologies as
he could; Morgan Neville offered Mrs. Blennerhassett
a place in his boat; and on December 17 they were off
down the river, lashed alongside the barge belonging
to Aaron Putnam, the part owner of Blennerhassett's
Island. A few weeks later, they had joined the
Tyler flotilla. . . .

CHAPTER V

BAYOU PIERRE

I

COLONEL BURR himself was still at Nashville, late in December, completing his arrangements. General Adair had gone riding off to New Orleans; General Jackson had finally made up his mind that there was nothing illicit in the Colonel's projects. Indeed, at the time—whatever his previous intentions or his eventual hopes—Colonel Burr can have had nothing in mind but the Bastrop colony. The news of General Wilkinson's Sabine treaty with the Spaniards had already reached him; he was "sorry for it" and felt that the General should have fought the enemy; but, at all events, he understood that war with Spain was again postponed, he realized, undoubtedly, that General Wilkinson had withdrawn his interest in the Mexican venture, there was nothing that he could do, temporarily, except proceed with his colonization scheme.

After various delays, he set out, therefore, on December 22, to join Mr. Blennerhassett at the mouth of the Cumberland. He took with him some horses

and thirty colonists, one of whom was a nephew of
Mrs. Jackson; in the two boats which alone were completed out of the five ordered from General Jackson's
yard, receiving seventeen hundred and twenty-
five dollars from the General for the unfinished
barges.   On December 23, he was at the rendezvous,
greeted by his aides, Blennerhassett, Tyler and
Floyd, and being introduced to the young men who
comprised the expedition.   The Colonel shook hands
with all of them, and told them that such objects of
the undertaking as had not already been explained
would be imparted to them at a more opportune time.
In other words, almost all of them had been enlisted
to settle the Bastrop lands, and for no other purpose,
and it was useless to talk to them about Mexico for
the present.   There were perhaps sixty of them, all
told, and nine boats—comfortable vessels, roofed
over and divided into sleeping and living compart-
ments.   In the hold of each were stores and imple-
ments for the colony, some necessary arms and
ammunition, and one of the rafts carried horses.

Such was the imposing and dread inspiring armada
which finally got under way, down the river.   A
little later, poking its nose out of some convenient
creek, perhaps, the boat containing Mr. Vidal and
his children went floating by. . . .

2

Ahead of them, unknown to the argonauts, at the
end of their journey, lay a Mississippi Territory already preparing for their coming, warned by proclamation of December 23 from Cowles Meade against
a conspiracy "directed by men of profound intrigue,"

ANDREW JACKSON

After the painting by Wheeler.

of which Governor Claiborne had advised him. To say nothing of a province of West Florida arrayed to resist invasion, for at no time do the Spaniards appear to have had any doubts concerning the nature of Colonel Burr's designs. Behind them, they left a panic-stricken, rumor-infested countryside through which the President's proclamation was slowly sifting, to be followed not long after by the report of his messages to Congress. And no better proof can perhaps be found of the fact that Colonel Burr had not intended a forcible separation of the Western States than the expressed unwillingness of those States to be so separated. As soon as the President's charges against Colonel Burr became known, editorial after editorial, resolution after resolution voiced the loyalty to the Union of a profoundly shocked and outraged population. Ohio was in a turmoil, Kentucky was up in arms, Tennessee was in a fury.

Many conflicting opinions exist as to the date on which the proclamation reached Nashville. Some historians have stated that the document was public in that city as early as December 19, others insist that it arrived by courier on December 23, on which day Mr. Graham also is said to have made his unhurried appearance. Mr. Parton, the biographer of Burr and Jackson, has only increased the confusion by supporting both theories—that the proclamation reached Nashville on December 19 in his *Aaron Burr*, and that it came after Colonel Burr's departure in his *Andrew Jackson*. There can be no doubt that the document must have reached the capital of Tennessee only after Colonel Burr had gone. It could not conceivably have been kept secret for

three days, and the fact that upon its announcement
the citizens of Nashville burned Colonel Burr in
effigy is evidence of the spirit in which it was received.
That the commotion was due primarily to the efforts
of General Jackson's enemies—the adherents of that
Mr. Dickinson whom he had killed in a duel the
previous May—only fortifies the certainty that no
connivance on the General's part in suppressing the
proclamation would have been tolerated. Nor would
such connivance on his part have been possible, since
he held no office other than that of General in the
militia, so that the paper would not have come
first into his hands.

Nor is it in the least likely that General Jackson
would have been disposed to lend himself to such
connivance. His own nephew was a member of the
expedition; he had already once been prepared to
wash his hands of Colonel Burr; he had told Governor
Claiborne that "I love my country and Government
—I hate the Dons—I would delight to see Mexico reduced; but I will die in the last ditch before I would
yield a foot to the Dons or see the Union disunited;"
and now, on January 1—for his own War Department orders sent from Washington at the same time
as the proclamation only reached him on that date,
revealing the curious sluggishness with which these
important government dispatches were moving—he
called out the militia; he warned Fort Massac against
a warlike flotilla; and, to a personal friend, he wrote
on January 15 that "the late denunciation of Aaron
Burr as a traitor has excited great surprise and
general indignation against Burr. . . . Should you
ever hear that I am embarked in a cause inimical to

my country, believe it not. . . . And if Burr had any treasonable intentions in view, he is the basest of all human beings. I will tell you why. He always held out the idea of settling Washita, unless a war with Spain. . . . If he is a traitor, he is the basest that ever did commit treason, and being tore to pieces and scattered to the four winds of heaven would be too good for him."

But General Jackson was never to believe that Colonel Burr had intended treason; any more than was John Adair, who, in March, 1807, was writing that the Colonel's intentions had been to lead an expedition into Mexico, "predicated on a war between the two governments. . . . On this war . . . he calculated with certainty. . . . This continued to be the object of Colonel Burr until he heard of the venal and shameful bargain made by Wilkinson at the Sabine . . . he then turned his attention altogether towards strengthening himself on the Washita and waiting for a more favorable crisis." Such were the opinions of two of the most prominent citizens of that region, Andrew Jackson of Tennessee and John Adair of Kentucky; and, had they stood face to face with Colonel Burr on the Nashville waterfront, proclamation in hand, it is doubtful whether either would have found in that state paper any reason for preventing the Colonel's departure.

General Jackson was later, in an angry letter to a certain James Landers, to express himself quite forcibly on the subject of his relations with Colonel Burr. "I had a hope," he told Mr. Landers, "whenever it was necessary to address you, that it would

have been in the language of that true friendship
which I thought existed between us, and on [a] subject more agreeable than the present.   I did flatter
myself that whatever might have been the conduct
of base and unprincipled enemies, who have had me
buried and entombed, who have, with all the ingenuity cf falsehood, been digging a pit for me which
they themselves have fallen into, that I never should
have found you in the list of those, under the cover
of falsehood of the blackest dye, trying to infuse into
the public mind, at a time when our country appears
to be endangered, jealousies respecting me well calculated to abate that patriotism that . . . ought to
pervade the mind of every true American.   Yes Sir,
I have heard that you should have said 'that I might
be engaged in the treason of Col. Burr.'

"As you have expressed yourself that I am capable
of perjury, it behooves you to give testimony to the
world that I am that base charleton, or attone for
the injury thus done my character, by expressing
publicly that you have no ground for the slander thus
expressed of me, or hold yourself answerable to me for
the expression.   I love my friend, and . . . tried to
foster that friendship that ought to have existed
between us.   On my part it has never been departed
from, but, Sir, when such declarations made are from
you, who the world believes to be my friend and capable of truth, the injuries resulting from them are such
that attonement must and shall be made.   I have
but one life to lose; that I have risqued in behalf of
my reputation: I will again—and he that is of your
standing, that will attempt to deprive me of it, is at
their own peril.   For, by the gods, I never will per-

mit such an attempt to assassinate my reputation to go unpunished.

"I did extend that hospitality to Col. Burr that I would and ever will to a man that I think a man of honour who is banished from his country and his home; and from the pledges he made (after my suspicions requested) I did think him a persecuted man, and when he returned under the acquittal of a respectable grand jury, I thought him as innocent as his declarations and pledges made him, and as such I did treat him as an innocent and deserving citizen of the United States. However, Sir, if I have done anything contrary to the law of the United States, I am answerable to my government, not to individuals, and I hold individuals answerable to me for any injury founded on falsehood that they may promulgate. I shall suspend any decisive action on the information I have rec'd. until I receive your answer, but as it appears you took but little time to denounce my guilt, I shall expect a speedy answer."

One may not, however, ignore current rumors to the effect that General Jackson had been aware of the proclamation—aware of it not only before Colonel Burr's departure from Nashville, but even before any official copy of the document had reached the city. The story was known in Washington, and in January, 1807, Senator Plumer was writing that Senator Giles had told him that "as soon as the President issued his proclamation, a friend . . . of Burr's rode express with a copy and delivered it to him in Kentucky some days sooner than it arrived by mail. In four days after Burr received it he rode from Frankfort . . . over the

mountains to Nashville. . . . He immediately
called upon Jackson and showed him the proclamation, and assured him it was agreed between him and
the President that such a proclamation should be
issued—but that the President had committed an
error, and issued it sooner than the time prefixed.
Jackson was again completely duped."

It seems more likely that Senator Giles was being duped, but the suggestion of connivance between the President and Colonel Burr is not without
its interest, and opens up a vista of Executive duplicity and treachery upon which one's gaze hesitates
to dwell. For if Colonel Burr was expecting the
proclamation, and understood it as an international
utterance intended to blind the Spaniards to his
future plans, officials throughout the country were
not expecting it, nor were they in any way dissuaded
from taking it quite seriously. And it is a curious
thing how *slowly* the proclamation, and the War Department orders, travelled into that region which was
the scene of Colonel Burr's activities, and through
which he must pass on his way down the river. . . .

These matters will probably never be explained,
but that no official copy of the proclamation had
reached Nashville before the Colonel's departure on
Monday, December 22, seems incontestable. His
embarkation on that date, in "two large flat boats
which did not appear to be loaded," was duly noticed
by the *Impartial Review* on Saturday, December 27.
No mention was made of the receipt of any proclamation, which would surely have found its place in the
newspaper's columns had it been public knowledge.
Only a week later, on Saturday, January 3, 1807, did

the *Review* print the proclamation. It would seem, therefore, to have arrived during the week following Friday, December 26—undoubtedly on December 27, as recorded by the committee which investigated the matter in 1828, at the time of General Jackson's presidential campaign, and which also found that the burning of Colonel Burr in effigy had taken place on December 30.

And perhaps the reason for this delay was merely that stated by the *Review*, in its issue of December 20, in which it explained that "the late rains have prevented the arrival of the Kentucky and southern mails, and our eastern papers are no later than received by the preceeding mail." And perhaps that was the reason, also, for Mr. Graham's leisurely progress through the land—for, like the Federal mails, this dignitary was not hurrying. . . .

3

On December 29, the Burr flotilla anchored just below Fort Massac. Courtesies were exchanged with the commander, Captain Bissell, and one of his sergeants, the notorious Dunbaugh, was granted a furlough to accompany Colonel Burr. The boats floated on. On January 5, Captain Bissell received General Jackson's warning—the only warning that had yet reached him, since on that incomprehensibly late date neither the proclamation nor the War Department orders had arrived. There had been no unlawful assembling of men or boats, the Captain replied. Colonel Burr had "passed this way with about ten boats . . . navigated with about six men each, having nothing on board that would even suffer a conjecture more than that he was a man bound to market." That was all. Captain Bissell did not mention Mr. Vidal and his children. . . .

On New Year's Day the boats were at New Madrid, and on January 4 at Chickasaw Bluffs. Lieutenant Jackson, in command, had received no proclamation, he had received no War Department orders. For a while, indeed, he thought of joining Colonel Burr and his hundred settlers—for some additional recruits had been picked up here and there along the river. On January 10, the armada was at Bayou Pierre, near Natchez, in the Territory of Mississippi. Colonel Burr went ashore, to the home of his friend, Judge Bruin. Whether or not he was handed a recent copy of the *Moniteur* containing his cipher letter to General Wilkinson, the news which awaited him was appalling. Mississippi considered him a rebel, the whole Territory was aroused, General Wilkinson had turned against him. Colonel Burr went back to his boats; he shifted them to the west bank, out of the Territory's jurisdiction; he encamped himself and placed sentinels. One would like to know what thoughts passed through his stoic's mind, what bitterness of rage enveloped him, what bewilderment of spirit.

A great dismay seized upon the adventurers, upon these youths who were going to Bastrop's, and who now learned that they were rebels against the United States. A great dismay; but no abandonment of courage, of confidence in their leader. They had done nothing wrong. They would defend themselves if necessary. They were very young, most of them, very resolute, very loyal, deeply hurt. . . .

WILLIAM CLAIBORNE

After the miniature by A. Duval.

4

Colonel Burr immediately issued a public statement in which he invited his fellow citizens to visit
him and see for themselves what manner of expedition he was conducting; he wrote to Cowles Meade
denying the rumors against his patriotism, and assur-
ing the Acting Governor that his boats were merely
"the vehicles of immigration." However, he would
resist unlawful molestation. Mr. Meade, for his
part, summoned the militia, and "with the promptitude of Spartans" some four hundred of them gathered at Natchez "prepared to defend their country,"
and were sent up the river to block Colonel Burr's
boats in Cole's Creek. On January 16, District
Attorney Pointdexter and Major Shields visited the
desperado encampment and agreed in writing with
the Colonel—this formal "capitulation" was later to
be used against him by the Government as an admission of his rebellious status—that "an interview
shall take place between [Colonel Burr and the
Honorable Cowles Meade] at the house of Thomas
Calvit . . . at two o'clock tomorrow." Mr. Meade
pledged himself to protect Colonel Burr, there were
to be no restraint on his person and no violence to
his boats, or to his people who promised to keep the
peace.

On January 17, therefore, the Colonel met the
Acting Governor, and submitted voluntarily to the
civil authorities of Mississippi, while a committee
was appointed to search his boats for military arma-
ments, none of which were discovered. That pack-
ages of guns and ammunition had previously been

sunk in the river was to be the subsequent testimony of Sergeant Dunbaugh—and it would perhaps be necessary to respect his affidavit, had it not been made at the instance of General Wilkinson, at a time when the sergeant was negotiating a pardon for the military crime of desertion, he having forgotten to return to his Captain Bissell to whom he eventually confessed that "with sorrow I take Pen in hand to inform you that I had to tell the officers that you sent me as a spy against Colonel Burr and had to make outt what I new againg him."

The boats moved down toward Natchez; the Colonel, accompanied by Major Shields and Mr. Pointdexter, went to Washington, the capital of the Territory, where Judge Rodney held him for the Grand Jury on five thousand dollars bail furnished by Lyman Harding and Colonel Osmun, old army friends. Colonel Burr was invited to Colonel Osmun's bachelor home at Windy Hill Manor, and with him, and Major Isaac Guion, an old Quebec comrade, "and other influential gentlemen, he had daily consultations. No sterner and truer patriots lived than these two veteran soldiers, and they reposed unshaken faith in [Burr]." As for the dreaded expedition, "this mighty alarm," Cowles Meade notified the Government, "with all its exaggerations, has eventuated in nine boats and one hundred men, and the major part of these are boys, or young men just from school. . . . They bespeak ignorance of the . . . designs of the Colonel . . . I believe that they are really the dupes of stratagem, if the asseverations of Generals Eaton and Wilkinson are to be accredited."

And Mr. Vidal was not impressed, after all his trouble. He had followed the expedition night and day, and what? It "resolves itself into nothing," he informed the Marquis Yrujo.

5

On February 2, the Supreme Territorial Court convened, and Colonel Burr appeared before Judges Bruin and Rodney.

To Judge Adams, who saw him then, he seemed "a man of an erect and dignified deportment—his presence is commanding—his aspect mild, firm, luminous and impressive. . . . The eyebrows are thin, nearly horizontal, and too far from the eye; his nose is . . . rather inclined to the right side; gently elevated which betrays a degree of haughtiness; too obtuse at the end for a great acuteness of penetration, brilliancy of wit or poignancy of satire, and too small to sustain his capacious and ample forehead. His eyes are . . . of a dark hazel, and, from the shade of his projecting eye bones and brows, appear black; they glow . . . and scintillate with the most tremulous and tearful sensibility—they roll with the celerity and phrensy of poetic fervour, and beam with the most vivid and piercing rays of genius. His mouth is large; his voice is clear, manly and melodious; his lips are thin, extremely flexible, and when silent, gently closed. . . . His chin is rather retreating and voluptuous. . . .

"In company, Burr is rather taciturn; when he speaks, it is with such animation, with such apparent frankness and negligence as would induce a person to believe that he was a man of guileless and ingenuous

heart; but in my opinion there is no human more reserved, mysterious and inscrutable. . . .   But alas
. . . Burr is an exemplary . . . instance of the
capriciousness of popular admiration, and the muta-
bility of human glory and felicity. . . .   The circumstance that has thus contributed to blast the
popularity and poison the peace and happiness of
this unfortunate man is lamentable indeed; but he
who will presume to ascribe it to a corruption or a
depravity of heart rather than the falibility of man,
and the frailty of human passions, must be blinded by
his own venom. . . . Yes . . . even Burr, the
inimitable, incomparable Burr, is disturbed, is un-
happy! Often did I mark the perturbation of his
mind, the agonizing sensations which rung his too
susceptible heart, and which . . . wrote themselves
in the darkest shades on his countenance; and when I
beheld the melancholy, the saturnine clouds which
often enveloped his bleeding, his magnanimous soul,
my feelings were melted with a thrilling, a sublime
sympathy. . . ."

One begins to appreciate the quality and degree of
fascination which Colonel Burr could exercise upon
his contemporaries; the attraction which caused so
many men to follow when he beckoned. . . .

6

It was the belief of the District Attorney that the
court had no jurisdiction over the case, but the Grand
Jury was instructed to proceed. On February 3,
the jury reported itself convinced that "Aaron Burr
has not been guilty of any crime or misdemeanor
against the laws of the United States or of this

Territory." On the other hand, the jury presented "as a grievance, the late military expedition . . . against . . . Aaron Burr;" it presented, as a further grievance, "the late military arrests made without warrant;" and it seriously regretted occurrences which "must sap the vitals of our political existence and crumble this glorious fabric into the dust."

The verdict was not without a certain humor, after all the uproar of treason which had prevailed in Mississippi. Almost everybody must have.laughed, except perhaps Mr. Graham who had come sauntering in a few days before, and Governor Williams who had just returned bristling with hostility to the accused. A banquet and ball were given to the Colonel. But on February 4, when he asked to be released from bail and discharged, Judge Rodney, for reasons best known to himself, refused to do so, and bound him over to appear daily in court. The Colonel must have realized then that he was in a desperate situation. A grand jury's verdict had been ignored by the civil judge; the Governor had announced his intention of seizing him at the first opportunity; attempts were being planned on his person, if not his life, by General Wilkinson who of course knew of his presence in Mississippi. Indeed, it was later to appear that the General had sent various officers in disguise, on different occasions, to kidnap the man he had betrayed. To Silas Dinsmore, he had promised five thousand dollars if he "cut off" Burr and Dayton. Lieutenant Peter testified that he had reached Natchez on February 2 with a party of five, "dressed in citizens clothing" and "armed with dirks and pistolls;" that they were acting under orders from

General Wilkinson "to seize Colonel Burr . . . and to return to New Orleans;" that there were no warrants from any civil authority to his knowledge; that the orders "did not specify any charge or crime against Colonel Burr;" that if the Colonel had resisted arrest "we certainly should have used our arms;" and that Governor Williams was cooperating with them. Colonel Burr knew himself to be between the military devil at New Orleans and the deep sea of civil persecution.

All his friends were of the same opinion, and urged him to conceal himself. On February 5, therefore, he did not appear in court; on February 6, Governor Williams proclaimed him a fugitive and offered a reward of two thousand dollars for his capture. Colonel Burr, writing from his hiding place which can not have been far distant, notified the Governor that he was ready to submit himself whenever his citizen's rights should be guaranteed, and again, on February 12, reminded him that he was only bound by law to appear if an indictment should have been found against him. The Governor replied that "from the judicial proceedings in this Territory you cannot be considered in any other light than as a fugitive from the laws of your country."

Colonel Burr knew what to expect now. A court-martial by General Wilkinson, the outcome of which would never have been in doubt, or seizure by the Governor of Mississippi, with perhaps the same result. In secret, he visited his boats and took leave of his men. They must keep the barges and go on to Bastrop's and settle there, or else sell them and divide the money. As for him, he had been tried and acquitted, but they were going to take him again, and "he was going to flee from oppression." The men did as he advised; many of them "dispersed themselves through the territory and supplied it with school masters, singing masters, dancing masters, clerks, tavern keepers and doctors"—so Mr. Claiborne, the historian of Mississippi, lists the professions. Pathetic young men. As the result of a spurious note alleged to have been addressed to them by the Colonel after his final disappearance—although clumsily enough the date given was on a day prior to the convening of the Grand Jury—some of them were arrested at Natchez; but they were soon released, with the exception of Mr. Blennerhassett, Mr. Tyler, Mr. Floyd and a Mr. Ralston. These were held for trial, but in April they were in turn released, for good, as they no doubt imagined. To the very end, most of them had not the slightest idea what it was all about. . . .

7

Colonel Burr returned to Windy Hill Manor; one of Colonel Osmun's best horses was waiting for him, and a friend, Chester Ashley, who was to go with him. They were bound for the coast, where the Colonel probably hoped to take ship. He was in disguise, "in a shabby suit of homespun with an old white hat flapped over his face," according to John Randolph who heard about it later.

They started, in the night, but the Colonel had to stop, wasting the precious moments, almost until daylight. At the door of Madeline Price's cottage at Half Way Hill, not far from Major Guion's, begging

her to follow him. One does not hesitate to record
the tradition of a whole countryside, vouched for
by Mr. Claiborne himself. It was a vine-covered
cottage, it seems, the residence of a once well-to-do
widow; and her daughter, Madeline, was "a miracle
of beauty, all that the old masters have pictured the
divine Madonna." In the midst of all his troubles,
the Colonel had found time to fall in love with her
and "the maiden had given him her heart." He
implored her, on that last night, to be his wife, to
accompany him on his desperate journey, but she
refused. He was "compelled to proceed, but promised to return, and carried with him the covenant
and pledge of the beautiful Madeline. . . . Fortunes and the homage of devoted hearts were laid
at her feet; but the Maid of Half Way Hill remained
true to her absent lover." But he never returned,
and finally he wrote, releasing her from her promise;
and in time she married, and departed from the
cottage.

Madeline, the Maid of Half Way Hill. . . .

8

It was hard going through the woods, the streams
were swollen, and they lost their way. Late on the
night of February 18, they stopped at a house in
Wakefield, Washington County—now in Alabama—
to ask the road to Colonel Hinson's, to whom the
man in the white hat had a letter of introduction. A
very tall gentleman called Nicholas Perkins, a lawyer
of that place, saw the eyes under the flapping white
brim. And just as in the Argonne, on their flight to
Varennes, Louis XVI and Marie Antoinette found

the busybody Drouet to recognize them and gallop across county to intercept them at the next stage, so at Wakefield Colonel Burr found Nicholas Perkins.

Mr. Perkins summoned the Sheriff, Theodore Brightwell, and perhaps reminded him of the Governor's two thousand dollar reward of which he was aware. At all events, these two citizens followed after the riders, and overtook them at Colonel Hinson's eight miles away. The Colonel was not at home, but Mrs. Hinson was serving supper to the travellers. The Sheriff went in, but after a long while the Sheriff did not come out, and the crafty Mr. Perkins cantered off through the rain to Fort Stoddert, where he told his story to Lieutenant Gaines. A man in a white hat who looked like Aaron Burr was at Colonel Hinson's, and the Sheriff was not doing his duty. He, Nicholas Perkins, had done his duty. The Lieutenant, who had received the proclamations from New Orleans and from the President, proceeded to do what he conceived to be his.

Early the next morning, on February 19, he took a file of soldiers and rode back with Mr. Perkins towards Colonel Hinson's. Some four miles from the house they met three horsemen—Mr. Ashley, the man in the white hat and the Sheriff who was quite evidently acting as their guide, having been, it seemed, completely won over by the fugitives. In the name of the United States Government, Lieutenant Gaines demanded, was this Aaron Burr? The man in the white hat replied that he had no right to question him, but he finally admitted his identity. He was immediately placed under arrest, on the authority of the presidential proclamation which did not mention Aaron Burr by name, and which was not directed against gentlemen riding quietly through the woods. Mr. Ashley and the Sheriff were not molested, and the cavalcade returned to Fort Stoddert.

"I was arrested a few days since," Colonel Burr wrote Charles Biddle, on February 22, "by a party of the United States troops. . . . This proceeding is the more extraordinary as the grand jury . . . acquitted me in the completest manner of all unlawful practices or designs. The report of this grand jury also censured the conduct of the government . . . and for this reason I am told that the printers have not thought it discreet to publish that report entire. The pretence of having forfeited a recognizance, though sanctioned by the proclamation of the Governor, is utterly false. The details of the prosecutions against me cannot be given—they are beyond all example and in defiance of all law. . . . What I write must be inspected by an officer of the guard."

And Captain Gaines—he had been promoted on February 28—was not so sure about his military arrest now. The people along the Tombigbee were criticizing his action, and protesting to the Government; and it was feared at the fort that Mr. Ashley would raise the countryside and effect a rescue. "They will assuredly find the inhabitants such as they could wish . . ." the Captain reported to General Wilkinson on March 4. "The plans of Burr are now spoken of in terms of approbation, and Burr in terms of sympathy and regard. I am convinced if Burr had remained here a week longer the consequences would have been of the most serious nature.

AARON BURR

From the original portrait by Vanderlyn in the possession of Walter Jennings, Esq.

Burr frequently . . . observed 'And yet my great offence and the only one laid to my charge was a design to give you the Floridas.'"

But Mr. Perkins had no misgivings.

9

And on March 5, 1807, Captain Gaines turned Colonel Burr over to Mr. Perkins—the zealous Mr. Perkins—for conveyance to Washington with an escort of nine soldiers. They went by boat to a point above Lake Tensau; there Perkins harangued his men, warning them against the wiles of the prisoner, and then they were off on horseback on their long, arduous journey, riding all day through torrents of rain, and sleeping on the ground in their soaking clothes. The man in the white hat—he was still in his disguise—never complained at the burden placed upon his fifty-one years. Only once did he show any emotion. They were passing through Chester, in South Carolina, and he jumped from his horse, crying to a group of bystanders that he was Aaron Burr, and claiming the protection of the civil authorities. But Mr. Perkins—the gigantic Mr. Perkins—seized him in his arms and put him back in the saddle. And for a while there were tears in the little Colonel's eyes. . . .

At Fredericksburg, in Virginia, Mr. Perkins received orders to proceed to Richmond. On March 23, they passed by John Randolph's door, at Bizarre. "So I am told," he wrote to Mr. Nicholson, "for I did not see him. . . . The soldiers escorting him (it seems) indulged his aversion to be publicly known and . . . he was accoutred in a shabby suit of homespun, with an old white hat flapped over his face (the dress in which he was apprehended). . . . His very manner of travelling, although under arrest, was characteristic of the man—enveloped in mystery —and should he be hanged for treason, I dare say he will . . . contrive to make posterity doubt whether he was actually executed. . . ." And on March 26 they had arrived, and Colonel Burr told Theodosia that "it seems that here the business is to be tried and concluded. I am to be surrendered to the civil authority tomorrow [March 28] when the question of bail is to be determined. In the meantime I remain at the Eagle Tavern." The first thing that he did was to change into very elegant clothes.

And Mr. Perkins went to Washington to receive the thanks of the President, and three thousand three hundred and thirty-one dollars. . . .

PART VIII

The Prisoner

1807–1808

"Weighing the whole of this testimony, it appears to me to preponderate in favor of the opinion that the enterprise was really designed against Mexico."

JOHN MARSHALL.

CHAPTER I

ARRAIGNMENT

I

THE news of Colonel Burr's arrival at Bayou Pierre was known in Congress on February 19, 1807. On February 27, the Cabinet decided to "discharge all the militia . . . from the mouth of the Cumberland upwards; to give up all boats and provisions seized, except Blennerhassett's . . . to institute an enquiry into the proceedings of Burr and his adherents from New York to New Orleans; and particularly to appoint good men . . . to take affidavits—the Attorney General to prepare the interrogatories." In due course, it was announced that the traitor had been captured.

The great conspiracy had collapsed. "I congratulate you, sir," the priceless General Wilkinson was writing to the President, "with my whole soul on the issue which the nefarious project has taken." How inspiring, he thought, had been the patriotism of the West and of Louisiana—those regions which, a few months before, he had seen ripe for rebellion. But there was always danger of a survival of activity against Spain—this subject, at least, could still be harped upon—and strong measures must be maintained. And "when the tempest has passed away," the General hoped that he would "not be left alone to buffet a combination of bar and bench." Mr. Jefferson must protect his General; and since the only way in which this could be done—in fact, since the only way in which Mr. Jefferson could save his own face after his loud proclamations of treason—was to bring about the condemnation of Colonel Burr, the entire machinery of government was set in motion with that end in view; public funds were expended without appropriation; a swarm of agents overran the country, gathering affidavits and answers to the Federal questionnaires; the President himself devoted his unremitting personal attention, the greater part of his time and the most brilliant ingenuities of his inventive mind to the consolidation of the case of the United States against Aaron Burr.

2

From the very first, it was inevitable that this trial should resolve itself into a political contest between Federalists and Republicans; into an arraignment of General Wilkinson and his protector. The prisoner at the bar of justice was Aaron Burr; the reputation at stake before the bar of public opinion that of Thomas Jefferson. Aaron Burr must be convicted or the President must emerge discredited and utterly ridiculous. The issue was never for a moment ignored at Washington; Mr. Jefferson's personal prosecution of Colonel Burr never at any

time to be denied. Other gentlemen were indicted
—Jonathan Dayton, Senator Smith, Comfort Tyler,
Davis Floyd, Israel Smith and Harman Blennerhassett—and all but the first two arrested, but it was
against Aaron Burr that the Government's utmost
effort was put forward, propelled by the tireless per-
sistence of the presidential hands.

It was the irony of circumstance, therefore, that
the case should have come before John Marshall,
within the jurisdiction of whose Virginia circuit
the act of war alleged by the Government had
taken place. John Marshall, the Federalist Chief
Justice whom Mr. Jefferson so feared and hated,
and who himself so despised the President. It was,
on the other hand—if the protection of the individual against governmental persecution is of any import to the community—a matter of public good fortune that the cause was tried before so impartial, so
wise and so fearless a judge; one whose sole concern
was the preservation of the Constitution, the maintenance of Law, the recording of evidence and
truth as opposed to rumor and perjury, and the
solemn dispensing of Justice.

Colonel Burr was charged with misdemeanor in
preparing an expedition against Mexico; and with
"traitorous compassings, imaginations and intentions," in that, on December 10, 1806, at Blennerhassett's Island, he had "falsely and traitorously"
joined and assembled "with a great multitude of
persons . . . to the number of thirty . . . and
upwards, armed and arrayed in a warlike manner,"
and "most wickedly, maliciously and traitorously"
ordained, prepared and levied war against the

United States. And in the presence of this document, as one stands at the door of the Eagle Tavern
at Richmond, in March, 1807—and in the presence of whatever other documents it may have
seemed profitable to Mr. Jefferson from time to time
to compose—one must never lose sight of his letter
of April 2, 1807, to Mr. Bowdoin at Madrid, in
which he explained that "no better proof of the good
faith of the United States [towards Spain] could have
been given than the vigor with which we acted . . .
in suppressing the enterprise meditated lately by
Burr against Mexico, *although*"—the italics are
not his—"*at first he proposed a separation of the
western country* . . . yet he very early saw"—
how long had Mr. Jefferson known that—"that the
fidelity of the western country was not to be shaken
and turned himself wholly toward Mexico. . . ."

How regrettable it is that this astonishing confession could not have been produced in court,
during the trial of Aaron Burr for accomplished
treason. How shameful it is, that such a trial should
ever have taken place. . . .

3

It is not intended, in these pages, to reproduce in
any detail the legal proceedings of the trial. The
endless arguments of counsel, the granting and denying of motions, the examination of witnesses and all
the intricacies of law involved are available in the
published records, and have been examined and
set forth in a number of volumes, not the least important of which is Mr. Beveridge's *Life of John
Marshall*. It is sufficient to remember that, having

JOHN MARSHALL

After the painting by J. Paul.

charged a levying of war, it was incumbent upon the
Government to prove that war had in fact been
levied, at the time, and in the place, and by the
persons alleged. And that, until evidence of such
"overt act" had been established, corroborative
testimony was out of order. . . .

On March 30, 1807, Colonel Burr was arraigned
before the Chief Justice, in a "retired" room at
the Eagle Tavern, and United States District Attorney Hay moved his commitment to jail on charges
of treason and misdemeanor, as set forth in the
record of the prosecution against Swartwout and
Bollmann. Mr. Perkins made the most of the opportunity allotted to him for the recital of the capture. Mr. Marshall then adjourned the hearing to
the Capitol, on the following day, and released the
prisoner on five thousand dollar bail. On March
31, adjournment had immediately to be made to
the hall of the House of Delegates, owing to the
enormous crowd of spectators, accommodation for
as many as possible of whom was insisted upon by
Mr. Hay. There followed hours of debate on the
motion to commit, in which Colonel Burr took a
leading part—emphasizing the conjectural nature of
the Government's accusations, and the astounding
irregularity of its recent conduct towards him—and
on April 1 Mr. Marshall delivered the first of his
celebrated opinions.

General Eaton's deposition, he stated, was merely
introductory to General Wilkinson's affidavit. Exclude from the latter the cipher letter of Colonel
Burr, "and nothing remains in the testimony which
can in the most remote degree affect Colonel Burr."

However, "I could not in this stage of the prosecution absolutely discredit the affidavit." There must, however—he had previously pointed out—be "a probable cause to believe there is guilt," nor was it the purpose of opinions quoted from Judge Blackstone to permit "the hand of malignity" to "grasp any individual against whom its hate may be directed or whom it may capriciously seize, charge him with some secret crime, and put him on the proof of his innocence"—and Mr. Marshall's gentle voice was meant to carry as far as Monticello if necessary.

Now "the fact to be proved in this case is an act of public notoriety. It must exist in the view of the world or it cannot exist at all. . . . It is therefore capable of proof. . . . Several months have elapsed since this fact did occur, if it ever occurred . . . why is it not proved?" Why had not the Government procured the necessary affidavits? From December until April was time enough. "I cannot doubt that means to obtain information have been taken . . . if it existed, I cannot doubt the practicability of obtaining it; and its non-production at this late hour does not . . . leave me at liberty to give to those suspicions which grow out of other circumstances that weight to which at an earlier day they might have been entitled. I shall not therefore insert in the commitment the charge of high treason."

Only that of misdemeanor. Bail was fixed at ten thousand dollars, and five sureties found—although few gentlemen were willing to come forward on the prisoner's behalf, so inflamed against him was public opinion—and the case was set for the next circuit

court for the District of Virginia, beginning on
May 22.

4

Mr. Jefferson was furious. The failure to commit Colonel Burr for treason was a resounding
blow to the prosecution, and the Chief Justice was
to blame. "The nation will judge both [Burr] and
the judges for themselves," the President wrote Senator Giles. "If a member of the Executive or the
Legislature does wrong, the day is never far distant
when the people will remove him. They will see
then and amend the error in our Constitution which
makes any branch independent of the nation. . . .
If their protection of Burr produces this amendment, it will do more good than his condemnation
. . . and if his punishment can be commuted now
for a useful amendment of the Constitution, I shall
rejoice in it." So, if Colonel Burr was not convicted,
perhaps the judge who tried the case would be removed. Now John Marshall himself was on trial,
as well as Mr. Jefferson and General Wilkinson.
And—one was almost forgetting—Colonel Burr. . . .

At Richmond, the Colonel was extremely busy.
Theodosia, for one, was in despair, and must be
written to. Some of her letters, he told her, indi-
cated "a sort of stupor;" she must "come back to
reason;" she must "amuse" herself collecting instances of virtuous men subjected to "vindictive
and relentless persecution," and write him an essay
with "reflections, comments and applications." Extraordinary man, to think of essays at such a time.

Then there were his lawyers. The Government

was to be represented by George Hay, acting as substitute for Attorney General Rodney—a little nervous, a little inadequate for his task; by Alexander McRae, Lieutenant Governor of Virginia, sour, belligerent and sarcastic; and by the fascinating, flowery, youthful William Wirt. To these Colonel Burr decided to oppose a peculiarly distinguished group of attorneys. For dignity and weight—he was even a trifle ponderous in argument—an ex-Secretary of State and Governor of Virginia, Edmund Randolph; for his acquaintance with jurymen, John Baker, "a lame man with a crutch, a merry fellow with plenty of horse wit and an infectious laugh, no speaker and no lawyer, but the best of good fellows;" for ridicule and satire, young Benjamin Botts; for his knowledge of the case acquired in the defense of Swartwout and Bollmann, an ex-United States Attorney General, Charles Lee; and "for a genius quick and fertile, a style pure and classic, a . . . beautiful elocution, an ingenuity which no difficulties can entangle . . . and a wit whose vivid and brilliant corruscation can guild and decorate the darkest subject"—the great John Wickham of Richmond. And Luther Martin was yet to come.

5

They set to work preparing their case; Colonel Burr went to Washington and asked for copies of the War and Navy Department orders concerning him, and of General Wilkinson's letter of October 21 to the President, all of which were refused him; the Grand Jury was summoned—"twenty democrats and four Federalists," the Colonel told Theodosia. Among them Mr. Nicholas, his bitterest personal enemy. "The most indefatigable industry is used by the agents of government, and they have money at command without stint. If I were possessed of the same means, I could not only foil the prosecutors, but render them ridiculous and infamous. The democratic papers teem with abuse of me and my counsel, and even against the Chief Justice. Nothing is left undone or unsaid which can tend to prejudice the public mind, and produce a conviction without evidence. . . . Machinations . . . are practised against me . . . not only with impunity but with applause; and the authors and abettors suppose, with reason, that they are acquiring favour with the administration."

And Senator Giles—he was a member of the Grand Jury—was urging Mr. Jefferson to bestir himself; any lack of evidence "would implicate the character of the administration." And Mr. Jefferson was writing back that witnesses would be produced who would "satisfy the world if not the judges;" and asking if "the bundle of letters . . . in Mr. Rodney's hands, the letters and facts published in the local newspapers, Burr's flight and the universal belief or rumor of his guilt" were not "probable ground for presuming the facts . . . so as to put him on trial?" Probable ground for presuming the facts of Colonel Burr's guilt—then it was no longer "placed beyond question," after weeks of the most painstaking research?

And in Richmond Colonel Burr was giving dinners, attended by all the elegant world of Federalist society. Superb dinners, "abounding in all the luxuries in which Virginia's generous soil yields in lavish abundance." Magnificent dinners at some of which "twenty ladies and gentlemen of rank, fortune and fashion graced the festive board," while the Colonel's "fascinating flatteries were lavished indiscriminately on the sex in general." And the lawyers were giving dinners—these legal banquets were a feature of Richmond life—and finally Mr. Wickham gave a dinner to which he invited his friend and neighbor John Marshall, forgetful of the fact that he had also invited Colonel Burr. And so the two of them "feasted" together "at the same convivial board," in the words of a Republican press roaring its condemnation of this "treason rejoicing dinner." As John Randolph was writing to Mr. Monroe, "the federalists have quenched the last ray of hope by their inconsistent and unprincipled support of Burr."

But on May 22, John Marshall was not thinking of the dinner any more, as he settled his long, loose-jointed frame into a seat on the bench beside Judge Griffin. . . .

CHAPTER II

A TRUE BILL

I

RICHMOND was packed, the court was jammed, the weather was sweltering. Thousands of persons, come from all over the country, were sleeping in tents, or in the wagons in which they had travelled, encamped along the river bank and on the hillsides. In the town, great throngs streamed up and down the Brick Row, elbowing each other in and out of tavern doors; up on the hill, hundreds waited for news on the green, while other hundreds fought and squeezed their way into the Hall, to stand on the window ledges, or on the big lock of the front door like young Winfield Scott, in order to catch a glimpse of the Chief Justice, of the great lawyers, of that celebrated Virginia jury, and of the quiet, dignified little gentleman in black silk and powdered hair. A great mob of men, sweating, smoking, spitting into the square sand boxes or wherever convenience might dictate; gentlemen in stocks and ruffled linen, in buckled breeches and silken queues; backwoodsmen, farmers, mountaineers, frontiersmen, in long hair, and deerskin coats, and red woolen shirts; almost all of them Republicans come to see a traitor convicted, aggressively partisan, inflamed by a screaming official press, bitterly hostile to the accused, clamorous and menacing. . . .

As soon as the court had been formally opened, at half past twelve, May 22, Colonel Burr objected to certain irregularities in the Grand Jury. The Marshal had excused two gentlemen and substituted two others, contrary to law. They were ordered removed. Colonel Burr then claimed a right to challenge the jury "for favour," and the point was finally conceded by Mr. Hay. Colonel Burr challenged Senator Giles and Mr. Nicholas, as having expressed views hostile to him. They were, as everyone knew, numbered among Mr. Jefferson's closest and most trusted adherents. After considerable discussion these gentlemen were permitted to withdraw; Doctor Foushee was excused; new jurymen were called, and, in spite of the fact that the majority of the gentlemen were notoriously prejudiced against the accused, Colonel Burr pronounced himself satisfied, since "the industry which has been used through this country to prejudice my cause leaves me very little chance indeed of an impartial jury."

The jury, as finally sworn, was perhaps one of the most distinguished ever assembled in America, a future Secretary of War, several Senators and three Governors-to-be of Virginia appearing upon its roster. John Randolph of Roanoke was appointed foreman; and if his known enmity for Mr. Jefferson might have given to his selection by Mr.

JOHN RANDOLPH

Marshall the semblance of partiality, he had also admitted in court that he was strongly prepossessed concerning Colonel Burr's guilt, and had asked to be excused.

2

The battle of motions and adjournments began, while the court waited for the arrival of General Wilkinson from New Orleans. John Randolph wrote to Mr. Monroe that Andrew Jackson—he had been summoned as a Government witness—did not scruple to say "that W. is a pensioner of Spain . . . and that he will not dare to show his face here"—although in the taverns they were betting that Colonel Burr would decamp as soon as the General came. Andrew Jackson was in Richmond —but he had not changed his mind about Colonel Burr. On the contrary, he was spending his time in violent harangues to the crowd on the State House green, in which he proclaimed the Colonel's innocence and denounced Mr. Jefferson's "political persecution." People hardly knew what to make of this fiery, uncouth frontiersman, with his hair all over his face and his queue tied in an eel skin; but his eloquence was having an effect, and the Government which had brought him east to testify was wishing him back in Tennessee again. As for the jury, they were dismissed early in June for several days, so that "they might go home, see their wives, get their clothes washed and flog their negroes"— according to a young man called Washington Irving who was reporting the trial for a New York newspaper.

In the meantime, the lawyers were at it. Mr. Hay moved once more to commit Colonel Burr for treason. Mr. Marshall entertained the motion, but concurred in the contention of the defense that the only testimony admissible was such as tended to prove an *overt* act of war. General Wilkinson's affidavit, for instance, contained no such proof. An affidavit of Sergeant Dunbaugh's was rejected for lack of proper certification. Mr. Hay was getting nowhere—his letters to Mr. Jefferson were filled with complaint—and he contented himself with securing an additional ten thousand dollars' bail, provided by four courageous gentlemen—extremely courageous, since the Chief Justice was of the opinion that even the jury itself would be in danger if an indictment was not returned.

And the Colonel's lawyers began to thunder against the Government and the whole course of its irregular procedure towards their client. "Six months ago," Colonel Burr himself reminded everyone, "he [the President] proclaimed that there was a civil war. And yet, for six months they have been hunting for it and cannot find one spot where it existed. There was, to be sure, a most terrible war in the newspapers, but nowhere else." In the newspapers, which printed the Government's affidavits secured by compulsory process, so that the Grand Jury might read them!

The defense had decided upon its campaign. It must attack the Government at every turn, and arouse in the public mind a revulsion against oppression and military tyranny, in order to counteract the carefully fostered popular hatred of Colonel

Burr. Just as the prosecution was doing its best to keep the country inflamed, and addressing two thirds of its speeches to the audience rather than to the judges—how difficult it is to remember that Judge Griffin was always present—so Mr. Botts, and Mr. Randolph, and Mr. Wickham were doing the same. And Mr. Martin, when he came voluntarily, out of friendship for Colonel Burr, on May 28; florid, convivial, pugnacious Luther Martin, "the rear guard of Burr's forensic army," a perfect mine of law, whose tongue was a sledge hammer and his voice a trumpet.

3

Mr. Hay was very worried, and kept asking his chief for orders, and while Mr. Jefferson was careful to assure people that any interference on his part in judicial proceedings would expose him to just censure, his countless letters to the District Attorney were garrulous with instructions. What to do with the testimony, how to circumvent the Chief Justice, why a previous opinion of Mr. Marshall's was in the President's estimation contrary to law. And what to do with the pardons. "Blank pardons are sent on," he had advised Mr. Hay, on May 20, already, "to be filled up at your discretion, if you should find a defect of evidence, and believe that this would supply it, avoiding to give them to the gross offenders unless it is visible that the principal will otherwise escape."

But Colonel De Pestre, for instance, was not a gross offender, and agents of the Government were offering to provide "handsomely" for him in the

army "if his principles . . . were not averse to
the administration." And Erich Bollmann was
not a gross offender. After his release in Washington, Doctor Bollmann had called upon Mr. Jefferson,
in the presence of Mr. Madison, and endeavored
to enlist his support for Colonel Burr's Mexican
expedition—the only project, Doctor Bollmann assured them, which the Colonel had in mind. Mr.
Jefferson had asked for his statements in writing,
after giving him "his word of honour that they
should never be used against himself and that the
paper shall never go out of his [the President's]
hands." But now the paper was in Mr. Hay's hands,
so that "you may know how to examine [Bollmann]
and draw everything from him;" and if the witness
should prevaricate, "ask him whether he did not
say so and so to Mr. Madison and myself." And in
order further to persuade his testimony, Mr. Madison was forwarding a pardon for him, "which we
mean should be delivered previously."

And when the time came to send Doctor Bollmann
before the Grand Jury—along with General Eaton,
and Commodore Truxtun, and the other witnesses—
Mr. Hay repeatedly offered him his pardon in open
court, only to have it invariably refused. "Cate-
gorically then I ask you, Mr. Bollmann," the District Attorney finally enquired. "Do you accept
this pardon?" And Doctor Bollmann replied that
"I have already answered that question several
times. I say no. I repeat that I would have refused
it before [prior to his appearance in court, when
the document had originally been thrust upon him]
but that I wished this opportunity of publicly de-

claring it." And the fearless Doctor Bollmann went
unpardoned and defiant to the jury.

In the midst of these unlovely manipulations,
Colonel Burr appeared day after day, calm, dignified,
restrained; impressive in his exact interpretations of
the law, in his lucid, dispassionate and frugal expo-
sitions. Only once, perhaps, at the very outset of
the trial, did he lose the self control which was to
render him so admirably conspicuous. He must
remember, Mr. Hay had remarked, that he stood
on the same footing as any other man charged
with crime. "Would to God," the Colonel exclaimed, "that I did stand on the same ground with
every other man. . . . How have I been brought
hither?"

4

And on June 11, General Wilkinson had not yet
arrived, but Colonel Burr had a matter to present
to the attention of the court. Copies of certain documents at Washington—military and naval orders,
and a letter of General Wilkinson's of October 21
to the President—had been denied him. These he
considered essential to his defense; the orders in
question, which had been published in the papers,
contained instructions to "destroy" his person as
well as his property; consequently Colonel Burr
felt it necessary to call upon the Court to issue a
subpoena to the President, "with a clause requiring him to produce certain papers; or in other
words, to issue the subpoena *duces tecum*." The
President must appear in person.

It was a petard for the prosecution. The President could not be ordered about that way, Mr. Hay insisted. Mr. Martin got going. The President had "let slip the dogs of war, the hell hounds of persecution;" would this President "who has raised all this absurd clamor" pretend to refuse papers which might be necessary to save a man's life? If so, he was "substantially a murderer, and so recorded in the register of Heaven." Was a man's life "to be endangered for the sake of punctilio to the President?" Were "envy, hatred and all the malignant passions" to pour out their poison against a citizen and not be enquired into? It was a big moment in the trial, and the Chief Justice granted the motion, although "gentlemen on both sides" had "acted improperly in the style and spirit of their remarks."

The President could be subpoenaed, Mr. Marshall decided. And should the present prosecution terminate as was expected by the Government, all concerned "should certainly regret that a paper which the accused believed to be essential to his defense . . . had been withheld from him." The circumstance "would justly tarnish the reputation of the Court which had given its sanction to its being withheld. Might I be permitted to utter one sentiment, with respect to myself, it would be to deplore most earnestly the occasion which should compel me to look back in any part of my official conduct with so much self reproach as I should feel, could I declare . . . that the accused is not entitled to the letter in question, if it should be really important to him." The utterance of a supremely honest gentleman.

The subpoena was issued, with an endorsement by

Colonel Burr to the effect that "the transmission to the Clerk of this Court of the original letter of Genl. Wilkinson and of copies duly authenticated of the other papers . . . described . . . will be admitted as sufficient observance of the process without the personal attendance of any . . . of the persons therein named; but in case of such transmission it is expected that the Copies of the orders . . . be accompanied by the Certificates of all the persons named . . . declaring that no other orders . . . have been given . . . respecting the said A. Burr or his property. . . ." As for the statement in the Chief Justice's opinion that the prosecution "expected" a conviction, Mr. Marshall subsequently admitted its impropriety and erased it. But Mr. Hay was very angry. There "never was such a trial," he wrote, "from the beginning of the world to this day."

And Mr. Jefferson was very angry, and perhaps a little alarmed. Public opinion, for once, was with the Court, and the incidents of the Smith-Ogden trial in connection with the Miranda affair had not been forgotten. Still, he felt secure enough—he had, perhaps, guessed that the process would never be enforced—to defy the writ. He could not be taken from his official duties, he told Mr. Hay; he could not be bandied from pillar to post; private Government documents could not be laid open to indiscriminate inspection. What could properly be divulged would be sent. And as for Mr. Martin, "this unprincipled and impudent Federal bulldog" who had presumed to attack the President—could not something be done about him? "Shall L. M. be sum-

moned as a witness against Burr?" Or "shall we
move to commit [him] as *particeps criminis* with
Burr?" A certain Greybell was available who would
"fix upon him misprision of treason at least."

But now the court had something else to think
about. . . .

<h2 style="text-align:center">5</h2>

General Wilkinson, accompanied by Mr. Graham
and Captain Gaines, had arrived, on June 13. The
"great accomplisher of all things," according to
Edmund Randolph; the man who was to "officiate
as the high priest of this human sacrifice," and support "the sing song and the ballads of treason and
conspiracy," whose torch was to "kindle the fatal
blaze." He came into court on June 15, in full uni-
form, obese, grandiloquent—strutting and swelling
like a turkey cock, it seemed to Washington Irving
—and testified for four days, discharging the won-
drous cargo of a mighty mass of words—Mr. Irving
again.

And Colonel Burr gave him just one look of with-
ering scorn, which did not prevent him from declaim-
ing to Mr. Jefferson that Burr, "this lion hearted
eagled eyed hero, sinking under the weight of conscious guilt, made an effort to meet the indignant
salutation of outraged honor, but it was in vain, his
audacity failed him, he averted his face, grew pale
and affected passion to conceal his perturbation."
Aside from that, the General had not dreamed "of
the importance attached to my presence . . . I
had anticipated that a deluge of testimony would
have been poured forth . . . to overwhelm [Burr]

LUTHER MARTIN

with guilt and dishonor. Sadly, indeed, was I mistaken, and to my astonishment I found the traitor vindicated and myself condemned by a mass of wealth, character, influence and talents. Merciful God, what a spectacle did I behold—integrity and truth perverted and trampled under foot by turpitude and guilt, patriotism appalled and usurpation triumphant. Did I ever expect it would depend on my humble self to stop the current of such a polluted stream? Never, never."

And never, never had he expected to be shouldered off the sidewalk into the middle of the street by Samuel Swartwout before all Richmond, and publicly posted in the papers as a traitor, a forger, a perjurer, a coward and a poltroon after refusing to consider Mr. Swartwout's challenge. But Mr. Jefferson assured his *protégé* that "your enemies have filled the public ear with slanders and your mind with trouble on that account. The establishment of their guilt will . . . dissipate the doubts of those who doubted for want of knowledge, and will place you on higher ground in the public estimate and public confidence. No one is more sensible than myself of the injustice which has been aimed at you." And for once, Mr. Jefferson was really quite sincere.

But the General was in worse trouble than that. For the defense was moving, though unsuccessfully, his attachment for contempt of court, on the grounds that he had "used unlawful and oppressive means . . . in abuse of the process of this court" to bring witnesses from New Orleans, and had "obstructed the free course of testimony, and the fair and regular administration of justice." And the

Grand Jury—which was to listen complacently to the fantastic tales told by Taylor, and Allbright, and Dunbaugh, and some of the other forty-eight Government witnesses, in the midst of whom the less fanciful testimony of such men as Commodore Truxtun, and Erich Bollmann, and Samuel Swartwout, had little effect—the Grand Jury was coming to some very disagreeable conclusions regarding the fat General. They had made him confess that he had altered parts of the famous cipher letter, and omitted sentences tending to incriminate him; "under examination," John Randolph reported to a friend, "all was confusion of language and looks. Such a countenance never did I behold. There was scarcely a variance of opinion amongst us as to his guilt. Yet this miscreant is hugged to the bosom of the government. . . . "

In fact, "W. is the most finished scoundrel that ever lived; a ream of paper would not contain all the proofs; but what of that? He is the man whom the King delights to honor." Even Mr. Hay was obliged to admit as much, with his own lips, to Mr. Randolph, and told him that when Daniel Clark had appeared in Richmond, the General had come to him, Hay, terrified beyond description, with the statement that Mr. Clark could ruin him. And Mr. Tazewell and other members of the jury had absolutely convicted him of forgery and perjury in his papers. But in spite of John Randolph's efforts— he was never to cease his pursuit of the Spanish pensioner—the Grand Jury failed to indict the State's chief witness; although it was only by a vote of nine to seven that he walked out of the jury room a free man, as he was to walk out of one courtmartial after another during the subsequent course of his unbelievable career.

So that the passing of years which had not yet witnessed the unsealing of the Spanish archives seemed to confirm his boast that at the last "angry passions will slumber, candor and truth will resume their empire, and posterity will do justice to my name and service." Indeed, he was right. Posterity, at the last, has done so. . . .

6

And on June 24, the Grand Jury finally brought in indictments for treason and misdemeanor against Aaron Burr and Harman Blennerhassett; followed, two days later, by indictments against Jonathan Dayton, John Smith, Comfort Tyler, Israel Smith and Davis Floyd. That the indictments for treason were the result of a misunderstanding on the part of certain jurymen of Mr. Marshall's opinion in the Swartwout-Bollmann case was afterwards frankly admitted by two of them to Mr. Blennerhassett, who was in Richmond then, writing everything down in his journal.

As for John Randolph, "the mammoth of iniquity escaped," he complained. "Not that any man pretended to think him innocent, but upon certain wire-drawn distinctions . . . W. is the only man that I ever saw who was from the bark to the very core a villain. The proof is unquestionable . . . suffice it to say that I have seen it, and that it is not susceptible of misconstruction. Burr supported himself with great fortitude. . . . Perhaps you never saw human nature in so degraded a situation as in the person of Wilkinson before the Grand Jury; and yet this man stands on the very summit and pinnacle of executive favor. . . ."

Indeed, the foreman had asked for General Wilkinson's letter of May 13, referred to in the Colonel's cipher, but Colonel Burr "rose immediately and declared that no consideration, no calamity, no desperation should induce *him* to betray a letter confidentially written." Even Mr. Hay had to confess that "the attitude and tone assumed by Burr struck everybody. There was an appearance of honor and magnanimity which brightened the countenances of the phalanx who daily attend for his encouragement and support."

Immediately after the indictment, Mr. Hay moved for the commitment to jail of Aaron Burr. The Colonel set forth that he would prove the charges to be founded on the testimony of perjured witnesses, and asked for his release on bail. But Mr. Marshall denied the motion, and Colonel Burr spent two nights in the common jail. On June 26, Mr. Botts declared that confinement in the jail would prove injurious to his health. Mr. Marshall therefore directed that the prisoner be lodged, under suitable guard, in the house of Luther Martin, but when the trial was postponed until August 3, to permit the summoning of a petit jury panel, he was finally removed to the State Penitentiary, a mile or so out of town, where they gave him three good-sized rooms on the third floor. But the only reason, Mr. Irving thought, "for immuring him in this abode of thieves, cut-throats and incendiaries" was to save the State the cost of guarding him elsewhere, and to "insure the security of his person."

7

"The scenes which have passed," Colonel Burr wrote to Theodosia, "and those about to be transacted will exceed all reasonable credulity, and will hereafter be deemed fables, unless attested by very high authority."

They were inclined to be quite severe with him at first, but the surveillance soon relaxed. General Wilkinson had not helped the Government's cause; General Eaton strutting about from tavern to tavern in a Turkish sash and a big white hat, placing drunken wagers on the prisoner's conviction, was an actual detriment to the prosecution; in Richmond, in elegant circles at least, public opinion was turning very strongly towards the accused. His rooms were thronged with visitors; it was as difficult, Mr. Blennerhassett complained, to get an audience "as if he really were an Emperor;" people swamped him with "messages, notes and inquiries, bringing oranges, lemons, pineapples, raspberries, apricots, cream, butter, ice and some ordinary articles;" and his secretary drove out daily from town "freighted with cake, confectionery, flowers, redolent with perfume, wreathed into fancy bouquets of endless variety."

But in the midst of all these amenities, while Mr. Dayton was conferring with him—to the intense annoyance of Mr. Blennerhassett, who could not understand how it was that the indicted gentleman seemed to enjoy the freedom of Richmond, in full

view of the United States Marshal who never did
arrest him—and while the Chief Justice was writing
to his colleagues for their advice on the law of treason, and good Republicans were drinking to an escort
of hemp for Colonel Burr "to the republic of dust
and ashes," and to "an honorable coat of tar and a
plumage of feathers" for Luther Martin—in the
midst of all this, the Colonel was lonely for his own
kin. And Mr. Martin had already done his best
towards a politic reconciliation.

For there was trouble with son-in-law Alston.
As soon as the President's accusations against
Colonel Burr had reached South Carolina, Mr. Alston
had written to Governor Pinckney, exonerating
himself as rapidly as possible of any connection with
his father-in-law's projects, of which, the Governor
might rest assured, Mr. Alston had had no suspicion. His wife and child had not accompanied
Colonel Burr, neither had he followed in October,
"with a corps of worthies," since they were, all
three of them, quietly sitting at The Oaks; and
Colonel Burr had had no right to make use of his
name in such a manner. Whatever the extent of
Mr. Alston's connection with the "conspiracy"—
and Mr. Blennerhassett was to have some interesting comments to make on that subject—his letter
to the Governor was as blatant a running to cover
as could be found throughout the ranks of the associates, and had had its share in influencing popular
estimation of the Colonel.

To counteract this, therefore, Mr. Martin had,
on June 26, written to advise Mr. Alston of Colonel
Burr's commitment to prison. "Never," he believed,

JOHN WICKHAM

"did any Government thirst more for the blood of a victim." The savagery of the prosecuting attorneys "would dishonor any beings but demons from Hell." That the Colonel was innocent of treason was positive; that a Bill had been found was due to "the jury not being well informed what facts constitute treason, and to gross perjury." That the Government "ardently desire to destroy Colonel Burr . . . I have not a doubt. And I am confident that Government does not believe him to have been guilty of a treasonable act." Under the circumstances, "it would be most pleasing, most consolatory to him, could you visit Richmond. He has many warm friends here . . . who . . . have not been deterred from proving their attachment to him in the hour of adversity." As for Mr. Martin himself, Mr. Alston could tell his "amiable lady" that "if on this occasion I had not come forward and offered my aid . . . I should have felt myself most deservedly liable to her eternal reproaches."

Mr. Alston could not help but read between the lines. And finally the Colonel sent for Theodosia, sick as she was at the time; but there must be "no agitations, no complaints, no fears or anxieties on the road, or I renounce thee." He wanted, he told her, "an independent and discerning witness to my conduct and that of the Government . . . I should never invite any one, much less those so dear to me, to witness my disgrace. I may be immured in dungeons, chained, murdered in legal form, but I cannot be humiliated or disgraced. If absent, you will suffer great solicitude. In my presence you will feel none, whatever be the malice or the power of my enemies, and in both they abound."

The Alstons came at once, bringing "Gampy" with them, and spent their first night on arrival at the Penitentiary. And if Mr. Blennerhassett, who reported having heard it from Colonel Burr, is to be believed, there was a very lively scene between the father and son-in-law, as a result of which Mr. Alston offered to print a public reconciliation but was spared the humiliation out of regard for Theodosia. There followed some extremely awkward days for Mr. Alston—marked by the constant, if unsuccessful, attempts of Mr. Blennerhassett to collect his money from him—while Theodosia went everywhere making friends, accomplishing more for her father in her own smiling way than all his attorneys put together, and earning for herself the affection of all Richmond, to say nothing of the unconcealed infatuation of Mr. Martin.

So the days passed, with the thermometer at ninety-eight. . . .

CHAPTER III

NOT GUILTY

I

On August 3, when Mr. Marshall opened the court at noon, Richmond was again packed, the Hall jammed, the crowd, except for a larger group than before of Burr adherents, hostile and menacing. It was unbelievably hot. Colonel Burr appeared on the arm of his son-in-law—an exhibition of cordiality the publicity of which may or may not have appealed to the diffident Mr. Alston—having walked from the home of Luther Martin to which he had been removed on August 2, for safe keeping in a room padlocked and barred, and guarded with sentries.

The great trial was beginning. The trial which was to decide whether or not the old pernicious English doctrines of constructive treason should prevail in America. From the first, the prosecution sought to establish the theory that assemblage with hostile intent was equivalent to an act of war, and that the actual presence of the instigator was not essential for conviction. It was not necessary, Mr. Hay insisted, that the persons assembled should proceed to hostilities, or that "they should be armed, or appear in military array." From the first, the defense maintained that under the Constitution only the proving by two witnesses of a definite overt act of hostility could constitute treason. The State, Colonel Burr himself proclaimed, held that "though there was no force used in reality, yet by construction there was force used; that though I was not personally present, yet that by construction I was present; that though there really was no military array, yet by construction there was military array." This was constructive treason, and "we totally deny all these things."

The conflict naturally involved a fundamental question concerning the admissibility of evidence, the State claiming the privilege of introducing testimony with regard to the previous general intentions and designs of the accused, the defense denying the validity of such collateral evidence. The Government must confine itself first to proving the overt act in question. An opinion on this decisive point was soon required of the Chief Justice—precipitated by the presence in the witness box of General Eaton with his affidavit, so much of which had nothing to do with the events on Blennerhassett's Island.

Mr. Marshall decided that "it is the most useful . . . ' and the natural order of testimony to show first the existence of the fact respecting which the inquiry is to be made." On the other hand, it was true "that the crime alleged . . . consists of the fact, and of the intention with which that fact was committed. The testimony disclosing both . . .

must be relevant." But this intention was "the intention . . . with which the overt act itself was committed—not a general evil disposition." This would be merely corroborative testimony, and it was "essentially repugnant to the usages of courts . . . that corroborative or confirmatory testimony should precede that which it is to corroborate or confirm." That part of General Eaton's testimony, for instance, dealing with alleged designs upon the city of Washington was "not relevant to the present indictment." However, Mr. Hay was "at liberty to proceed according to his own judgment, and the Court feels itself bound to exclude such testimony only as at the time of its being offered does not appear to be relevant."

The prosecution was to have every latitude, every opportunity of producing its evidence, but the Chief Justice had clearly set forth the limits beyond which it might not presume to pass. That his opinion was of vital comfort to the defense was undeniable; that it was founded on the most irreproachable principles of law, in harmony with the most solemn provisions of the Constitution in the matter of treason, was equally incontestable. "Marshall faced a problem of uncommon difficulty," Mr. Beveridge points out. "It was no small matter to come between the populace and its prey—no light adventure to brave the vengeance of Thomas Jefferson. Not only his public repute—perhaps even his personal safety and his official life—but also the now increasing influence and prestige of the National Judiciary were in peril. However, he must do justice no matter what befell—he must, at all hazards, pronounce the law truly and enforce it bravely, but with elastic method. He must be not only a just, but also an understanding judge."

2

When the court convened, the Government was not ready, necessitating a series of adjournments, and it was only on August 10, after Mr. Blennerhassett had been arraigned, that Colonel Burr was given access to the jury. For four days, scattered through a week of further adjournments, the examination of talesmen continued; in the midst of a brilliant running debate concerning the nature of opinions formed which might exclude individuals from service, during the course of which Mr. Martin accused the prosecution of wishing to "deprive Colonel Burr's counsel of an opportunity of defending him, that they might hang him up as soon as possible, to gratify themselves and the Government;" to which characteristic outburst Mr. Hay replied that he wished "argument to proceed without hearing [the Government attorneys] grossly insulted."

Meanwhile, juror after juror had formed an opinion of the prisoner's guilt, juror after juror had openly expressed the hope that he might be hanged. Of the first venire of forty-eight, only four were retained. Out of the second venire, none were really qualified to serve, but Colonel Burr remarked that "either . . . I am under the necessity of taking men in some degree prejudiced against me, or of having another venire. I am unwilling to submit to the further delay of other tales, and I must therefore encounter the consequences." Ten men were sworn on August 15; the Colonel gave notice of a motion to issue a second subpoena *duces tecum* against the President if General Wilkinson's letter was not produced; and the court adjourned until Monday, August 17. On that day, two more jurymen were chosen, the indictment was read, and General Eaton was sworn, his name bringing on that discussion relating to evidence reference to which has already been made.

The General observed that "concerning an overt act which goes to prove Aaron Burr guilty of treason, I know nothing. Concerning certain transactions which are said to have happened at Blennerhassett's Island, or any agency which Aaron Burr may be supposed to have had in them, I know nothing. But concerning Colonel Burr's expressions of treasonable intentions, I know much." Mr. Marshall ruled that "any proof of intention formed before the act itself, if relevant to the act, may be admitted." General Eaton then began his lugubrious revelations, and "strutted more in buskin than usual," Mr. Blennerhassett was told, so that "the effect was as diverting to the whole court as it was probably beneficial to the defense."

3

It is not intended to report the details of the testimony given during the trial. With few exceptions, it was all of the same character, calculated to prove treasonable intent. Some of it was notoriously false. General Eaton was the first of a long line of witnesses—Taylor, Allbright, the Morgans, Toms, Dicks and Harrys, gardeners, boatmen and grooms, which the Government had gathered together to the number of more than a hundred—who told the same story of fantastic conversations with Colonel Burr, of contemptuous references made by him to the Government, of sinister projects against the Union, of warlike manifestations at Blennerhassett's Island. In rare cases only, such as in the testimony of Commodore Truxtun, was it brought out that the Colonel had never proposed anything further than an expedition to Mexico. "In all his conversations with me," the Commodore asserted, "he [Burr] said that this expedition was to take place only in the event of a war with Spain."

The testimony of Jacob Allbright was, perhaps, the most important, since on his evidence, had the Government been able to find anyone to corroborate it, the whole question of the overt act depended. He had, he stated, been a laborer at the island, and on the night in question, "a man by the name of Tupper laid his hands upon Blennerhassett and said 'Your body is in my hands, in the name of the Commonwealth.' Some such words as that . . . When Tupper made that motion, there were seven or eight muskets leveled at him," and after further conversation "Tupper then changed his speech, and said he wished him to escape safe down the river, and wished him luck."

Here was the Government's act of war—if only another witness could have been found to swear to it. And the one best witness of all for the purpose was in court—he was in Richmond throughout the trial—General Tupper himself, but he was never called to testify. Because his version was utterly different from Allbright's. From his subsequent deposition—the original of which was found many years later in Ohio, and quotation from which has already been made in these pages—one learns that had General Tupper been put on the stand, and the defense was loud in its condemnation of the prosecution for its failure to do so, he would have proved the "swearer from Wood County" to be a perjurer, or at any rate an unreliable witness; he would have told the jury that he had gone to the island by invitation, with no intention of apprehending anyone, that he had been in no way molested, that no one had leveled any muskets at him, and that nothing out of the ordinary had happened.

But General Tupper was not called; and aside from Allbright, the best the State could do for its overt act was to produce a servant, William Love, who stated that there had been "about betwixt twenty and twenty-five" men on the island, and that "some of the men had guns, some had dirks." And Israel Miller, who agreed that Comfort Tyler's men had "five rifles and about three or four pairs of pistols," while at the island he had seen "one blunderbuss, two pairs of pistols and one fusee." And another man, Morris Belknap, who had observed some twenty men on the island, two or three of whom were cleaning rifles. "These were all the arms I saw." The place could hardly be called an arsenal. So it went. No one even pretended that Colonel Burr had been present during these momen-

tous occurrences.   Attempts to persuade Mr. Blennerhassett to turn State's witness had failed.   The
Government's case was a farce.

"If the gentlemen have done with the overt act,"
Colonel Burr remarked, already on August 19, "or
when they have done, I will thank them to inform
me, for then we shall have some considerations to
offer to the court."   And there was no doubt in
anyone's mind concerning the character of these
considerations. . . .

4

It was on August 20 that Mr. Wickham formally
presented the motion calling for the suspension of
further testimony, on the grounds that the prosecution's witnesses were none of them able to prove
an overt act.   The evidence had "wholly failed to
prove that an overt act of levying war had been
committed on Blennerhassett's Island; and hence
no evidence could be received to charge Colonel
Burr, by relation, with an act which had not been
proved to have been committed."   Mr. Wickham
spoke for nearly two full seven hour days, followed
more briefly by Mr. Randolph.   The Constitution,
he reminded everyone, was meticulously clear on the
subject of treason.   The Supreme Court opinion
in the Swartwout-Bollmann case, incriminating a
person even remotely connected with treasonable
acts, had been delivered in a case of commitment
only—Mr. Martin was later flatly to pronounce it
an error.   "If Blennerhassett and Tyler were not
guilty of treason, then it was impossible that Colonel
Burr could be guilty of treason in aiding, advising

BENJAMIN BOTTS

Now reproduced for the first time from an original portrait in the possession of the family.

or procuring them to commit a crime." Let the prosecution withdraw their present indictment and bring in a new one, if they wished to try Colonel Burr for treason.

The prosecution merely asked for an adjournment, which Mr. Marshall granted. On August 24, Mr. McRae, almost breathless with rage, did his thundering. According to Mr. Blennerhassett, the gentleman had only succeeded in sinking his reputation, but on August 25, Mr. Wirt raised his own "as high as McRae sunk his." Mr. Wirt's speech was a magnificent effort, as an exposition of law and as a piece of oratory, parts of which have become classics of elocution, and the whole of which kept a suffocating audience in uncomplaining and fascinated attention. The motion, he observed, was "a bold and original stroke in the whole science of defense. . . . It cuts off from the prosecution all that evidence which goes to connect the prisoner with the assemblage on the island, to explain the . . . objects of the assemblage, and to stamp beyond controversy the character of treason upon it." Mr. Wirt would answer Mr. Wickham. He would not "complain of flowers and graces where none exist"—Mr. Wickham had previously criticized Mr. Wirt for his superfluous verbal ornamentation of arguments. "I cannot give you a squib or a rocket in every period. . . . I have always thought these meteors of the brain which spring up with such exuberant abundance in the speeches of that gentleman . . . no better evidence of the soundness of the argument with which they are connected . . . than those vapors which start from our marshes and blaze with a momentary combustion." Mr. Wirt would not subdivide the proposition into small sections and then take one of them and "toss it with an air of elephantine strength and superiority." Mr. Wirt, young, impudent and superb, would answer Mr. Wickham.

He did so for the greater part of the day, attacking Mr. Wickham's conclusions concerning the liability of a conspirator who remained absent from the actual scene of treason with a profound logic and a brilliant mastery of the law which were still vivid in Mr. Marshall's mind when he remarked that "a degree of eloquence seldom displayed on any occasion has embellished a solidity of argument and a depth of research by which the Court has been greatly aided in forming [its] opinion." How ridiculous, Mr. Wirt exclaimed, any attempt to make of Mr. Blennerhassett the principal and of Colonel Burr a mere accessory. And then Mr. Wirt declaimed the paragraphs of that delightfully idiotic oration, that valedictorian's description of the innocent recluse in his island paradise, which brought down upon him the merciless arrows of Mr. Botts's satire, in a speech which had the entire courtroom in convulsions.

But Mr. Botts was not there only for the purpose of making people laugh. He was there to examine the evidence, to review the whole course of the Government's scandalous behavior. He did so fearlessly, and with terrible clarity. It was common knowledge, he proclaimed, that "if Aaron Burr should be acquitted it will be the severest satire on the Government." The prestige of the administration was at stake, and no falsehood, no insult, no persecution was too despicable for use against the accused. Mr. Hay replied, with an address which lasted nearly two days, in which, among a number of other observations, he so far forgot himself as to remind Mr. Marshall that Judge Chase had been impeached for having wrested the decision of a case from the jury and prejudged it before hearing the evidence. Mr. Lee, who answered him on August 27, was not slow to expose the indiscretion. "It was very kind in the gentleman," he told him, "to remind the Court of the danger of a decision of the motion in favor of the prisoner: a decision like that which had already produced the impeachment of another judge." Mr. Hay denied any idea of coercion, and Mr. Marshall assured him that he had not considered the allusion as personally intended. But the Chief Justice did not forget.

"That this Court," he said in his opinion, "dares not usurp power is most true; that this Court does not shrink from its duty is not less true. . . . No man is desirous of becoming the peculiar object of calumny; no man, might he let the bitter cup pass from him without self-reproach, would drain it to the bottom; but if he has no choice . . . if there is no alternative presented to him but a dereliction of duty or the opprobrium of those who are denominated the world—he merits the contempt as well as the indignation of his country who can hesitate which to embrace."

In the recorded annals of a trial noted for many distinguished utterances, these words must always preserve their own transcending dignity. . . .

5

Mr. Randolph had still to speak, but the climax of the long argument was undoubtedly Mr. Martin's fulminating address begun on August 28 and completed the following day. Mr. Martin had been drinking—he had been drinking steadily throughout the trial—Mr. Martin's delivery was ungraceful, his arguments were poorly arranged, but the fire of his eloquence was never more flaming, the penetration of his judgment never more searching, the force of his personality never more compelling.

With tremendous sentences he demolished the prosecution's claim that the defense was attempting to impede the course of justice, or to suppress the truth. The prosecution had been a persecution, and "I shall ever feel the sincerest gratitude to Heaven that my life has been preserved to this time, and that I am enabled to appear before this court in [Colonel Burr's] defense;" and if the joint efforts of himself and his colleagues should be successful "in wiping away the tears of filial piety"—he never missed a chance to proclaim his devotion to Theodosia—"in healing the deep wounds inflicted on the breast of the child by the envenomed shafts of hatred and malice hurled at the heart of the father—if our efforts shall succeed in preserving youth, innocence, elegance and merit from a life of unutterable misery, from despair, from distraction—it will be to me the greatest pleasure. What dear delight will my heart enjoy! How ineffable, how supreme will be my bliss."

And he was thankful that when a great question,

so "awfully" important as that respecting the prin-
-ciples of treason, was to be decided, he was to have
"an opportunity of exerting . . . my feeble talents in opposing principles which I consider so
destructive as those which are advanced on the
present occasion;" and if they were able to establish in the mind of the Court the propriety of principles the reverse of those contended for by the
prosecution—the reverse of constructive treason
—"I shall think that I have not lived in vain."

It was not a question of who was the principal and
who the accessory. There had been no treason whatever committed by anyone anywhere—except in
the newspapers. And "I have with pain heard it
said that such are the public prejudices against
Colonel Burr, that a jury . . . must have considerable firmness of mind to pronounce him not
guilty. . . . God of heaven! Have we already
under our form of government . . . arrived at
a period when a trial in a court of justice where life
is at stake shall be but a solemn mockery, a mere
idle form and ceremony to transfer innocence from
the gaol to the gibbet, to gratify popular indignation excited by bloodthirsty enemies. . . . "

6

On August 31, the Chief Justice delivered his
opinion. It was one of the longest he ever rendered,
and required three hours in the reading.

With regard to the Swartwout-Bollmann decision, he stated, it had since been argued that the
Supreme Court had adopted the whole English doctrine on the subject of accessories to treason. This

was not the fact. ' "Those only who perform a part,
and who are leagued in the conspiracy, are declared
to be traitors." Both circumstances must concur;
they must "perform a part which will furnish the
overt act, and they must be leagued in conspiracy."
In any case, the overt act of war must be proved,
and sworn to by two witnesses. And the assemblage which levies war must be "a warlike assemblage, carrying the appearance of force, and in a
situation to practice hostility."

It was "the opinion of the Court that this indictment can be supported only by testimony which
proves the accused to have been actually or constructively present when the assemblage took place
. . . or by the admission of the doctrine that he
who procures an act may be indicted as having performed that act. It is further the opinion of the
Court that there is no testimony whatever which
tends to prove that the accused was actually or
constructively present when that assemblage did
take place; indeed, the contrary is most apparent."
The legal guilt of the person who planned the assemblage on Blennerhassett's Island depended "not
simply on the criminality of the previous conspiracy,
but on the criminality of that assemblage. If those
who perpetrated the fact be not traitors, he who advised the fact cannot be a traitor." His guilt depended on theirs, and could not be established in a
prosecution against himself.

Ought the Court to sit and hear testimony which
could not affect the prisoner, or ought the Court to
arrest that testimony? The present indictment
charged the prisoner "with levying war against the

United States, and alleges an overt act of levying war.   That overt act must be proved . . . by two witnesses.   It is not proved by a single witness" —everybody knew, then, what was coming—"The presence of the accused has been stated to be an essential component part of the overt act in this indictment . . . and there is not only no witness who has proved his actual . . . presence, but the fact of his absence is not controverted. . . . The conclusion that in this state of things no testimony can be admissible is so inevitable that the counsel for the United States can not resist it. . . . If the overt act be not proved by two witnesses . . . all other testimony must be irrelevant. . . . No testimony relative to the conduct or declarations of the prisoner elsewhere, and subsequent to the transaction on Blennerhassett's Island can be admitted; because such testimony being . . . merely corroborative . . . is irrelevant until there be proof of the overt act by two witnesses."

And the result was "a conviction, as complete as the mind of the Court is capable of receiving on a complex subject, that the motion must prevail. . . ."

7

That the motion must prevail.

Mr. Hay had nothing to say—the Government had only one Jacob Allbright—and on September 1, the case went to the jury.   In a short while they were back, with their obstinate verdict.   "We of the jury say that Aaron Burr is not proved to be guilty under this indictment by any evidence submitted to us. We therefore find him not guilty."   There was a

tremendous discussion over this irregularity—the
foreman stating that most of the jurymen were
willing to put the verdict in more formal idiom,
since it was intended for one of acquittal—and
finally Mr. Marshall directed that it remain on the
Bill as reported by the jury, and that Not Guilty
be entered on the record.

The trial was over. "The knowledge of my
father's innocence," Theodosia wrote at once to a
friend when they brought her the message, "my
ineffable contempt for his enemies, and the elevation of his mind have kept me above any sensations bordering on depression." All during the
anxious weeks, it had been the Colonel who cheered
them up. Mr. Hay entered a *nolle prosequi* to all
the other treason indictments, and reported his failure to the President. Mr. Jefferson was very angry.
Very angry. The event, he replied, was what had
been intended from the beginning by the Chief
Justice—not only to clear Burr but to keep the evidence from the world. Mr. Hay must collect it all,
and preserve it most carefully. "These whole proceedings will be laid before Congress." Perhaps an
impeachment would be in order. . . .

There was still the indictment for misdemeanor.
On September 3, Colonel Burr was admitted to five
thousand dollar bail provided by William Lang-
bourne, and Jonathan Dayton who was still at
large in Richmond, and on the point of going quietly
to Ohio. The Alstons went home. Colonel Burr
was walking to court now every morning with an
escort of two hundred gentlemen. In the evenings
there were dinners—at least, at Luther Martin's

WILLIAM WIRT

and John Wickham's—and the Colonel was talking
unconcernedly of reviving his plans for the Bastrop
colony. Mr. Hay was having influenza. . . .

From the very first, everyone understood that the
misdemeanor trial was more an attempt to catch
John Marshall—to gather further instances of what
the Government considered his partiality and arbitrary attitude—than a serious prosecution of the
accused. But the Chief Justice was not to be
caught, and listened patiently to testimony while
Colonel Burr's counsel were arguing about another
subpoena *duces tecum* for the President—a process
concerning which Mr. Jefferson was preparing fever-
ish instructions for Mr. Hay. Judge Griffin—he was
there, was he not—must be induced "to divide [the]
court and produce a truce." The United States
Marshal must "take no part in the exercise of any
act of force" ordered in the case, and the Executive
would "cover" him. And this, and that. And
when the subpoena was issued, he returned it, refusing to "sanction a proceeding so preposterous."
And there the matter remained, with the President
in contempt of court. . . .

The misdemeanor trial went on. Some fifty witnesses were examined; General Eaton was made
to look more of a fool than ever; General Wilkinson
acted like "a sergeant under a court-martial;" and
there was no evidence to speak of at the end of it
all—no evidence which Mr. Marshall could allow—
to show that Colonel Burr had ever planned anything hostile to Spain except in the event of war
between the two countries. Mr. Hay did his best
to enter a *nolle prosequi* and prevent a verdict, but

the case was sent to the jury, and on September 15, in half an hour, it reported Not Guilty.

Mr. Hay could then enter his *nolle prosequi* to all the misdemeanor indictments—but he moved to hold Colonel Burr, Harman Blennerhassett and Israel Smith for trial in the District of Ohio this time, on the charge of treason. It was all to do over again. Mr. Marshall listened once more to endless testimony; incomprehensibly it seemed to the accused who were furious with him, so that Colonel Burr could not trust himself, at the end of each day, to "sum up and condense . . . into compact columns" the "forces" displayed by his attorneys, as had been his custom. But after listening to all the testimony, Mr. Marshall decided, on October 20, that the enterprise had been directed solely against Mexico, and that it would "be improper in me to commit the accused on the charge of treason." He would commit Aaron Burr and Harman Blennerhassett—not Israel Smith—for misdemeanor in preparing an expedition against Spain, and he required a three thousand dollar bond. After all, what did the Colonel expect! But for the second time, if not the third, John Marshall had pronounced Aaron Burr innocent of treason.

But no one was satisfied. Mr. Jefferson and Mr. Hay were more and more convinced of Mr. Marshall's "chicanery;" the Government was bound to get its precious testimony before the world, and the Chief Justice was trying to prevent it. Actually, the Ohio trial never took place, even Mr. Hay having advised the President "to desist from further prosecution." The public, of course, saw nothing in all this—in all these opinions which it did not, or would not, understand—but the fact that Mr. Jefferson's traitor had escaped, and drank damnation to the judges. And Colonel Burr was disgusted. "After all," he wrote Theodosia, "this is a sort of drawn battle. [Marshall's] opinion was a matter of regret and surprise to [his] friends . . . and of ridicule to his enemies—all believing that it was a sacrifice of principle to conciliate Jack Cade [Thomas Jefferson]."

The Colonel was unjust—he was even extremely rude to Mr. Marshall—but it was exasperating, of course, after having been exonerated of high crimes and misdemeanors by five juries in Kentucky, Mississippi and Virginia. . . .

CHAPTER IV

AFTERMATHS

I

RICHMOND emptied itself; Colonel Burr went north; the Chief Justice galloped off to the Blue Ridge, content in the knowledge that he had obeyed the "public law" rather than the "public will" in the "most deplorably serious" business which he had just completed—although Mr. Blennerhassett could see in his latest decision only an attempt "to pacify the menaces and clamorous yells of the cerberus of Democracy." And Mr. Jefferson was talking seriously about impeachment.

His message to Congress was emphatic on the subject, even though the Cabinet had not allowed him to retain in that document such paragraphs as he had originally composed concerning his belief that "wherever the laws were appealed to in aid of the public safety, their operation [in the Burr trial] was on behalf of those only against whom they were invoked." The great Republican papers, the Philadelphia *Aurora* and the Richmond *Enquirer* in particular, took up the Executive cry of impeachment and filled their pages with attacks on Mr. Marshall. "Lucius"—William Thompson whose earlier criticisms of the Justice had been submitted to Mr. Jefferson and enthusiastically endorsed by him—began to write his "Letters to John Marshall" in the *Aurora*, from which they were copied in all the administration gazettes. Mr. Marshall had erected tyranny upon the tomb of freedom; he was a disgrace to the bench of justice; he had prostrated the dignity of the Chief Justice of the United States; he had exhibited a culpable partiality towards Aaron Burr, and a "shameless solicitude . . . to implicate the government . . . as negligent of their duty."

In fact, Marshall and Burr were "traitors in heart and in fact;" few countries had ever produced such a criminal and such a judge; Mr. Marshall and Colonel Burr together were "forever doomed to blot the fair page of American history, to be held up as examples of infamy and disgrace, of perverted talents and unpunished criminality, of foes to liberty and traitors to [the] country." Mr. Marshall had screened a criminal and disgraced a judge, and he ought to be removed from the elevation which he had dishonored by his crimes.

So, in the fall of 1807, the Chief Justice was being publicly villified by the President's mouthpiece, while the President himself was urging on the House a repetition of the earlier proceedings against Judge Pickering and Judge Chase—proceedings which would without doubt have been instituted had not Congress found more pressing international affairs to attract its partisan attention.

And at Baltimore, in November, the populace was hanging them all in effigy—John Marshall, "His Quid Majesty" Aaron Burr, Blennerhassett, "the chemist, convicted of conspiracy to destroy the tone of the public Fiddle," and "Lawyer Brandy Bottle" Luther Martin. They were all in town at the time, except Mr. Marshall; Mr. Blennerhassett at the Evans Hotel, in the attic of which he hid during the popular commotion, and Colonel Burr, with Samuel Swartwout, at Mr. Martin's house, preparations to defend which had been made by the attorney's law students.

Out in the streets the crowds went roaring by—the tradition that Colonel Burr appeared at a window and bowed, supposing the manifestation to be in his honor, is scarcely credible—dragging after them the carts containing the effigies to be "executed," and escorted by a troop of cavalry who were present, "not to disperse the mob, but to . . . behold their conduct." And the next day, after the "hangings," crowds began to gather again around the taverns, and there was violent mischief in the air, so that Colonel Burr who was out walking with a Mr. Barney was advised by another friend, Mr. Hughes, to "take your departure without further civil or military honors being conferred upon you."

They put the Colonel in a hack, and Mr. Barney drove off with him to a stage stop outside of Baltimore, while Mr. Hughes followed them a little later with the baggage and the reservation. And at first Colonel Burr would have objected to these arrangements, saying that he was too old a soldier to be frightened by a mob, but "that is all fine bravado,"

the practical Mr. Hughes told him. "Barney and I
have no desire to shoot down or be shot by our fellow
citizens. You may throw your life away, Colonel,
but this bright world has too many attractions for
us to throw ours in defending you, when a pleasant
ride of half an hour will save you from danger and
restore us to our affectionate parents."

In other words, Mr. Barney and Mr. Hughes were
quite anxious to be rid of his perilous company. . . .

2

The Colonel went to Philadelphia and hid himself
away in a French boarding house in which Charles
Biddle found him in the evenings "generally alone
with little light in his room. He was very pale and
dejected, how different from what he had been a
short time before . . . It would not have surprised me on going there to have found he had
ended his sufferings with a pistol."

And one evening Colonel Burr was taken by the
Sheriff, at the suit of a Mr. Wilkins of Pittsburgh—
one of the gentlemen whom he had interested in the
Bastrop project. "Late at night," Mr. Biddle reported, "he [Burr] was brought to my house, and the
Sheriff waited a considerable time with him and
Mr. Pollock for me to come home. Mr. Pollock is a
highly respectable gentleman, intimate in my family, a relative and friend of Colonel Burr, and a
man of large fortune . . . Colonel Burr was perfectly composed; at this time scarcely anything could
disturb him. At length one of my neighbors was
sent for. Mr. Holwell, a gentleman of the bar, who
. . . pledged himself to be answerable for Mr.

Burr's appearance in the morning. In the morning Mr. Pollock was accepted as the bail." But the plaintiff's attorney had made a mistake, and the case was dismissed.

As for the Spanish schemes, although they were still running in the Colonel's mind, he would have been grateful for "any appointment that would have made him independent. My reason for thinking so," Mr. Biddle wrote, "is that on the resignation of Judge Shippen he requested me to speak to Governor McKean, and endeavor to get him appointed in his room. This, as Colonel Burr then stood, I thought would be improper, and told him so. However, I spoke to the Governor's son . . . who being of the same opinion . . . the Governor was not spoken to."

Colonel Burr did not yet seem to have realized that, so well had the administration done its work, in the public estimation he was a condemned man. . . .

3

And if at Washington there was not time, in the face of approaching trouble with England, to impeach the Chief Justice, the Senate still found opportunity to attempt one conspicuous demonstration of administrative vengeance—aside from Senator Giles's proposal of legislation for the punishment of accessories to treason whether personally present or not.

On November 27, 1807, Senator Maclay of Pennsylvania offered a resolution, subsequently adopted as amended by Senator Thurston of Kentucky, to the effect that "a Committee be appointed to inquire whether it be compatible with the honor and privileges of this House that John Smith, a Senator from . . . Ohio, against whom bills of indictment were found . . . for treason and misdemeanor, should be permitted any longer to have a seat therein; and that the Committee do inquire into all the facts regarding the conduct of Mr. Smith as an alleged associate of Aaron Burr, and report to the Senate."

It was known that Senator Smith was a friend of Colonel Burr, that he had been in communication with him during the period of the conspiracy, and that he had been abortively indicted for treason and misdemeanor. It was also a matter of record that Senator Smith had offered to pay one half of the expenses of the Ohio militia at the time of their service against the conspirators, and that an effort to indict him at Chillicothe had failed. Now the United States Senate proposed to try its hand against him. On December 31, the Committee, in the person of John Quincy Adams, reported that "the conspiracy of Aaron Burr and his associates against the peace, union and liberties of the United States is of such a character, and that its existence is established by such a mass of concurring and mutually corroborative testimony," that no person engaged in it should be permitted to hold a seat in the Senate.

Whether or not Mr. Smith was involved was for the Senate to decide, but it was clear that a great part of the testimony essential to Colonel Burr's conviction had been withheld from the jury at Richmond—Mr. Adams, who was preparing to turn

from Federalist into Republican, was taking his
fling at Mr. Marshall—and that the actuality of
Mr. Smith's complicity had been obscured as a
result of the decisions rendered from the bench during the course of the trial. "If the daylight of evidence . . . be not excluded from the mind by the
curtain of artificial rules," Mr. Adams observed,
"the simplest understanding cannot but see . . .
crimes before which ordinary treason whitens into
virtue." Therefore the Committee moved that
Senator Smith be expelled.

Senator Smith asked for, and obtained, the privilege of counsel, Mr. Key and Mr. Harper appearing
for him—the Senate having refused its consent,
naturally enough, to Luther Martin—and on April
4, 1808, the defense produced its evidence. "No
actual or fancied depravity in our judicial tri-
bunals can impose on this House the necessity of
inquiring into indictable offenses committed by any
of its members," Mr. Key asserted. "There is little
difference between punishing a man without a trial
and destroying the purity of that trial," and an
adverse decision by the Senate would naturally influence any subsequent trial of the Senator in a court of
law. Aside from that, the Senate's testimony against
Mr. Smith was all circumstantial, except that of a
certain Elias Glover, who had been shown "to be
absolutely unworthy of credit," and concerning
whom it had been proved that "he had long felt
. . . the most malignant animosity toward Mr.
Smith." Mr. Harper also protested against "the
admission of this clandestine and furtive testimony [in
the form of depositions] which shuns the light of day."

AARON BURR

From the original portrait by Vanderlyn in the possession of the New York Historical Society.

Mr. Adams replied in a long speech reviewing Mr. Smith's relations with Colonel Burr, stating that to him it was irreconcilable that the Colonel should have been the Senator's guest in Ohio "without making to him any communication of his real views, while he was so liberally disseminating them to others far less intimate to his acquaintance and far less important to his purposes." Senator Hillhouse of Connecticut attacked all this. "If all Mr. Smith's conversations and confessions are taken together," he proclaimed, "there can remain little doubt of his innocence. . . . Where . . . is the evidence whereon we can ground . . . a vote which is to disrobe a Senator of his office and of his honor? Nothing but jealousy, that jealousy which frequently attaches itself to a charge of treason . . . and must in this case have taken hold of the mind of the gentleman from Massachusetts, could have induced a belief that there was evidence to prove on Mr. Smith a participation in the conspiracy of Aaron Burr." Senator Giles was equally opposed to the resolution to expel. He would vote against it, "solely from the conviction of the innocence of the accused."

Not even the administration leader could bring himself to any other opinion, and his was the deciding vote which defeated the resolution by ten nays to nineteen yeas. Mr. Smith was free to resign his seat, withdraw from Ohio to Louisiana, and return to the preaching of the Gospel which had been his occupation in early life. Mr. Dayton, too, disappeared from the public view, while misery and ruin awaited Mr. Blennerhassett. So the jealousy which

frequently attached itself to a charge of treason
pursued these three.

But for Colonel Burr there was reserved a more
fantastic ordeal. . . .

4

Neither the Colonel nor Mr. Blennerhassett had
appeared at the January court in Ohio, and their
bonds were forfeited. That the Government might
at any time, in spite of its failure to continue the
prosecutions, seize upon his person—to say nothing
of the possibility of similar action on the part of
his numerous creditors—determined Colonel Burr's
resolve to leave the country. There was no security for him in America; in England he might conceivably awaken a renewed interest in his Mexican
projects—the idea of revolutionizing the Spanish
dominions was never to perish from his mind—to
England, therefore, he would go, with the last
dollars he could scrape together.

And so, in April, 1808, there came secretly to New
York a certain Mr. Edwards—there were still
indictments pending in New Jersey and New York
against Aaron Burr—who sought a vagrant shelter
in the homes of various old friends of the same
Aaron Burr, and in that of a Mrs. Pollock, in which,
for a short while, a Miss Mary Ann Edwards—in
Charleston they called her Theodosia Burr Alston—
also found refuge.

He was to sail in the packet *Clarissa Ann*, "having paid sixty dollars for the cabin . . . and also
for a pilot boat to put me on board." Theodosia
arrived "at —— where I lodged" on June 1, and

he was to have gone aboard the next day, after
spending the night on Long Island, but the pilot
boat did not come. On June 3, he was at the house
of Mr. Kemble in New Jersey. On June 6, he was
back in New York with the Swartwouts. Whenever
they could do so in safety, Miss Edwards and her
"brother" contrived to meet, and there seem to have
been several false partings. And Theodosia was
in despair—"the moment of separation," on one
occasion, "was embittered by tears and reproaches."
Reproaches, from Theodosia. . . .

In the midst of it all she took his instructions, she
received his messages, she arranged to take charge
of his affairs and of his precious papers. "Put all
my papers and manuscript book into some one
box (you may get one made for the purpose if you
please) and leave it with Mrs. P. keeping yourself
the key. Tell her . . . that they are yours.
Willie"—the secretary was still there—"will do
the labor for you." And when he had gone she was
to give it out publicly that Colonel Burr had passed
through a certain place on his way to Canada "accompanied by one Frenchman and two Americans
or Englishmen. On the same day Mrs. Alston
passed on her way to Saratoga for her health (or
some such thing)." It was all very mysterious, and
abounding in cipher names and blanks. And then,
"my dear creature, I regret sorely that we cannot
meet this evening; but somehow and somewhere
tomorrow absolutely we will. Perfect arrangements
are made for the grand Hegira, and all seems well.
Sleep; refresh and strengthen yourself."

Theodosia gave him all her time, all her energy,

all her attention, all her desperate affection during those wretched days, those anxious nights of clandestine and often deferred meetings. And finally, on June 6, "Ten P.M. met T. At eleven A.M." —June 7—"went on board pilot boat." They had parted for the last time. On June 8 there was no wind. On June 9, "at seven P.M. set sail."

"This is the commencement of my 26th year," Mary Ann Edwards wrote to H. E. Edwards on June 21, from Ballston Spa—where Mrs. Constable was being so friendly because little "Gampy" had "obtained [her] good opinion and won a place in [her] heart." Miss Edwards had been alarmed, "after your departure, my dear brother . . . with a report that you had been taken by the French; but as it was immediately contradicted, I yielded to my belief in the superiority of the English at sea, and to my reliance in the protection of your friend Neptune. . . . Never were hopes brighter than mine. To look on the gloomy side would be death to me, and without reserve I abandon myself to all the gay security of a sanguine hope.

"Do not imagine that my spirits are low, or that I am so weak as to wish you back. Do me more justice. I am cheerful always, and if my feelings ever amount to great gayety, your present voyage is the source of it."

The gay security of a sanguine hope—a magnificent pretense for Theodosia, who had known for some years that she was dying; the superb artifice of a matchless courage. . . .

PART IX

The Exile

1808–1812

"I suffer and freeze . . ."

AARON BURR.

CHAPTER I

ALIASES

I

THE next four years were to be, in many ways, the most extraordinary in a life of many extraordinary moments; and the account of their passage spread upon the pages of the journal kept by Colonel Burr—in the form, frequently, of imaginary conversations with Theodosia—is an astonishing record of vicissitudes and pleasures, of desperate dilemmas and shameless subterfuges, of public pretences and private depravities. And at the same time of amazing fortitude, of unconquerable tenacity, of immeasurable spirit.

That during these years one is to see him at his worst, is undeniable; that occasionally, for a laugh flung at adversity, for a splendid gesture in the face of ruin, he is to compel an almost incredulous admiration, is also incontestable; that a less guarded, a more spontaneously genuine revelation than ever before of his mysterious personality—a truer conception of the processes of his mind and of the complexities of his character—are to be obtained, will perhaps become apparent. One is to see great

235

courage, great folly, great suffering, great degrada-
tion—although an adequate comprehension of them
can only be furnished by a perusal of the original,
unexpurgated journal itself—and in the midst of
it all, shining upon his whole life, the sinister illum-
ination of an inevitable conclusion. . . .

The *Clarissa Ann* stopped at Halifax, where a
Prevost relative at Government House gave Mr.
Edwards a passport allowing the bearer to "proceed
without delay from Falmouth to London . . .
having dispatches for . . . Lord Castlereagh, at
whose office he is immediately to present himself on
his arrival in London." And Mr. Edwards would
also have liked to purchase a Newfoundland dog,
but none could be found to suit his taste, and he
was obliged to content himself with smaller pets
which he subsequently acquired in Europe.

A month afterwards he was at Falmouth, and
three days later, on July 16, 1808, in London. The
Colonel found lodgings in Craven Street, and at
first his prospects seemed encouraging. He delivered his letters to Lord Castlereagh, he interviewed
Lord Mulgrave and Mr. Canning, he outlined to
these dignitaries his plans for an invasion of the
Spanish dominions in America. And if these prudent
Ministers were not consumed with eagerness—if,
indeed, at the moment, the prevailing governmental
policy·was one of friendship for Spain and its now
dethroned monarch—in private circles, and among
the more adventurous young noblemen, Colonel
Burr's proposals were enthusiastically discussed.
And the excellent Mr. Merry was again appealed to,
and his interest enlisted; until, in November, he

was obliged to notify the Colonel that "although I could not see Mr. Canning yesterday . . . I conversed with another person of nearly equal authority, who told me he was sure that what you proposed to me . . . could never be consented to, pointing it out in every way to be impracticable."

But long before that, in August already, the British Government had begun to show in Colonel Burr's presence in England that interest which it had withheld from his schemes. He was summoned to Lord Liverpool's Home Office and required to make application for an alien's license. "For what reason or purpose are you come?" they asked him. "I am known personally to Lord Mulgrave and Mr. Canning," he replied, "to whom the motives of my visit have been declared. These reasons have long been known to Lord Melville." They gave him his license, but in November he returned it to Mr. Reeves of the Home Office, and "claimed the privileges of a British subject as a birthright, which I had a right to resume, and gave him notice that I should go where I pleased." On his application Colonel Burr had stated that he had been "born within the King's allegiance and his parents British subjects," which was perfectly true. But this "violent measure" grew out of the suggestions of Mr. Reeves who promised to have the case examined.

The report of this action was of course widely discussed and criticized in America, so that several years later Colonel Burr thought an explanation of it necessary. A rumor, he wrote Erich Bollmann, had been "industriously circulated" that he had "claimed protection as a British subject, having

had some difficulty with the Home Department
. . . about passports and permission to travel.
. . . It was strongly recommended to me by a
man of very high consideration, enjoying an important place under government, but hating personally
Lord Liverpool, to defend myself against his persecutions by claiming my birthright as a British
subject. It was presumed I would cheerfully seize
this mode to disengage myself from thralldom. . . .
It became a topic of conversation and many distinguished persons took a very lively interest in the
question. . . . My rights were demonstrated beyond a doubt." However—in spite of his statement
to Mr. Reeves—"I refused to suffer myself to be
called a British subject, for a single day, for any
purpose, under any circumstances; nor did I at any
moment swerve from this determination."

Colonel Burr was very positive about that in
1812; but in November, 1808, he was writing in his
journal that he had called on Reeves who reported
that "Dampier has given opinion" concerning his
"pretensions as a British subject" that he might
"resume at pleasure. The Lord Chancellor . . .
that I cannot and am forever an alien. The Attorney General is doubting, Lord Hawkesbury thinks
the claim monstrous. I begin to think the policy of
this movement very doubtful." It was just one of
many subterfuges, of which he may well have been
ashamed subsequently. . . .

2

In the meantime, in spite of the restrictions placed
upon him by the authorities—so that he concealed

his movements under a variety of aliases, Edwards, Melville, Kirby, Dunbar and others, until "you see I have as many names as any thief or nobleman in England"—Colonel Burr was enjoying himself.

He made trips into the country; he went sight-seeing; he visited the Tower of London, which might "do very well to keep the lions and state prisoners;" he stopped to see the railway at Croydon, where "four horses were drawing sixteen wagons . . . being eleven tons to each horse." He was taken into the home of Mrs. Prevost—the mother of the Halifax official—at Weybridge, and cordially received by Mrs. Achaud and Mr. Mallet, cousins of his stepsons. "Mrs. Prevost and Achaud are ladies of very superior understanding and knowledge of the world," he informed Theodosia. "The houses of Achaud and Mallet are frequented by literary men, and foreigners of literary fame and acquirements."

Colonel Burr was absolutely in his element in such gatherings, William Godwin and Charles Lamb being numbered among his friends, while William Cobbett, the "Peter Porcupine" of earlier American days, wished him to run for Parliament. In military circles he was no less welcome, and accepted countless courtesies at the hands of numerous Generals and Colonels; in society he was much sought after, and constantly entertained by Lords and Ladies—Lady Holland, Lady Affleck, Lord Bridgewater—to say nothing of "*les dames* Bartlett," and the fair Mrs. Onslow, and a certain Corsican widow, and a French lady of high degree, and a celebrated Italian beauty, and many other nameless recipients of his temporary attention. . . .

But in the midst of all these attractions—all this scented correspondence and all these delightful interviews—Colonel Burr derived the greatest pleasure ot all, perhaps, from his intimate association with the aged Jeremy Bentham, of whom he had always been the most ardent admirer, and whom he placed "second to no one, ancient or modern, in profound thinking, in logical and analytical reasoning." For several months the Colonel lived with Mr. Bentham who received him "with something more than hospitality," both in Queen's Square Place in London and at Barrow Green, and lost himself in philosophical discussions concerning such advanced subjects as tatooing, infanticide and crimes against Nature, so that for a while he almost forgot Mexico.

A complete set of Mr. Bentham's works was of course shipped to Theodosia, together with a bust of the gentleman—executed, it may be, by that same Italian artist who was making a mask of the Colonel, "a most hideous, frightful thing, but much like the original," the taking of which had left a distressing purple mark on the original's nose which interfered for several days with his social engagements. . . .

3

But the news from home was not good. "There are a thousand vague reports about you," Theodosia wrote. "The world begins to cool terribly around me. You would be surprised how many I supposed attached to me have abandoned the sorry, losing game of disinterested friendship. Frederick [Prevost] alone, however, is worth a host." John Swartwout, too, was "true, invariably and nobly conspicu-

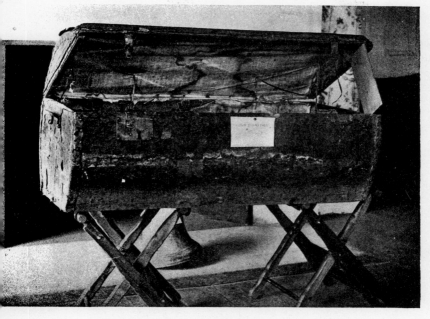

AARON BURR'S TRUNK

ous as the sun." And she was worried about her
father because he seemed to have abandoned the
Mexican expedition. "No doubt," she told him,
"there are many other roads to happiness, but this
appeared so perfectly suitable to you . . . so
entirely coincided with my wishes relative to you,
that I cherished it as my comfort, even when illness
scarcely allowed me any hope of witnessing its completion." However, "you will not remain idle . . .
my mind is anxious . . . in regard to your future
destiny. Where you are going, what will occupy
you, how this will terminate, employ me continu-
ally. . . . You, or rather circumstances, have deprived me of my greatest support during your
absence. . . . Tell me you are engaged in some
pursuit worthy of you."

She knew him so well, and that he must be kept
busy at something. . . .

And Theodosia was extremely ill. "Oh, my guardian angel," she exclaimed, "why were you obliged
to abandon me just when enfeebled nature doubly
required your care . . . how often when my
tongue and hands trembled with disease, have I
besought Heaven either to reunite us, or let me
die at once. . . . As soon as relief from pain
restored me in some measure to myself, I became
more worthy the happiness of being your daughter.
Now . . . if the disorder did not so strongly
affect my head I should feel almost well. No doubt
the mercury will remedy all my evils"—she took
quantities of mercury all the time. It was probably
cancer, of which her mother had died. "I long to
visit a region where the muses and graces have

some favorites. . . . Nothing would gratify me more than a visit to Europe."

And Colonel Burr begged her to come; he consulted physicians; he arranged to have her received by Mrs. Prevost; he set aside for her use four hundred guineas of the money available for his own expenses. All this he explained to Mr. Alston; "Gampy" would be educated with the children of General Bentham, "incomparably the best educated children I have ever seen;" he had "provided for her reception at every port at which she may probably land . . . we have provided a small house for her. It is probable that her fate will be determined within six or eight months. If she survives, I shall return with her to the United States. I have now discharged my duty; it remains for you to fulfill yours. It would be as insulting as unnecessary to address anything to your feelings, as to claim your sympathy with mine."

They did not get on together, those two. And Theodosia did not come. . . .

4

And in December the Colonel went to Scotland, to secure access to Lord Melville.

In the coach there was "a very pretty, graceful, arch looking girl about eighteen." She was "reserved and distant," but during a *tête à tête* breakfast at the first relay she was "all animation, gayety, ease, badinage," and the other passengers were "kept three quarters of an hour cooling in the coach." Leaving Oxford, the "only article of any interest was a pretty, comely little brunette," who, upon her arrival at her destination, was handed in by him "at a very respectable farmhouse." At Stratford there was a barmaid. At Birmingham, the Colonel missed his stage, because he got drunk—he was drinking a good deal now, all the time. "Still at Birmingham. Full of contrition and remorse. Lost my passage. Lost or spent twenty-eight shillings and a pair of gloves. . . . What business had I to go sauntering about the streets of a strange place alone and unarmed. . . . Truly I want a guardian more than at fifteen." However, in order to redeem the twenty-eight shillings, "I will take passage outside."

He had a splendid time at Edinburgh. He was entertained by Lord Justice Clerke, and Lord and Lady Hope, and Sir Alexander McKenzie, and the Baron Hepburn; he was waited upon by the Lord Provost of Edinburgh, and given the freedom of the library; he was introduced to Sir Walter Scott, and Madame Bruce, and Judge Hume, and Mr. Jeffery of the *Edinburgh Review;* and he fell in love with the Duchess of Gordon. "I lead a life of the utmost dissipation," he informed Mr. Bentham. "Driving out every day and at some party almost every night. . . . But in the midst of folly and dissipation, some little, little thing has been accomplished in the way of business." He found things "good and cheap here, and the peculiarities of the Scots and Scotesses amuse me greatly." At all events, "the time passed at Edinburgh was a continued round of dissipation, dinners, suppers, balls, routs. Edinburgh is the most hospitable and social place I have been. They meet to amuse and be amused, and they succeed."

He had to borrow money to pay his tavern bill
and engage his return passage in the coach. But he
could always find means to purchase a toy for
"Gampy." In Gravesend, for instance, in March,
1809, "this silly thing," he wrote him, "is the best
I can get in this dirty little place for my boy. You
and Grandpassa may puzzle at it for a month. . . .
I wish you would beat that cross little mother of
[yours] for me. The great ugly thing, she never
writes me a word about you, no more than if you
were a dead dog—beat her I say and tell her it's
for Gampis."

5

And in London there was trouble.

A claim, first, on the part of bookseller White, for
an unpaid bill; so that Colonel Burr hid himself,
under his Kirby alias, in James Street, in the house
of a certain Dunn, huckster. And when the matter
was at last adjusted amicably, it was the Government again. At about midnight, on April 4, 1809,
the Colonel's room was invaded by four worthies,
bearers of a warrant from Lord Liverpool, who seized
all his belongings and papers, and hustled him off
to the Alien Office. Mr. Reeves did what he could,
and Colonel Burr was finally taken by one of the
government messengers to his home in Stratford
Place. There he remained in close confinement for
three days, during which he spent most of his time
playing chess with his host and with his host's pretty
young Welsh wife. "They have got everything,"
he complained. "No plots or treasons, to be sure,
but what is worse, all my ridiculous journal, and all

my letters and copies." However, at the end of
the three days, Lord Liverpool apologized for his
action and the prisoner was released.

But in the same breath Lord Liverpool informed
him that his further presence in England would be
embarrassing to the Government, which proposed to
provide him with transportation to some other local-
ity. The place selected was Heligoland. Colonel
Burr was not slow to guess at the influence behind
Lord Liverpool. "Mr. Jefferson," he wrote, "or the
Spanish Junto, or probably both, have had influence
enough to drive me out of this country." He had,
he told Theodosia, "the honour of being a state
prisoner as a dangerous alien; an attempt, probably,
to conciliate the Government of the United States."
But Heligoland must be avoided, and in the end,
owing to the efforts of the Swedish Minister, the
authorities consented to issue a passport for Sweden.
"The mail coach," the Colonel notified Mr. Mallet,
"will take me . . . to Harwich, whence I shall
embark . . . for Gottenburgh, in obedience to
the sentence of ostracism declared by the benign
Lord Liverpool." Behind him, he left a good many
unpaid debts. . . .

CHAPTER II

PRUNES AND VERMICELLI

I

COLONEL BURR was now to spend some nine months in Sweden, Denmark and Germany. Nine months of social festivities, of association with artists and scholars, of precarious existence on borrowed funds, and, above all perhaps, of indiscriminate gallantries.

At Stockholm there were Madame de Castre, the singer, and the Countess de Gyllanstolp—a hard name, he thought, for such a beautiful woman. At Copenhagen there were other ladies. At Altona, near Hamburg, there was Janiva, the daughter of his landlady, with whom he drank champagne, and who frequently "filled up the evening" for him. At Weimar—where he met Mr. Wieland and Mr. Goethe—he had an affair with a lady of the court. "De Reizenstein is a sorceress," he recorded. "Another interview, and I might have been lost, my hopes and projects blasted and abandoned"—those precious projects! So he fled to Gotha, where he had another affair, with the Princess Louisa who did not, however, give him a garter as a souvenir. . . .

He was simply wandering from place to place, sometimes alone in countries of which he did not speak a word of the language, sometimes with American friends who had crossed with him in the *Clarissa Ann;* putting up at dreary inns where he suffered cold and discomfort; enjoying the reprieves of such private hospitalities as came his way; living only himself and his laundress knew how on his slender handful of borrowed pennies, managing an appearance of self-respect and dignity as flimsy as his worthless notes of hand; ever an object of governmental suspicion and police surveillance. The ex-Vice President of the United States. When all was said and done, a shabby gentleman who never paid his debts. Of course, he was always fascinating at first, so graceful, so charming—so glib. A pitiful figure. . . .

At last he obtained his passports for France. They had made a fuss about them at Hamburg, and at Frankfort—where he was kindly received by some cousins named Vandervalten—and the French authorities had ordered his arrest upon the slightest pretext; but Mr. de Bourrienne could find nothing against him, and finally procured the necessary papers, nor did he ever hear that "this dangerous citizen had compromised the safety of the state in any way." The Colonel had no other object, he had himself assured Count Volney, but "that of gratifying the very natural curiosity of seeing the capital of the world." However, "the publication more recently of a message from the Emperor to the

Senate"—Napoleon had consented to the independence of the Spanish possessions in America—
"has furnished a . . . more imperious motive. It
has led me to believe that I can, better than any
other man, perform a service greatly desired by the
Emperor and by another country. . . . To avoid
misconception, I would add that the . . . proposal
which I desire to make [has] no reference to the
United States, its government or politics."

To what extent this statement was untrue must
shortly become apparent. . . .

2

And at home, in America, the wretched Theodosia
was working so faithfully.

"Your removal from England," she told her
father, "was first announced to me . . . in the
newspapers, and for some minutes I remained stupi-
fied. . . . Thus, then, has vanished all the pleasure I derived from reflecting on the advantages of
your late residence." Without Mr. Alston's knowledge she had written to Mr. Gallatin to obtain some
assurance of security for Colonel Burr if he should
return, and to her former friend Mrs. Madison whose
husband was now President, "but no answer has
reached me, and this delay strengthens my apprehensions as to success."

The gazettes were still printing calumnies and
fanning "every spark of animosity," and "this
looks ill. Our best and most numerous collection of
friends is in New York. There are many there who
wish to see you once more established at home."

Theodosia was quite right; indeed, the time had come when the great De Witt Clinton himself had attempted an alliance with the Burrites and Martlings, for the purpose of regaining that political control which factions in his own party were wresting from him; an alliance approached at a banquet at Dyde's Tavern, in 1806, during which toasts were drunk and cheers given for Aaron Burr—but a great Clintonian mass meeting had finally rejected the proposed union, which Mr. Clinton then renounced.

And Theodosia was right when she wished that Colonel Burr were home again. "My dear sir," one reads in an incomplete letter in the possession of the New York Public Library, "it is necessary that Colonel Burr's friends should know something about him. That they should have it in their power to say he is in such a place, and that he will be at such a place at such a time. That if the sovereign people decree that his valuable talents should be appropriated to the public good they may know where to find him. Or that his friends may point to his habitation and say there resides in solitude the man whose talents and virtues were above estimation; he was greater and better than his country deserved. Or that his friends should point the public attention to such or such a tribunal, where the thunder of his eloquence and the lightning of his genius in the defense of the rights of his fellow citizens shall convince them of the wrong his country has suffered by the intrigues of demagogues in depriving it of such talents.

"But this candid proceeding . . . is denied, and a few young men . . . have the address . . . to give to Colonel Burr the air of a poor vagrant, without friends or home, flying from justice and himself. And with the suspicious they have conjured him up in the magic mantle of intrigue by which the best men, and those too who love the man, dare not come within the vortex of his fortune. This picture is no fancy . . . and must be remedied or Colonel Burr by prudent men will be viewed as a man lost to political life. . . . I am jealous for what I esteemed a righteous cause, and think that cause sacrificed. I have only to lament that men whose happiness I held so nearly connected with my own [have] by a narrow timid policy sunk so low. And if it has been my fortune to fall with them I only lament it because it disables me on a future occasion to make an effort to serve, first my country, and lastly my friends. I have therefore made up my mind no longer to struggle against the political tide, but with the most ardent attachment to Colonel Burr . . . I must, as a duty that I owe myself, my family and friends, act with any party who may sincerely oppose the Livingstonianism of this state, and Virginianism of the United States."

One can only regret the lack of any signature to this contemporary document. . . .

At the same time Theodosia was struggling with creditors, and trying with all her power to raise funds for her father. "I have written a second time to the gentleman who promised us the supply of funds," she informed him, "but there is little to be hoped from him. . . . I find his character does not stand very high as a man of punctilious honour in money dealings"—Colonel Burr should have winced at

AARON BURR

From the original portrait by Sharpless in the possession of Independence Hall, Philadelphia.

that. "Perhaps he may be teased into a performance of his engagements." And again, in another case, "I have written a second time to Judas. My letter cannot fail to reach him. It is written openly, in my own name. Perhaps he may be driven to compliance with his engagements. I mean to try . . . [Mr. Alston] of course has no part in my correspondence with Judas. Oh that he could prove to be a Peter, and repent of his sins!" One would so much like to know who "Judas" was. . . .

And in the midst of it all, those splendid sentences which destroy all criticism and silence all disdain. "I witness your extraordinary fortitude with new wonder at every new misfortune. Often, after reflecting on this subject, you appear to me so superior, so elevated above all other men; I contemplate you with such a strange mixture of humility, admiration, reverence, love and pride, that very little superstition would be necessary to make me worship you as a superior being, such enthusiasm does your character excite in me. When I afterwards revert to myself, how insignificant do my best qualities appear. My vanity would be greater if I had not been placed so near you; and yet my pride is our relationship. I had rather not live than not be the daughter of such a man."

Perhaps it is a sufficient justification of his whole life that he should have been the father of such a daughter. . . .

3

In February, 1810, Colonel Burr was at Paris, with his little dogs, waiting for some answer to his proposals to the French Ministers, and to beguile his waiting there were ladies.

There was "*la belle cordonnière;*" there was Albertine, "*la belle Allemande;*" there was Adele Fleury, his "*belle amie;*" and there was Madame Paschaud, who was "about the size and form of Mrs. Madison . . . very black hair and eyes. A fine, clear, fair brunette. . . . Her husband is at Geneva." He met her on March 12, in her absent husband's book shop, and for several months they strolled, and dined, and drove, and quarrelled a little together. In August she was off to Geneva, but in September she was back again, inviting the Colonel to dine, "as she does almost every day." But his interest in Madame Paschaud had begun to fade, and the husband's return from Geneva was perhaps not unwelcome.

In other circles he found Miss Williams, who entertained him in her country home; and Madame St. Clair, who was "really ladylike and handsome;" and Madame Récamier, with whom religion was "lovely," and who was "an angel of benevolence;" and Mrs. Fenwick, who was "really an extraordinary woman," and always amused and interested him; and the elderly Mrs. Robertson, widow of the historian, who often sent him her carriage and had him to dine, frequently for the purpose of consulting him professionally. "She always keeps me about half an hour while she makes her toilet," he recorded, and was usually in a hurry for her law papers, "as all women always are"—but she was very kind to him, and gave him presents for Theodosia.

And among the new friends that he seemed

to make so easily—the Duke de Bassano, Mr. Denon, Mr. Roux, Doctor Swediaur, the dentist Fonzi, the deceptive Mr. Crede—he came upon an old acquaintance, the painter Vanderlyn, with whom he was to spend much of his time. It has usually been said that Colonel Burr discovered John Vanderlyn while, as a country boy at Kingston, the latter was drawing pictures on a coach panel; that the Colonel told him to put a clean shirt in his pocket some day and come to him in New York; and that the young artist took him at his word. The facts, as recorded in Robert Gossman's unpublished biography of the great American painter, would appear to be quite different.

While he was still at Kingston Academy, John Vanderlyn had been taken to New York by his brother, Doctor Peter Vanderlyn, where he visited his relative Governor Clinton, and purchased some colors and a manual of drawing. In 1792, he was again in New York, and this time his brother secured for him a position as assistant to Thomas Barrow, a dealer in artists' materials, in whose shop he came in frequent contact with such men as Trumbull and Stuart. At the same time he was taking drawing lessons from Alexander Robertson, whose school he attended for two years. Finally, in 1794, Mr. Stuart gave him two portraits to copy; one of them was of Aaron Burr, and so good a reproduction did the young man make that it was purchased by Congressman Van Gasbeck, who subsequently told Senator Burr about it. It was in this manner that Colonel Burr "discovered" John Vanderlyn, who had, meanwhile, gone back to Kingston.

Upon his return to the city, in 1795, Colonel Burr

sent for John Vanderlyn and offered him the means
of continuing his studies. He was dispatched, consequently, to Philadelphia, to the studio of Mr.
Stuart, in whose home he lived until the older man
confessed that he had done all that he could for his
pupil who was now ready for European masters.
John Vanderlyn went back to Richmond Hill, where
Colonel Burr gave him letters both of introduction and credit, and sent him to Paris. In 1801, he
was back again, and painting the famous portrait of
Theodosia which he always considered his best work,
and which the Colonel took with him on his own
journey to Europe. And in 1805 he was once more
in Paris—where he was to win the Emperor's gold
medal with his picture of "Marius Amid the Ruins
of Carthage"—and Colonel Burr was writing him
that "you say nothing of coming out, at which I
marvel—if you are to spend some years in portrait
painting, this is the best country, for here is the
rage for portraits." And now, in 1810, the *protégé*
was perhaps become patron—at all events they were
much together, and the painter was receiving notes
from Colonel Burr to the effect that "*ma belle amie*
cannot honor your *atelier* by her presence today,
nor can we now agree on a day," and that "it was
not in my power to . . . give you reasonable notice, having slept too late."

4

The negotiations with the French Government
had soon come to nothing—one is to examine them
attentively on a later page—and in the spring of
1810 Colonel Burr was asking for passports to Amer-

ica. But they would not give him a passport. "In my affairs no advance," he was writing in August. "No passport, no money." And no doubt there was a reason for the French refusal, for General Armstrong, an old Livingstonian enemy of the Colonel, was American Minister at Paris, and Alexander McRae, one of the Government's attorneys in the Richmond trial, was Consul! And Jonathan Russell, *chargé d'affaires*, a frequent guest at Richmond Hill in the old days, was not any more friendly.

And there was not only official hostility—a hostility dictated in part perhaps by the State Department—to be encountered, but "the Americans here have entered into a combination against Aaron Burr," the Colonel noted. "That every man who speaks to him shall be shunned as unworthy of society. That no . . . person shall take any letter or parcel for him, or other like benevolent things." All sorts of stories were being circulated concerning him, and in January, 1811—he was still in Paris—he was told "by a gentleman who had offered to forward letters for me, that the messenger was instructed to take no letter or parcel from Aaron Burr, and that every person who handed him a letter for transmission must pledge his honour that it contained nothing from Aaron Burr. That is that Jonathan Russell whom you have known." As for the passport, Mr. McRae and Mr. Russell had both stated that as a fugitive from justice Colonel Burr was not entitled to a passport.

Colonel Burr's situation was desperate. "My affairs are quite stagnant," he wrote in October, "and I have no other prospect but that of starving in

Paris." Already in August he had explained to his friend Edward Griswold that he had only brought with him sufficient funds for a month's stay; could Mr. Griswold loan him "from six to one thousand dollars," or "to be more precise, one hundred and fifty guineas. . . . All this vexation arises from the machinations of our worthy minister, General Armstrong." But on August 16, the Colonel was obliged to note that he had heard about the loan from Mr. Griswold, and "he cannot! This matter is rather grave. Winter approaches. No prospect of having leave to quit the empire, and still less of any means of living in it. So must economize most rigidly my few remaining *louis*."

And he tried to, but somehow there were always books to buy, or a trinket for Theodosia, or some *sous* to a beggar, or the famous antique coins he was collecting for "Gampy;" and if he bought only a pound of sugar a month and restricted his consumption of segars, he turned around and purchased "a nosegay for m'lle." But in September Mr. Griswold finally let him have two thousand francs, and the Colonel was soon happily throwing money out of the windows again.

5

He took to speculating and promoting. He would raise merino sheep; he would manufacture vinegar from the sap of trees; he would supply Charleston with water with a special apparatus of Mr. Cagniard's; and lastly he would make his fortune in a renewed venture in the old Holland Company lands, concerning which he had once fought a duel.

For several months the matter filled his mind, with its fluctuations of optimism and depression; Swediaur, Fonzi, Crede, they were all to come in on it; maps and prospectuses were sent for from Amsterdam; Mr. Griswold made him "a most liberal proposition" which would clear him ten thousand dollars in two weeks. The Colonel pawned some of his presents for Theodosia, and with the balance of Mr. Griswold's loan, gathered together twenty-five hundred francs with which he purchased shares in the Company. "On casting up my remains," he found that he had left "just twenty-one dollars." A few days later, "I have now exactly three francs, four *sous* . . . my boots are at the shoemaker's and I cannot redeem them." And the next day, "on my way home gave ten *sous*, so got home with one *sou* in my pocket." And a little later again he was borrowing money from the Paschauds, fourteen francs of which he immediately spent on a bouquet for Adele Fleury, which was perhaps not exactly what Madame Paschaud would have preferred. The following day, Mr. Griswold gave him fifty francs, with some of which he paid two months' arrears to his servant Jeanette, while a part of the remainder was expended on a dinner for Adele. . . .

He was now in constant trouble. "Nothing from Amsterdam," he complained, "and verily I shall starve. Four or five little debts keep me in constant alarm, altogether about two *louis*"—and the American papers were saying that he was receiving a pension of two thousand pounds a year from the Emperor! Once, in December, he was dunned "for four *sous* which I had not." He was obliged to sell

"Gampy's" coins, to part with his books, to pawn
his possessions and most of the presents he had
accumulated for Theodosia. Once in a while—all
too frequently in their opinion—people had to lend
him money to buy food.

But at last there was good news from Amsterdam. Mr. Griswold would help, Mr. Crede was
interested. "I will send you a million of francs
within six months," Colonel Burr wrote in his journal to the absent Theodosia, "but one half of it
must be laid out in pretty things. Oh, what beautiful things I will send you. Gampillus, too, shall
have a beautiful little watch, and at least fifty trumpets of different sorts. . . . Home at ten, and
have been casting up my millions and spending it.
Lord, how many people I have made happy!"
Dreams, illusions, fantasies. In the meantime, he
went out and ordered a portrait of Theodosia to
be enamelled on a watch. But on February 10, 1811,
it was all over. "I am sick at heart, having [dis-
covered] the perfidy of a friend. . . . I had con-
fided to him my speculation . . . disclosed every
circumstance . . . I had built on it the hopes of
fortune"—and Mr. Crede had "disclosed the whole,
and associated himself with another to take it
wholly from me. The object is irrevocably lost."

He then possessed exactly sixteen *sous*, which he
promptly loaned to Mr. Fonzi. . . .

6

It is a marvel that he survived. Of course he
borrowed right and left, pitiful little sums which
were never to be repaid, most of them. In 1815 he

still owed money to John Vanderlyn, and to Mr. Fonzi, and to "our amiable friend B——t . . . which is most mortifying." He dined on stewed prunes, on sweetened barley water, on a "mess of vermicelli," on baked pears and milk. And yet he often declined invitations in society; Mrs. Robertson asked him to stay, "refused. Asked me for tomorrow . . . said I was engaged." Another time he "took a bowl of soup but refused to dine." But he enjoyed his bottle of wine whenever he could get one; it helped him "to bear poverty."

And it was not only the food. There was the cold. On December 31, "yesterday was cold, and today colder. Quite winter. The gutters all froze hard. Put on my flannel waistcoat . . . as I wear no surtout for a great many philosophical reasons; principally because I have not got one. The old great coat which I brought from America still serves in travelling, if I should ever again travel." And his room—"my room is up two flights of stairs, about fourteen feet square, paved with brick; very coarsely furnished; a large, very large, ill constructed fireplace. No quantity of wood can warm the room." And it was "still hard winter. With my great chimney and small room ventilated at a thousand crevices, and wood at twenty-five *sous* for five small sticks, I suffer and freeze." Finally, it was "very cold and no fire." He could not have his coffee one morning, "having no coal." Another time it was "very chilly. A fire would be comfortable." But at the same time, whenever there were a few coins in his pocket, he was paying nine francs for an evening at the theatre, and buying an opera glass,

and giving all his change to beggars. He must always
be spending, and giving, and running after women,
and getting himself befuddled. He must be boun-
tiful—on borrowed money. . . .

He was penniless, he was starving, he was freez-
ing, he was proscribed, he was shunned except by a
few acquaintances. In November, already, he had
not heard from Theodosia for fifteen months; the
letters had been lost. But in these darkest hours, in
all this misery and graceless behavior—some of the
pages of his diary are distressingly candid—there
was always courage, there was always resignation,
there was always humor. One frequently laughs
over his journal. . . .

CHAPTER III

THE OPEN DOOR

I

IMMEDIATELY upon his arrival in Paris, in February, 1810, Colonel Burr had called upon Count Volney, the Prince de Benevet and Mr. Adet—one time Minister to the United States—and obtained an interview with the Duke de Cadore, Minister of Foreign Affairs. He was not, however, permitted closer access to the Emperor than a sight of him one evening at the theatre;. and Jerome Bonaparte and Mr. de Talleyrand, forgetful of Richmond Hill hospitalities, denied themselves to him. He turned, therefore, to the policeman Fouché, now Duke d'Otrante, with a request for an audience in which to explain to him the details of the project towards which the Emperor remained so indifferent. Mr. Fouché granted the audience—Mr. Fouché was always ready to listen—but Mr. Fouché did not help Colonel Burr. Another attempt to see Mr. de Talleyrand at his home brought from the latter to his visitor a suggestion that he look upon the portrait of Alexander Hamilton hanging on the wall,

should he be at any loss to understand Mr. de
Talleyrand's refusal to receive him. . . .

But some of the officials appeared to be interested,
and were discussing Colonel Burr's long memorial
to the Emperor, and exchanging reports which were
eventually to vanish in the archives of the Ministry
of Foreign Affairs, where Professor Isaac Cox, of
Northwestern University, was to come upon them
long years after and make possible the publication of
the details of this hitherto obscure negotiation.

2

The plan outlined by Colonel Burr to Mr. Roux,
Chief of the Division of Foreign Affairs, and reported
by the latter on March 1 to the Duke de Cadore,
involved the occupation of the Bahamas by an army
of five hundred French, Danish and German volunteers, to be transported in American ships; the seizure of the Floridas, on behalf of the United States,
by a force to be recruited by Colonel Burr from the
provinces themselves and from the Western States;
and, if the Emperor so desired, the raising in the
Floridas of some ten thousand men, chiefly Louisian-
ans, to cooperate with a French army in the liberation of Louisiana and Mexico. In such an event,
Colonel Burr would be disposed to lead a contingent
from Florida to Halifax, through Canada—which was
also eager for liberation—across the Great Lakes,
and down into the valleys of the Ohio and Mississippi, to join the detachments raised in the American
Southwest in an attack on Upper Louisiana, while
another expedition crossed Lower Louisiana and pro-

ceeded along the coast. Colonel Burr was assured of an enthusiastic reception in Louisiana and Mexico, but if the Emperor preferred, these troops could be used against Jamaica.

On March 12, the French Foreign Office was again examining the project of liberating the Spanish colonies, with especial reference to a Canadian base as opposed to one on the Isthmus. Ten or twelve thousand men should be taken from Florida to Nova Scotia, and it was quite possible that the United States would assist in the enterprise. But first the Floridas must be severed from Spain, or there would be no chance of success in Jamaica, Mexico and Nova Scotia. On March 19, they were writing about it again. Then, four months later, on July 24, Mr. Roux had another interview with Colonel Burr, which assumed the Emperor's interest in the emancipation of the Spanish dominions. The Floridas, he was positive, were discontented under Spanish rule and would place themselves under the protection of the United States if France did not come to their assistance. Mexico, with French support, would close its ports to British and Spanish commerce.

As for Louisiana, according to Colonel Burr, the spirit of independence in that region was more lively even than in Mexico. The inhabitants were almost wholly French, and disliked the American Government. The same was true, with regard to England, in Lower Canada, which would have rebelled in 1778 had there existed any local representative government as in the American Colonies. . . .

Such was the character of the proposals which Colonel Burr was making to the Emperor's Ministers, and which they seem to have considered for a while in solemn credulity. Proposals reported from Paris to Mr. Madison, in an anonymous document dated December 10, 1810, as envisaging the conquest by one hundred thousand French troops of the northern portion of the United States, coincident with insurrections in Mexico, Texas and the Floridas under the leadership of Colonel Burr— from which it would appear that some of Mr. Madison's agents were doing their best to earn their salaries.

3

It is not necessary to indulge in exclamations over these French archives, to point out the inconsistencies which manifest themselves, to underline the fantastic aspects of their contents. It was the old story—the liberation of the Spanish dominions, all the Miranda aspirations brought to life, with a touch of Genêt for French eyes, the harmonious repetition of two fond names, Canada and Louisiana, for French ears. It was such a project as that other which had not insulted Mr. Merry's intelligence, nor seemed extravagant to the Marquis Yrujo. It was Colonel Burr at his old money raising stratagems.

How much of this project was the expression of any serious intention of his own is, perhaps, a matter of greater concern, since the recovery by France of Louisiana was included in his aims. Hitherto, in these pages, one has vigorously denied any motive of treason in Colonel Burr's enterprises, any contemplated action inimical to the welfare and integrity of the United States. Throughout the discussion of his Mexican expedition, and of his trial for treason, one has purposely excluded any reference to this forthcoming memorial to the Emperor, because in 1806 and 1807 the memorial had not been written, because it was necessary to confine oneself to those events alone which occurred within those years, and because the case of the United States, and of public opinion, against Aaron Burr could, in one's estimation, be permitted to rest only upon the evidence producible against him at the time. Mr. Jefferson was not trying Colonel Burr in 1807 for something which he may have decided to do in 1810.

But in 1810 it is incontestable that Colonel Burr was, on paper at least, meditating treason. Louisiana, an American territory, was to be invaded and seized by foreign troops, aided by a force of malcontents organized by himself in the Floridas. This was treason. And one may not evade the fact that his willingness to commit treason in 1810 jeopardizes the whole structure of his innocence in those earlier years, with its revelation of a subsequent guilt establishing the possibility of a previous intent. When a man has been suspected of one murder, and then is caught planning another, it is difficult not to assume that the first suspicion, however unjust actually, was well founded.

In the case of Colonel Burr, however, one stands in the presence of an even more absorbing possibility. His—one can no longer conceal the conviction—his is, perhaps, a case for the alienist. . . .

4

The matter was one of contemporary comment, doubts concerning Colonel Burr's complete sanity having been expressed on two occasions at least by men who had had an opportunity of observing his conduct in critical situations.

At the time, for instance, of the Colonel's interview at Bayou Pierre with Cowles Meade, the latter had reported that Colonel Burr had talked insanely to him, and that he appeared mentally deranged. And later on, during the trial, Mr. Blennerhassett was of the same opinion. He had visited Colonel Burr and found him "as gay as usual"— Theodosia herself had called their sojourn in Richmond a party of pleasure, and stated that "our little family circle has been a scene of uninterrupted gaiety." But there was nothing gay about the proceedings in Mr. Blennerhassett's estimation, and he could not understand how the Colonel could continue to be "as busy in speculations on reorganizing his projects for action as if he had never suffered the least interruption." He was insisting, then, that "in six months our schemes could all be remounted." Everything was rosy, the trial was a bagatelle, as soon as it was over they would all start for Mexico again. This seemed idiotic to Mr. Blennerhassett. "Whatever feeling [Burr] possesses," he declared, " is confined within the sensuality of his temperament, if indeed his conduct . . . does not warrant the suspicion of Cowles Meade."

Indeed, the matter would seem to have been a sort of family jest in his early years; at all events, there is a letter from Colonel Burr to Tapping Reeve, written prior to 1782, in which the young man urged his brother-in-law to "think of the Carolina enterprize . . . but if that plan is too vast for you, I have a more moderate one in store, and which I think I shall be able to make appear a pretty rational one, for a *madman*"—and the italics are his own.

One has seen enough, surely, of the Colonel's sanguine temperament during the days of the conspiracy, to sympathize with Mr. Blennerhassett's attitude. The Mexican expedition had become a mania with Colonel Burr; it was, until his closing years, always to remain a mania, a patriotic fixed idea, an obsession of his mind. As great a mania as that other which so possessed him, the mania for instruction, for fault finding, for correction, for ordering people around, to which a certain space has already been devoted in these pages. And both of them were only manifestations, perhaps, of an even greater mania—his mania for grandeur, for self-importance, for impressing his associates. The gentleman who could at times talk so grandiosely and so fantastically; who exhibited his little daughter's letter after changing a misspelled word; who was so touchy about his honor, so insistent upon his integrity, so conscious of his reputation—when actually so often lacking in all three.

So many other corroborating symptoms of mental instability come to mind. His secretiveness, his mania, again, for mystery and intrigue. His jealousy, in army days, of his superiors, of those who were promoted above him. His professed scorn of

public opinion, contrasted with his intense resent-
ment of criticism, his acute consciousness of persecution—however real—his willingness to beg favors
from an enemy, as on two notorious occasions. His
incredible extravagance and spendthrift habits; his
mania, once more, for liberality, for ostentation,
for accumulating books and pictures, for acquiring
objects with which to gratify his passion for giving.
His so frequently injudicious choice of associates and
confidants, his facile intimacy with casual acquaintances, he who was supposedly so fastidious, so reticent, so reserved. His extremes of enthusiasm and
depression, for all his stoic's philosophy; at Richmond all gaiety, at Philadelphia a little later on the
verge, so it seemed to Charles Biddle, of suicide;
the Mexican venture boiling in his mind, the Mexican venture abandoned, the Mexican venture revived, refurbished, magnified beyond all reason;
millions to be made in Holland Company lands, the
whole project hopeless and discarded.

Empires, colonies, embassies, revolutions, expedi-
tions, canals, banks, merino sheep, real estate,
vinegar, water works. Schemes, plots, enterprises—
some of them sound, practical, touched with a
brilliant genius; some of them dreams, delusions,
fantasies, the exotic flowering of an uncontrolled
imagination. . . .

5

It is for the pathologist to decide, but one seems
so inevitably to detect the indications of a deranged
mind, of a hapless personality incapable of orienta-
tion when freed from the restraint of an attractive

routine, of a flattering responsibility, of a sympathetic task.

One looks at that curious, masklike countenance, at those somber, mysterious eyes; one remembers a delicate childhood, an astounding precocity, a reckless industry which so often denied sleep, an arduous physical effort, accompanied by accumulating exposure and exhaustion, followed by months of illness, of listlessness, of "hypochondria;" one is aware of a constant expenditure of energy, bodily and mental, a constant strain of worry and contrivance in private affairs, a constant battering of pride and sensibilities in public life; one recalls the ordeal at Richmond, the indignities in London, the ills and discomforts of Sweden, and Denmark, and Germany, the famished plight at Paris. Aaron Burr was fifty-four in 1810; he had endured, and hazarded, and suffered much; if the door guarding his sanity had ever been the least ajar, then was the time, perhaps, for it to swing slowly open.

And while heredity is often a deceptive guide, one may not forget that on one side of his house Colonel Burr's direct ancestry, however remote, was tainted with active insanity. The thing was in the blood which flowed through his veins, and is not denied in family annals. At all events, it may well be prudent to consider the record of Aaron Burr's life—the years already disclosed and the years to come—in the light of such a surmise. It will, in some instances, be most charitable.

CHAPTER IV

INSULA INHOSPITABILIS

I

THE long denied passport to leave the Empire was finally issued. Colonel Burr had strong friends at court in Mr. Denon and the Duke de Bassano; the French Government was just as well satisfied to have him out of the country; and Mr. Russell was at last persuaded to grant the Colonel's request. But the matter was not to be so simple. It was early in March, 1811, that Mr. Russell had consented to draw up the document; late in April the passport had been mislaid in some of the French bureaus, and a new application became necessary.

While he was waiting for the governmental red tape to unwind itself, Colonel Burr went on a trip to Amsterdam to interview the officials of the Holland Company, his interest in the land project having been temporarily revived. He also visited the Persian church, in which three Persians were "singing very loud and in the most horrible discord," and had a ridiculous adventure at a crowded inn, involving an embarrassing nocturnal domestic arrangement with a lady passenger. But most important of all was his meeting with Captain Coombs, of the ship *Vigilant*, who, after having suffered confiscation, was waiting for permission to sail, and who offered to take the Colonel aboard and provide him with a cabin. Colonel Burr, who had just returned to Amsterdam from a sightseeing tour through Holland, abandoned his previous plan of sailing from Bordeaux, and went back to Paris, where he arrived on June 22.

John Vanderlyn was in some sort of trouble, so that "if he does not go to the United States he will be in jail here in a year," and the passport now had to be changed to apply from Amsterdam instead of Bordeaux, an alteration to the securing of which the Duke de Bassano consequently applied his patient energies. In the meantime, the Colonel was spending money, buying presents for Theodosia, interesting himself in schemes for preserving milk, eggs and fruit, calling on Albertine, and renewing the overtures to the Holland Company. It was June time in Paris, and the Duke had loaned him ten thousand francs. . . .

But the Duke was very busy in the Colonel's behalf—perhaps it was in his mind to avoid lending him any further sums if possible—and when Mr. Russell began to raise objections to the change in the passport, Mr. de Bassano knew just what to do. "The person," he wrote Mr. Denon, on July 18, "through whom I have communicated to Mr. Russell that he should not have refused a new passport to Mr. Burr was in the country. I wrote to her yesterday to return. She arrived at the moment your note was received. I shall have the passport in the

course of the day, and shall forward it immediately
to the Duke [de Rovigo] and I am convinced that
you will receive it tomorrow to transmit to Mr.
Burr." And later on the same day, "I have received
the passport from Mr. Russell for Mr. Burr, and
have sent it to the Duke de Rovigo, requesting an
immediate return of it. It ought to reach me this
evening. Thus there is nothing to prevent the
departure of the Colonel tomorrow, unless the police
should throw those obstacles in the way which I
think I have prevented."

With the help of the "person" it was all arranged,
and on July 19, accompanied by a secretary, Colonel
Burr set out in a *cabriole* for Amsterdam. Behind
him he left a whole catalogue of debts, some tearful
ladies, the portrait of Theodosia which John Vanderlyn was copying, and a list of errands for the
latter's attention. He was glad to go—for he was
"weary of Europe"—and no doubt many people in
Paris were glad to see him go. . . .

2

But Colonel Burr might just as well have stayed
in Paris, for nearly three months were to pass before
the *Vigilant* finally sailed. Three months of delays,
and postponements, and false alarms, due to governmental indecision and the repeated assembling of
new passengers; for the Colonel, three months of
anxiety and increasing distress, since he had been
obliged to sell some of his presents in order to pay
his four hundred and fifty guilders passage money,
and the officials of the Holland Company would
hold no further traffic with him.

And all during those weeks Colonel Burr wrote incessantly to John Vanderlyn, and fussed at him to finish the new portrait of Theodosia; to send him this, that and the other; to supply him with seeds of certain plants which he proposed to introduce in America, and with drawings of Mr. Doolittle's new washing machine; to give him news of, and carry messages to, various beautiful ladies—"the beautiful D. C. . . . after having settled your own business with her I give you permission to kiss her more than twenty times for me"—"Always say something of *la belle* C., etc., etc."—to reform his ways and be a little ashamed of himself—"I can't help pitying you a little for the Violette *affaire*. You deserve, however, to be castrated, you rascal! To leave Ambrosia and Nectar to feast on tripe and small beer! To descend from Venus to a yahoo! Oh, if I were only there I would endeavor to inspire *La Belle* with the idea of a *douce vengeance*"—and to pack up his portmanteaux and come to America on the *Vigilant*.

"If you could leave Paris within forty-eight hours after having this," the Colonel assured him, "there is no doubt you would be in time for the *Vigilant*." If he could "instantly come on, I have no doubt you would be in season and your passage would cost nothing—that is if you would work, for you might paint it twofold." Exclusive of the crew, "we shall be about 50 passengers of which abt 40 of this city, among whom, as is said, several accomplished young ladies, all of whom you would have painted if you had been on board." But John Vanderlyn did not come, and on September 29, 1811, "we got under

weigh at 6 this afternoon, the wind ahead and light.
Made about half a league and have to come to anchor
again. At the return of the ebb, at 6 tomorrow,
hope we shall make sail, and if the wind allows us
to get out of the harbor, will continue on our voyage."

Two days later they were seized by a British frig-
ate, and sent in to Yarmouth for a prize court
decision. "Imagine to yourself, my dear Sir,"
Colonel Burr wrote to Mr. Reeves of the Foreign
Office, in his letter asking for permission to go to
London, "on board a small ship, very badly accom-
modated, fifty-four passengers, of whom a majority
women and children; thirty-one sailors, thirty-
three hogs and about one hundred other quadrupeds
and bipeds. With this picture in your mind, I am
sure you will hasten to reply and to furnish me some
sort of passport or privilege of locomotion."

On October 16, he was in London, with two shillings in his pocket.

3

"How am I to get to the United States?" he wrote
in his journal. "If I had rino could get out in twenty
days. I will walk to any port in the kingdom."

The case of the *Vigilant* was postponed time after
time, the Colonel was in daily need of "rino," not
only to procure another passage, but to house and
feed himself! Many of his former associates—except
the Godwins, and Hubert Koe, and Jeremy Bentham
—were now disposed to ignore him; Mrs. Prevost
was dead; men like Peter Irving and Robert Morris
called on him but offered no assistance; but in the
midst of all his necessitous manipulations, Colonel

Burr would not borrow from Mr. Bentham or accept his hospitality. To the very end he preserved his dignity in the presence of that friend he so revered.

One by one he began to sell his presents for Theodosia and "Gampy;" he tried to economize, with the usual lapses—"have spent fourteen shillings and sixpence magnificently, i.e., like an ass"—and he turned once more to his promotions and speculations. "My occupation for the moment," he told Theodosia, "is making a chymical experiment. . . . If I should hit on it, which seems probable, it will be of value here, and of much greater in the United States. A chymist of science and fortune assists me, and allows me the use of his laboratory." It was the old French vinegar scheme, the product to be made from a certain acid, and a wealthy manufacturer named Brunell was interested, but the foreman at the laboratory finally reported the result of his experiment to "take the bad smell out of the acid," and while "it did effectually take out the smell . . . at the same time, it took out the acid, and the residuum was neither more nor less than simple water. So that won't do."

An attempt to introduce some of Mr. Fonzi's novelties in false teeth, moulds of which he had secured through John Vanderlyn, was equally unproductive. Another invention of his own was for a while much more so—on paper. He had, in fact, "made more than a million guineas" one night, thinking about it. It was not his only flight of inventive imagination; in 1773, already, Tapping Reeve had been congratulating him, a little ironically perhaps, "upon the success of your Invention;"

and in 1824 Colonel Burr was still at it, and exhort-
ing his friend Flandreau "to think of our Gasses and
to note all your thoughts. . . . Ask Mr. Jennings
how and for what sum he will make the Pistons etc.
which may be required for the experiment and set
him at Work." He was, apparently, always contriving something, and in 1811 it was a simplifica-
tion and improvement of the steamboat. The
Colonel "found it perfect," and applicable to "everything that floats. Sails, and masts, and rigging, and
the whole science of seamanship are become useless.
My vessels go at the rate of twenty miles an hour,
and am in hopes to bring them to thirty." Suddenly,
however, "an objection occurred to me; it struck me
like electricity; my poor vessels lay motionless;"
but during the night "I found a complete remedy,
and now away we go again." And of course, "so
soon as I get this million, Lord! What pretty
things will buy for thee [Theodosia] and Gampillo.
Laid out, however, a great deal of the money last
night. Thought of the faithful in the United States.
Then succoured the G's and made an establishment
for A."

4

And in the meantime he was roasting some potatoes by the fire on which to dine. In one fortnight
he had "only half a pound of meat, six pounds of
potatoes, and four pounds six ounces of bread."
He found his appetite "in the inverse ratio to my
purse; and I now conceive why the poor eat so much
when they can get it." On January 20, 1812, he
had "two pounds of bread, which will last me three

THE EXILE

THE EXILE

and then the rent, eight shillings per week, is due,
and must be paid on Wednesday morning or Gam
[Burr] goes into the street." He was "never at a
loss to know Wednesday, for it is my pay day, and
comes in terror"—the rent for his room in Clerken-
well Street, and two shillings to the maid Eliza.

On February 7, "the cash has got down to seven-
pence; and I have no tobacco; and coffee, and coal,
and bread only for tomorrow." And the next day,
"instead of having bread for the day, had not a
mouthful, and was sick for want of tobacco. To
dine and drink a pint of ale would just ruin me. So
sent my little maid for fourpence worth of bread and
an ounce of tobacco, three pence half-penny; for
which had to borrow a penny and a half of her; and
having only coffee for the morning, and very scant."
A few days later he was ill, with only two farthings
in his pocket, so that he was unable to purchase
any medicine. He was doing without meat, dinner
was often a bowl of soup or some rice, his usual
drink "toast and water." In March, he had "left
in cash two half pence, which is much better than
one penny because they jingle, and thus one may
refresh one's self with the music." He went out to
try and sell Theodosia's enameled watch, and gave
the two half pence to a little girl.

But the worst trouble was his umbrella. He lost
his umbrella, and "it is impossible for me to buy one
or do without one." He searched for it everywhere,
and it "hung heavy on my heart," but "it is finally
lost, and I must submit to the inconvenience of getting wet and spoiling my clothes."

5

Colonel Burr was trying all the time, of course, to secure a passport, but with Jonathan Russell now acting as *chargé d'affaires* in London the undertaking was no easier than before. "Since my arrival here," the Colonel wrote Edward Livingston in February, "I have already been twice disappointed in passages, which I ascribed to the caprice or malevolence of the respective captains, but no doubt it emanated from [Russell's] influence." The *Vigilant* had been released, and while Captain Coombs had decided to sail for New Orleans, which was awkward, he was prepared to pay Colonel Burr's passage from that port to the Atlantic Coast. Otherwise he would only refund ten pounds of the passage money. But the United States Consuls at London and Yarmouth forbade him to take Colonel Burr on board, and he sailed, the richer by the greater portion of the money paid him in Amsterdam.

"The Captain . . . finally resolved to go to New Orleans, and urged me very much to go with him," the Colonel told Charles Williamson. "This was greatly out of my way; but . . . having paid my passage, I at length agreed to sail with him . . . and I was just about to announce to you my approaching departure, when I received a letter from him stating that the American Consul had warned him not to take me, and had menaced him with the displeasure of the United States Government, if he dare to do it. He . . . therefore begged to be excused from receiving me. . . . The malice of these agents of a feeble and timid administration did not stop here; for to their influence may be ascribed also that the Captain refuses to pay me here the amount of my passage, and a sum which I had advanced to him at Amsterdam, which has put me to serious inconvenience. You will be at no loss to conjecture the motives to this interposition on the part of the American Government. It has, however, convinced me more thoroughly that I ought not to lose a day to be there."

But at last Colonel Burr found a Captain Potter, whose ship, the *Aurora*, was at Deal, who was willing to take him to Boston for thirty guineas; and Mr. Reeves finally sent him a passport, made out in the name of his alias Arnot, "and if you are tired of the name of Arnot, and wish any other, you may have it." The only thing left to do was to obtain the necessary cash, all the more so since out of the ten pounds received from Captain Coombs he had spent twenty shillings for "a pair of pantaloons which I did not want." He sold and pawned the rest of his gifts; he sent his *eighteen* pieces of baggage down to the ship—"trunks, boxes, portmanteaux, bundles, rolls," filled with Heaven knows what—he borrowed ten pounds from Mr. Reeves. But he still needed twenty pounds.

He went, on March 24, to Mr. Reeves, and "gave a hint of the state of the treasury, but he did not take it. . . . How very awkward would be my position if the *Aurora* should sail without me. Without a rag of clothes, or a penny of money, or anything to make money of. . . ." And so, on March 25, he went back to Mr. Reeves and explained his predicament, and this time his long suffering

friend gave him the money. Like the Duke de
Bassano, he was perhaps anxious to be rid at any
price of the ex-Vice President of the United States.

"And now," Colonel Burr recorded, "I repose,
smoking my pipe and contemplating the certainty
of escaping from this Country. . . . As to my
reception in my own country, so far as depends on
the government, if I may judge from the conduct of
their agents in every part of Europe, I ought to
expect all the efforts of the most implacable malice.
This, however, does not give me a moment's uneasi-
ness. I feel myself able to meet and repel them.
My private debts are a subject of some little solicitude; but a confidence in my own industry and
resources does not permit me to despond, not even
to doubt. If there is nothing better to be done, I
shall set about making money in every lawful and
honorable way. But again, as to political persecution. The incapacity for every purpose of our present rulers, and their total want of energy and firmness, is such that it is impossible that such feeble
and corrupt materials can long hold together, or
maintain themseves in power or influence. Already
there are symptoms of rapid and approaching decay
and dissolution."

And as for his Mexican schemes—whether or not
he knew that in 1810 revolts against the Spanish rule
had broken out in several provinces, including West
Florida and Mexico, which the Spaniards ascribed
to his influence, and that, already in 1808, General
Wilkinson himself had written to Mr. Jefferson that
"the scenes which are now passing . . . inspire the
liveliest hopes that the emancipation of Mexico and

South America is not distant"—for his own part, Colonel Burr was telling Mr. Bentham that "there is a possibility . . . that I may mingle personally in the affairs of Spanish America. . . . It is also probable that I may be capable of rendering [Miranda] or his countrymen service in the United States, whither I am now about to return, and certainly I should do it with pleasure and zeal."

He did not understand yet that the management of such enterprises had passed forever out of his hands. . . .

6

On March 26, accompanied by Mr. Reeves—the courtesy was to cost the latter another three guineas for a boatman—Colonel Burr drove to Gravesend. The *Aurora* had sailed with the tide. But they found a wherry, and after a twenty-seven mile journey down the river, in a cold southwesterly wind, the Colonel was finally put aboard his ship. "I shake the dust off my feet," he wrote. "Adieu, John Bull. Insula inhospitabilis, as it was truly called eighteen hundred years ago."

And the Captain—"our two captains, Potter and Nicholls"—feared that there would be war between England and America, but "I have no such apprehensions. I believe that our present administration will not declare war. If the British should hang or roast every American they can catch, and seize all their property, no war would be declared by the United States under present rulers." The war talk was all to influence elections, "but J. Madison and Co. began this game too soon, and I doubt whether all the tricks they can play off will keep up the farce till the month of May. I treat their war prattle as I should that of a bevy of boarding house misses who should talk of making war; show them a bayonet or a sword, and they run and hide. Now at some future day we will read this over, and see whether I know those folks."

But this time Mr. Jefferson's passion for peace had made war inevitable, and if J. Madison and Co. were to run, it was to be from the battlefield of Bladensburg. . . .

The *Aurora* sailed, and off the Isle of Wight a boarding party from a British sloop wanted to insist that Mr. "Adolphus Arnot" must be a Frenchman, but permission was finally given to proceed. And now that he had left England once and for all, the Colonel would have liked to put in again, in order to purchase some bread, and lemons, and tobacco—for he had only a handful of segars and there was no tobacco to be had aboard—but the Captains would not consent to it. Captain Potter gave his passenger two ounces, however—"being all he had; an effort of generosity of which I should not have been capable towards an indifferent person"—and they were off across the Western Ocean.

They made an uneventful voyage of it, although for a while it was rough, and Colonel Burr was ill, and "the tossing was so great we didn't attempt to put anything on the table, but eat off the floor." And the steward was "a dirty, negligent, morose rascal as I ever met," until the Captain "beat [him] till he was quite disfigured; also made him strip off his waistcoat, and beat him with a rope's end till

he howled most piteously and promised reformation."
Colonel Burr himself was "not known or suspected
on board, save by Captain Potter, in confidence.
Mr. Arnot is a grave, silent, strange sort of animal."
Mr. Arnot was also letting his whiskers grow.

And on May 4, 1812, they were in sight of Boston
Light. . . .

CHAPTER V

I

COLONEL BURR remained quietly aboard the *Aurora* that first night, and the next day, trusting to his whiskers and a wig, he stepped ashore and found lodging in the boardinghouse kept on Cornhill Square by Mrs. Goodrich, a sea captain's widow. The door never opened "but I expect to hear the comer exclaim out Colonel Burr;" but nothing happened, he had not been recognized, the newspapers did not announce his arrival. He notified Samuel Swartwout in New York, and faced the problem of redeeming his baggage from the Custom House.

"Now here occurred a dilemma," he wrote. "Dearborn, the Collector (son of the General) knows me as well as you do, having seen me hundreds of times. . . . For me to go direct to him . . . and demand a permit in the name of Arnot seemed to be an experiment that promised little success, and, in case of discovery, might expose me to serious inconveniences, as the family of Dearborn have been extremely vindictive against me. . . . On the other hand to spend twenty dollars out of thirty-two, which is my whole stock, in going to Newburyport and returning my things by land, might disable me from ever getting out of Boston." So he took a young man with him to show him the way "entered with all possible composure; passed under the nose of Mr. Dearborn into the adjoining room, where the first part of the business was to be done." But when the clerk directed him to take the permit to be signed by the Collector, "here was the rub. I told the young man . . . to take it . . . and I got out as fast as I could, passing again under the nose of Dearborn. I do assure thee that I felt somewhat lighter when I got into the street."

And on the wharf there was every chance of his being recognized, and his real name was written in many of his books, and on the superscription of letters—for all his wig and whiskers the Colonel would appear to have managed matters very badly —but, again, nothing happened. One wonders, however, whether anything would really have happened if he *had* been recognized, or whether much of this mystery was not gratuitous. . . .

2

Back on Cornhill Square the Colonel began to look around. He sent for an old army subordinate, Benjamin Fessenden, and "the old soldier" proved loyal and helpful. He made himself known to a Mrs. Pollard, with whom he had once lodged—or rather, she recognized him the moment he stepped through the door—but her son, "young P.," was not in a position to do anything publicly for the Colonel as he was then running for an office, although he assisted him in many private ways.

And the Colonel wrote to Jonathan Mason, a friend since college days. "I pray you not to conjecture aloud who may be the writer," he told him. If he would come to Mrs. Goodrich's he would find an old acquaintance. Mr. Mason sent word that his position was very delicate and that, after thinking it over, he would either call or write. "Now I engage he will neither do one nor the other," Colonel Burr remarked. "Did you ever hear of such meanness? This very J. Mason was at Richmond during the trial . . . came often to see me, and openly avowed a friendship for me. He is immensely wealthy, and not a candidate for any office. What should restrain such a man from expressing his feelings? Timidity." Just the same, Colonel Burr was not ashamed to ask Mr. Mason for a loan and to suggest to him that he purchase some of his books. Mr. Mason informed him that he had withdrawn from commerce, and that it would not be convenient for him to make advances.

On the other hand, Samuel Swartwout in his reply was all enthusiasm. The Colonel had nothing to fear except from his creditors, and as for them, let him come to New York and go on the jail limits, and be done with it. Colonel Burr was afraid that Theodosia's "little heart would sink to hear that Gamp. was on the limits"—although if she could see him there, and "be supported by the light of his countenance and catch inspiration from his lips," she would "forget that he was not in paradise"—and besides, the jail limits would interfere with a project

JOHN VANDERLYN

which he entertained "of entering into . . . matrimony. . . . The fair object is a worthy lady, some few years older than myself, with fortune enough, and, I think, good nature enough to make that appropriation of it."

But the receipt of a year old letter from Theodosia herself suggesting the very thing, "terminated his indecision." She had advised him to come home, "land in New York"—nothing could be done for him in South Carolina—"Make your stand there. If you are attacked, you will be in the midst of the Tenth Legion. Civil debts may be procrastinated, for a time, by confinement to the limits. There you can take breath, openly see your friends, make your arrangements. . . . I confess I augur ill of government . . . but I believe differently of the citizens generally. At all events, it is better to brave any storm than to be leading your present life. . . . If the worst comes, I will leave everything to suffer with you."

But how to get to New York. "Have left one five cent piece," he was writing, and "my drink is toast and water. I shall soon be pure as an angel." He must pay his board, and twenty dollars for a passage on a sloop, and they were only offering him some thirty dollars for the watch which he was trying to sell. But Mr. Fessenden took the Colonel to see Doctor Kirkland, the President of Harvard College, and that good gentleman finally paid him forty dollars for some of his foreign books. The Colonel was to redeem them from the College library whenever he chose—so that now each of the larger colonial Colleges had served him in some capacity, Prince-

ton as his *alma mater*, Yale as a comrade in arms, and
Harvard as his pawnbroker.

Colonel Burr paid his bills; he embarked his effects
aboard the sloop *Rose*—"it has cost me four trips
through State Street, and the whole length of the
long wharf in open day, amid thousands of idlers"—
and early in June Mr. De Gamelli left Boston. As
for the jail limits project, Theodosia seemed to
"consider it as temporary. It might be, probably
would be, during life;" and so he wished to reach
New York incognito and reserve his decision.

3

The *Rose* sailed—and she was of Fairfield, Connecticut, as were the Captain and several of his
passengers, and the Captain's wife was actually a
cousin of Colonel Burr's! But it did not occur to
her that she might also be a cousin of Mr. De
Gamelli's. . . .

They put in at the Mill River, near Fairfield, and
after breakfasting at the Captain's house, Colonel
Burr strolled out into that countryside which he
knew so well. "Every object," he recorded, "was
as familiar to me as those at Richmond Hill, and
the review brought up many pleasant and whimsical
associations. At several doors I saw the very lips
I had kissed and the very eyes which had ogled me
in the persons of their grandmothers about six and
thirty years ago. I did not venture into any of
their houses lest some of the grandmothers might
recollect me. The instance of Mrs. P. at Boston
will make me cautious of old ladies whom I knew
when they were younger."

It was a long, long time since Colonel Burr had been in Fairfield. This was, really, his homecoming —but after all, it was only Mr. De Gamelli walking down the lane.

He gave his cousin an ivory nutmeg grater, which she received "with more coldness than you would have received an apple from a servant," and the *Rose* departed—but "this giving," it suddenly occurred to him, "is a very unprofitable business, and I have twenty times determined to quit it, yet am perpetually seduced into the perpetration of it." Perhaps because that door in his mind was always swinging open. . . .

4

The Colonel had hoped to reach New York after nightfall, but the Captain was not disposed to take the *Rose* through Hell Gate in the dark, and anchored her off a wharf near a tavern, the keeper of which Colonel Burr recognized as an old crony. If he went ashore there he would certainly be identified—but instead, he had himself transferred to a small sailing vessel which was passing, and whose owners agreed to take him to the city. The wind dropped soon after, however, and it seemed as though they might go drifting all night, when "I heard the noise of oars, and hailed. It proved to be two vagabonds in a skiff. They were very happy to set me on shore in the city for a dollar, and at half past eleven I was landed."

So, on June 7, 1812, exactly four years after his parting with Theodosia, Aaron Burr returned, in secret and in doubt, to the city which had once made him Vice President of the United States. He went at once to Samuel Swartwout's, at 66 Water Street, "cheerfully, and rejoicing in my good fortune. I knocked and knocked, but no answer. I knocked still harder, supposing they were asleep, till one of the neighbors opened a window and told me that nobody lived there. I asked where lived Mr. S. Of that she knew nothing. I was now to seek a lodging.

"But few houses were open. Tried at two or three taverns, all full; cruised along the wharf, but could find no place. It was now near midnight, and nobody to be seen in the street. To walk about the whole night would be too fatiguing. To have sat and slept on any stoop would have been thought no hardship; but, then, the danger that the first watchman who might pass would take me up as a vagrant and carry me to the watch-house was a denouement not at all to my mind. I walked on, thinking that in the skirts of the town I might meet at that hour some charitable [person], who for one or two dollars . . . would give me at least half a bed; but seeing in an alley a light in the cellar of a small house, I called and asked for a lodging; was answered yes; shown into a small garrett, where five men were already asleep; a cott and sort of coverlid was given me, I threw open the window to have air, lay down, and slept profoundly till six."

Remarkable man—or was it that such turns of fate simply made no impression on him, summoned no memories, stirred no feelings. . . .

The next morning, "being already dressed, I rose, paid for my lodging twelve cents, and sallied out to

66 Water Street, and there had the good luck to find
Sam alone. He led me immediately to the house of
his brother Robert, and here I am in possession of
Sam's room in Stone Street, in the City of New York,
on the 8th day of June, anno dom. 1812."

Some of his darkest hours were still before
him. . . .

PART X

The Outcast

1812-1836

"I am severed from the human race."

AARON BURR.

CHAPTER I

THE MIGHTY WATERS

I

COLONEL BURR remained hidden in the Stone Street house for some three weeks, while the Swartwouts busied themselves arranging for his immunity from arrest.   Government officials were sounded, the creditors were persuaded to leniency, a paragraph was inserted in the papers stating that the Colonel had been in Boston and was on his way to New York. The news did not unduly disturb the city.   A further notice then appeared one morning to the effect that Colonel Burr had returned, and that he had opened an office for the practice of the law at 9 Nassau Street.   More than five hundred persons called to see him before nightfall, and Robert Troup, his old personal friend and sometime political enemy, placed his own law library at the Colonel's disposal.

Colonel Burr possessed ten dollars in cash.   He was fifty-six years old.   He tacked up a little tin sign outside his door, and prepared to resume his long interrupted practice, thinking that little by little enough clients would come to him to bring him a living.   They came immediately, and by the

score, and during his first twelve days of business
he earned two thousand dollars. He was not to be
shunned, then, as a lawyer; his office was crowded;
several clerks had to be installed to assist him; the
future seemed secure. And then two letters came
from South Carolina.

Two terrible letters. The boy, "Gampy," the
precious grandson, had died, on June 30, 1812, at
Debordieu Island, of the fever. "One dreadful blow
has destroyed us," Mr. Alston wrote. "That boy
on whom all rested . . . he who was to have re-
deemed all your glory and shed new lustre upon our
families—that boy at once our happiness and our
pride—is dead. We saw him dead . . . yet we
are alive . . . Theodosia has endured all that a
human being could endure, but her admirable mind
will triumph. She supports herself in a manner
worthy of your daughter." There was no more joy
for her, she told her father. "The world is a blank.
I have lost my boy. . . . May Heaven, by other
blessings, make you some amends for the noble
grandson you have lost. . . . Of what use can I
be in this world . . . with a body reduced to pre-
mature old age, and a mind enfeebled and bewildered.
Yet . . . I will endeavor to fulfill my part . . .
though this life must henceforth be to me a bed of
thorns. . . ."

2

Theodosia was desperately ill, and the Colonel
insisted that she should come north. And since Mr.
Alston was prevented by law from leaving the State—
he was now Governor of South Carolina—Mr. Timo-

THEODOSIA BURR ALSTON

Now reproduced for the first time from the original portrait by Vanderlyn, formerly in the possession of the Alston family, now in the possession of Dr. J. E. Stillwell.

thy Green was sent down to escort her; an elderly retired lawyer with some knowledge of medicine, whose presence was a little resented at The Oaks. In his opinion Theodosia was too feeble to undertake the journey by land—the Colonel would find her very emaciated, and a prey to nervous fevers—and he took passage for her, therefore, in a schooner-built pilot boat which was refitting at Georgetown.

She was the privateer *Patriot*, Captain Overstocks, a vessel noted for her speed. She had discharged her privateer crew, hidden her armament under deck, and was preparing for a dash to New York, richly laden with the proceeds of her raids concealed beneath the covering of an ostensible cargo of rice. Her departure was not unknown along that piratical coast, and there was danger, of course, not only from the wreckers—the dreaded "bankers" of the Carolina beaches—but from the British fleet, since the two countries were now finally at war. Mr. Alston did what he could; he gave Captain Overstocks a letter to the British Admiral, asking free passage for his sick lady; and at noon, on December 30, 1812, the *Patriot*, with Mr. Green, Theodosia and her maid aboard, crossed the bar off Winyaw Bay. Early in January—but this was not known until much later—the *Patriot* fell in with the British fleet off Hatteras, presented her letter and was courteously granted passage. That night a terrific storm arose; the *Patriot* was never heard from again.

For a few weeks they hoped against hope, while Colonel Burr walked pathetically up and down the Battery at New York, waiting for the *Patriot*, or for some rescuing vessel, and answered Mr. Alston's

despairing letters. "Tomorrow will be three weeks
since, in obedience to your wishes"—the son-in-law
had to put that in—"Theodosia left me. . . .   My
mind is tortured . . . Gracious God! Is my wife,
too, taken from me? I do not know why I write, but
I feel that I am miserable." But thirty days were
decisive—"My wife is either captured or lost."
There was no news, and in February, "My boy—my
wife—gone both! This, then, is the end of all the
hopes we had formed. You may well observe that
you feel severed from the human race. She was the
last tie that bound us to the species. What have
we left. . . .   You knew those we loved. . . .
Here, none knew them; none valued them as they
deserved. The talents of my boy . . . made his
death regretted by the pride of my family; but,
though certain of the loss of my not less admirable
wife, they seem to consider it like the loss of an
ordinary woman. . . .   The man who has been
deemed worthy of the heart of Theodosia Burr, and
who has felt what it was to be blessed with such a
woman's will never forget his elevation."

3

There was no news, but Colonel Burr would not
believe that Theodosia was dead. "I am filled with
the most gloomy apprehensions," he wrote to
"Kate;" undoubtedly his cousin, Mrs. Catherine
Bartow Howes; "my hope is that the vessel may have
been taken and carried into Bermuda . . . but
indeed I am wretched, and the utter impossibility
of doing anything for her relief or my own makes me
still more so. When or how this dreadful suspense

will terminate, God only knows." But the most striking thing in this letter is that the Colonel, who knew that the *Patriot's* master's name was Overstocks, refers to him as "Capt. Soustocks." The word *sous* is French for "under;" Captain Overstocks, Captain Understocks—what sort of trick was the Colonel's mind playing him; was it necessary to be mysterious about the Captain's name. . . .

He hoped that she had been captured, but when rumors of capture began to reach him, he would not believe those. Rumors of piracy, of mutiny, of Carolina wreckers. The *Patriot* had been captured by the celebrated pirate Dominique You; she had been captured by the infamous "Babe;" Mrs. Alston had been forced to walk the plank with the entire ship's company; something dreadful had happened on Kitty Hawk, near Hatteras, that stronghold of the wreckers; Theodosia had been taken at sea, and carried off. But the Colonel would not believe any of those stories. "No," he kept insisting now. "She is indeed dead. She perished in the miserable little pilot boat. Were she alive, all the prisons in the world could not keep her from her father."

He would not believe, but the rumors persisted, until long after his death, in 1850 and thereafter, more substantial versions began to take shape, found in the deathbed confessions of sailors, in the scaffold statements of executed criminals. A schooner-built pilot boat had come ashore in a storm on Kitty Hawk; she had been boarded by the wreckers; some said that they had found the boat abandoned, and a lady's effects scattered about the cabin; there was a portrait of a lady taken ashore, and discovered some fifty years later, along with some of her clothes, in a cottage on Nag's Head, a cottage inhabited by an old woman who had been the wife of one of the most notorious wreckers in those old days of "the English war;" a portrait which still exists, and is believed by many to be that of Theodosia Alston. Some said that the pilot boat had not been abandoned when the wreckers came aboard. . . .

One is inclined to believe the latter version. A storm off Hatteras—it was so violent that it scattered the British fleet—a schooner-built pilot boat, all the accounts agree on that, driven ashore on Kitty Hawk; the Manns, and the Tilletts, and the rest of the "banker" brotherhood going out to her; and then— the secret lies hidden, perhaps, in the sands of Kitty Hawk. On the other hand, one may not ignore the statement made, in 1910, by Mr. J. A. Elliott, of Norfolk—himself personally acquainted with the gentleman to whom he refers—that "in the early part of 1813, the dead body of a young woman, with every indication of refinement, drifted upon the shore of Mr. ——, at Cape Charles . . . on the sea coast of Virginia. . . . She was buried on the farm of the gentleman who found her, and has remained there unidentified and undisturbed the past ninety-seven years. . . ." And so the secret lies hidden, perhaps, in that forgotten and nameless grave on Cape Charles; and it is there, after all, that one would be tempted to stand for a moment, in respectful memory of that very excellent lady.

But these things were all unknown to Colonel Burr. He knew only that she was dead; Theodosia the incomparable was no more; the world had become "a blank to me, and life had then lost its value." From henceforth he was to stand in adversity—like the storm beaten rock on the seal which he used for his letters—steadfast and aggressive; no one was to suspect the chasms of despair into which he had been plunged; but the soul within him had perished, foundered with the pilot boat *Patriot* in the overwhelming waters of affliction. . . .

CHAPTER II

THE PATIENT YEARS

I

"What have we left?" Mr. Alston had asked. Nothing, only some trinkets of Theodosia's, and a letter addressed to her husband; a letter written to him in 1805 already, to be read at her death, in which she had told him that "something whispers me that my end approaches . . . Adieu, friend of my heart. May Heaven prosper you, and may we meet hereafter. . . . Least of all should I murmur . . . whose days have been numbered by bounties, who have had such a husband, such a child, such a father. . . . Let my father see my son sometimes. Do not be unkind towards him whom I have loved so much, I beseech you. . . ." There was nothing left of the old days—even Colonel Burr's papers had all been lost with Theodosia in the *Patriot*—nothing, except a letter from Mr. Blennerhassett.

He had written before, in 1811, to Mr. Alston, when the latter was running for Governor, and his letter related to various sums of money to which Mr. Blennerhassett still considered himself entitled. "Having

long since despaired," he had observed, "of all in-
demnity from Mr. Burr for my losses, by the confederacy in which I was associated with you and him,
I count upon a partial reimbursement from you. . . .
The heroic offer you made to cooperate with your
person and fortune in our common enterprise, gave
you . . . a color of claim to that succession in
empire you boasted you would win by better titles.
. . . But I confess, Sir, I attached a more interesting value to the tender you so nobly pledged of your
property to forward and support our expedition,
together with your special assurances to me of reimbursement for all contingent losses of a pecuniary
nature I might individually suffer."

And so, having already paid twelve thousand five
hundred dollars of the original fifty thousand advanced by Mr. Blennerhassett, would Mr. Alston
now pay fifteen thousand more, or else Mr. Blennerhassett was of the opinion that the electors of South
Carolina would be interested to learn of candidate
Alston's share in the confederacy, of his intention of
joining it at New Orleans with three thousand men,
and of the manner in which he had committed "the
shabby treason of deserting from your parent by
affinity and your sovereign in expectancy," vilified
him in a letter to Governor Pinckney, and perjured
himself by denying all connection with his projects.
Unless the fifteen thousand dollars were forthcoming,
Mr. Blennerhassett would publish all his correspondence and interviews with Mr. Alston, and the latter might rest assured that Mr. Blennerhassett had
no intention of abandoning "the ore I have ex-
tracted . . . from the mines both dark and deep,

not indeed of Mexico, but of Alston, Jefferson and Burr."

Mr. Blennerhassett was simply boiling with revelations, but somehow he did not publish anything, and Mr. Alston did not pay, and in 1812 he was elected Governor. But in April, 1813, Mr. Blennerhassett was writing again, to Colonel Burr this time; and it seemed to him very probable that nothing short of the publication of his book, "hitherto postponed only by sickness," would bring him any part of the balance due him from Governor Alston. "His well earned election to the chief executive office of his state," Mr. Blennerhassett continued, "and your return from Europe will . . . render the publication more effective. . . . I would still agree to accept . . . $15000 . . . and of course withhold the book, which is entitled *A Review of the Projects and Intrigues of Aaron Burr, during the years 1805, 6, 7, including therein as parties or privies, Thos. Jefferson, Albert Gallatin, Dr. Eustis, Gov. Alston, Dan. Clark, Generals Wilkinson, Dearborn, Harrison, Jackson and Smith, and the late Spanish Ambassador, exhibiting original documents and correspondence hitherto unpublished, compiled from the notes and private journal kept during the above period by H. Blennerhassett, LL.B.*"

It would have been a fascinating volume, no doubt, but its publication was always unaccountably delayed, and on September 10, 1816, Mr. Alston himself was dead. And in time Mr. Blennerhassett died, leaving a destitute widow to whom Colonel Burr found the means of sending a little money on one or two occasions. . . .

2

The question of money was to be a constant embarrassment to Colonel Burr during all his remaining years.

In Europe, of course, he owed considerable sums, few of which were ever repaid. But aside from these more recent debts, there were a number of older judgments against him, his protracted failures to satisfy which caused him on several occasions to be required to give bail for the jail limits, and, at least once, to institute proceedings to recover his office furniture which had been distrained for rent. When the Colonel arrived in New York in 1812, there were outstanding against him—in addition to private loans and the countless claims of his associates in the Mexican venture—judgments and suits to the amount of twenty-three thousand dollars, including the Saltonstall estate claim of some eight thousand dollars which he satisfied in 1815, and the Le Guen claim of nearly seven thousand dollars.

They had, it will be remembered, been arguing about it ever since 1801, Colonel Burr insisting that part of the remaining debt had already been paid by him, and that certain securities of his had never been returned to him; and in June, 1817, he was writing to Mr. Le Guen that "I am constrained again to ask whether you admit the payment of $1250 . . . on the 2nd May 1805—and whether you will deliver up the securities, or account for the value of them. If you will do this, I will pay any balance . . . but if you have appropriated those securities to your own use, it is manifest that a very large balance must be

due to me." Mr. Le Guen was prepared "to arrest
the further progress of the suit . . . by an amicable
adjustment," but he had "no knowledge of any payment made in 1805," and was "certain that nothing
had been received for which credits have not been
claimed and allowed." Colonel Burr was equally
certain that "if Mr. Le Guen would make diligent
search I have no doubt he would discover how he had
disposed of [the] securities and the money recd. on
them," but he could "find no list of them, nor can I
give further particulars."

No satisfactory arrangement was arrived at, and
in 1823, after Mr. Le Guen's death in France, his
widow came to America to continue the controversy.
Colonel Burr offered some parcels of land which he
still owned in lieu of cash, but in November, 1824,
Mrs. LeGuen heard that "Colonel Burr has lately
gained a Law Suit which it is thought will be of
advantage to him. . . . We should therefore take
the opportunity to urge the payment of his debt
. . . I insist upon an immediate compliance with
my demands. I own to you had I known he had
such good prospects I should not have been so lenient
towards him."

But the Le Guen judgment was never satisfied. . . .

3

And his other creditors were no less troublesome,
naturally—although they were not all as persistent
as Mr. and Mrs. Anthony Borowson, his Richmond
Hill coachman and cook from whom he had borrowed
a considerable sum at the time of his flight from New
York in 1804, and who now harassed him for pay-

ment while retaining possession of many valuable
portraits and other pieces of personal property which
they had appropriated as security for their loan.
But in May, 1815, Colonel Burr was writing to Mr.
Lathrop in his office "Do not allow any person in the
office to receive any papers for me in cases in which
I may be defendant"—for sometimes people came
breaking in to make disagreeable and even threatening scenes—and in October he was telling Mr. Alston
that "for the present it will suffice to say that my
business affords me a decent support. . . . My old
creditors (principally the holders of the Mexican
debts) came upon me last winter with vindictive
fury. I was held to bail in large sums, and saw no
probability of keeping out of prison for six months.
This danger is still menacing but not quite so imminent; I shall neither borrow nor receive from any
one, not even from you; I have determined not to
begin to pay, unless I see a prospect of paying all."

But he always did his best to help the men who
had suffered financially from their association with
him in the Mexican venture, and to assist the countless relatives and friends who had advanced him
money for that project, and who now, many of them,
found themselves in ruinous circumstances. And he
remembered those who had been kind to him in the
great emergencies of his life. He did what he could
to succor an indigent relation of Doctor Hosack; late
in life he gave to a son of Benjamin Botts a farm
which he had acquired near Jamaica in return for an
annuity of five hundred dollars, so that for a quite
nominal sum Mr. Botts eventually became owner of
the property which he had desired, but the outright

purchase of which he could not have afforded; and
in 1822 the Colonel took Luther Martin—now broken
in health and feeble of mind—into his own inadequate home, and cared for him faithfully until his
death. Because Luther Martin had once come forward voluntarily to stand at the Colonel's shoulder
through the ordeal of a Richmond summer; and, one
feels quite certain, because this wretched old man—
for whom the State of Maryland had recently decreed that every lawyer in the State should pay an
annual license fee of five dollars to be placed in trust
for him—had once loved Theodosia.

And it is interesting, in this connection, to remember that the dockets of the New York County
Clerk's office reveal the fact that on October 24, 1817,
Luther Martin had secured a judgment against
Colonel Burr of twenty thousand and thirteen dollars, presumably for his legal services, which was
satisfied on July 22, 1833. But that the suit was
friendly, and mutually agreed upon, in order to fore-
stall other creditors, there can be no doubt, since
Luther Martin's attorney in the case was that Mr.
Lathrop who was an intimate friend of Colonel Burr's
and had worked in his office. The gentleman to
whom he once wrote that "your drunken letter and
your sober one have both been [received]. It is with
pleasure I remark that your frolic did not render you
inattentive to business—at this rate one may now
and then venture on a debauch."

4

Colonel Burr was generous, throughout those years;
poor as he was, and often in the most straitened

circumstances, he was always ready to help others, to be charitable, to bestow his slender bounty. The money which came to him from his law cases, and his Colonel's pension of six hundred dollars—a belated effort to secure from Congress repayment of expenditures incurred by him during the Revolutionary War was not successful, in spite of the apparent justice and legality of his claim—and an annuity of fifty pounds which he had purchased somehow in England, and, during his very last years, the five hundred dollars from Mr. Botts's farm. But the trouble was that he was too generous; he forgot his creditors and helped strangers, or stray acquaintances who had no call upon him except that they had once been soldiers; he was charitable to beggars, and always buying sweets for all the children of the neighborhood, but often in his own house there was not food enough.

The old mania for giving had, if anything, increased. His liberality was obviously a malady. He was in the habit, it is said, of contriving a space among the books on his table into which he put all the cash of which he was at any time personally possessed— for it was strictly understood that the firm moneys were handled by someone else in the office—and then he gave it away as fast as anyone came asking for it. He was simply incapable of saving money, of denying himself the pleasure of prodigality, of resisting the temptation of a gratifying munificence. He once disposed in this manner of fifteen hundred dollars in three days, until there was not a cent left in the house; on another occasion, when he had been able to deposit a considerable sum in his old Manhattan

Bank, a clerk sent around to ask if he were paying
off the poorhouse, so frequently were cheques of his
to nondescript persons being presented at the cash-
ier's counter.

That door was always swinging open. . . .

And of course he was, sometimes, atrociously im-
posed upon.   As in 1828, for instance, and for several
years thereafter, by the twenty year old daughter of
a New York widow; "a lovely and voluptuous looking
woman"—one quotes from the account of Charles
Burdett, who saw her frequently at the Colonel's
house in Nassau Street, to which he had then moved
back from Reade—"faultless in figure, with a face
of surprising beauty, and manners which might have
captivated *the mind of a man much stronger than was
Colonel Burr's after he had passed threescore years
and ten*."   The italics are not Mr. Burdett's.   The
"syren" was then at the boarding school of "Mrs.
N——," undoubtedly the celebrated Mrs. Nau, and
during Mr. Burdett's stay in the city—he was on
furlough at the time from a military academy at
Middletown—he was "daily dispatched to the school,
with notes and presents.   The notes invariably contained money; the presents consisted of fruits or
flowers, and . . . she called almost daily at [Colonel
Burr's] office.   Wine from his own cellar (claret, the
only wine which he really loved) was sent upon her
requirement, and . . . nothing was denied. . . .

"He was utterly blind to her faults. . . . It was
'give,' 'give,' 'give,' without cessation."   And she
was an erratic young woman, who once attended a
ball attired as a ballet dancer, "in fact attired as no
lady, having one particle of self-respect, would dare

to be in private, much less in public." She "harassed him daily with clamorous demands for money. Bills against her came in to him with terrible rapidity and frightful in amount . . . all were sent in to him"—she was passing herself off in the shops as the Colonel's ward—"and each was put off with some vague promise, while she was actually monopolizing every dollar of ready money that he could command." But finally she got into serious trouble with Mrs. Nau, whose own bills were not being paid; she left the school; the tradesmen came to the conclusion that she was deliberately defrauding them; and it became necessary for her to leave town with her mother and sister, and take ship for the South.

"To the last the interest of Colonel Burr in this syren was manifested. All the arrangements for the voyage were made through him. The private stores were furnished by him, and to me," Mr. Burdett remarks, "was committed the honor of seeing them on board. . . . If I did not properly estimate the honor thrust upon me . . . I derived very great pleasure from their departure." And Mr. Burdett has further observations to make concerning the subsequent adventurings, apparently at Charleston, of this enterprising Calypso. As for the Colonel, "he must have, his nature demanded, something to love, something to cherish, something on which to lavish his store of feelings."

Something on which to lavish his store of cash . . .

5

And there were other *protégés* of a more pleasing character. Charles Burdett himself—born in 1814—

who was understood to be an adopted son of Colonel
Burr's, and who worked as a boy in his office, was
sent by him to be tutored in Albany by Mr. O'Sha-
mussy, and to the school of Doctor Hazelins at
Cooperstown, and to Captain Partridge's military
academy at Middletown, after which he entered the
Navy for a while. And the Eden girls, Rebecca and
Elizabeth, daughters of a "Mistress Eden," and
members of that family on whose behalf Colonel
Burr undertook one of his most celebrated litigations.

In 1825, they were all three—Rebecca, Elizabeth
and Charles—domiciled under the private tuition of
Mr. O'Shamussy in the Selden mansion at Albany,
which the Colonel made his headquarters during his
frequent visits to the law courts of the capital. The
girls were "as lovely in character," Mr. Burdett
records, "as pure in life, as virtuous in thought, and
word, and purpose, as ever lived." And of course
the Colonel supervised their education. "Having
somehow imbibed an idea," he was writing to one of
them in 1823, already, when they were living at
Troy, "that you had engaged in study with that
zeal and determination, without which little is acquired and nothing well acquired, I have proposed to
myself to have the honor of visiting you on Wednesday . . . when I shall hope to find, even yet, something new to admire and applaud. A single week of
idleness is always betrayed by a vacuity of countenance, and incoherence, precipitancy and hesitating
volubility of speech, and a careless and undignified
deportment and manners."

They studied "not only the classics and the modern
languages, but astronomy and navigation. . . .

Nothing was neglected. Their studies were regulated
by system; their health was cared for by incessant
injunctions"—Rebecca was a "small, delicate, frail
looking" girl. One of them "became an excellent
violinist; the other was a good performer on the
flageolet." Rebecca herself was sent to Cooperstown
in 1826, where she lived in the family of Doctor
Hazelins, and perfected herself in the German language. "While there, her every movement was
directed by the Colonel. She walked daily the
distance prescribed by him"—it was the old days of
Theodosia over again. The mania for controlling,
for arranging, for superintending. . . .

Colonel Burr was "perfectly wrapped up in them
. . . they were the only human beings who ever
filled the void caused by the death of Theodosia. . . .
They loved and honored him. They looked for his
visits, as children separated from an affectionate
parent would watch for his return. His word was
their law. . . . He loved them, and . . . they
loved him with true filial affection. . . . He was
the most affectionate, the most indulgent guardian
any *protégés* ever had, and exacting as he was, stern
as he was, in demanding implicit obedience to the
rules he laid down, there never was one more de-
votedly beloved than he was by these young ladies."
In 1827 the girls were both living, with their mother,
in the Colonel's house in New York; "nothing was too
good for them. No request denied, no favor withheld, when . . . deserved;" and then in 1828,
Elizabeth, and in 1829, Rebecca, were married; the
girls went away, Mrs. Eden soon followed them,
and the separation caused Colonel Burr "more

pain than anything since the death of his beloved daughter."

But one cannot help wondering what John Reeves and the Duke de Bassano, for instance, would have thought of such boundless generosity. . . .

6

The years passed. Colonel Burr plodded on through his law cases—landed property suits, many of them—and won his share of verdicts, in spite of deliberate attempts in the courts to slight him with discourtesies and affronts. But he paid no attention to them. To a judge who once harangued him, criticizing his methods, he quietly remarked that "I am sorry that your Honor is not feeling well today." And to a lady who was asking how to get through a troubling emergency he replied "Live through it;" and when she still insisted that she would not be able to survive, he finally exclaimed "Well, die then, Madam; we must all die, but bless me, die game!" He had no patience with self-pity and lamentation; he was proud—as proud as on that day in London when he had answered "Sir, I met him!" to a questioner who had desired to know if Alexander Hamilton was a gentleman—he outstared the scornful, outcountenanced the haughty, outscored the impertinent and went about his business. And whatever the reactions of his mind to other interests, he was already in his very late sixties when he won that series of important and extremely complicated suits, known collectively as the Medcef Eden case—a suit in chancery to recover an estate for the heirs of Medcef Eden—the successful negotiation of which

THE JUMEL MANSION

Mr. Hamilton had, at an earlier date, declared impossible.

Until almost his very last years he remained hale and vigorous, industrious and active. With Charles Burdett, or with his secretary, John Pelletreau, he made frequent, and often fatiguing, business trips; he boasted that he "had not taken a single dose of medicine from the time he was twenty-one . . . until he had passed sixty "—he was forgetting various illnesses in Europe—"and he attributed his marvelous preservation of health to the fact that when he felt in any wise unwell he would . . . utterly abstain from food." He was known "to go for twenty-four hours without tasting a mouthful and then his hunger would be appeased by some plain rice or samp and milk, of which latter dish he was really fond."

Socially, of course, they ignored him. One reads of his sitting, silent and neglected, in the corners of Albany parlors, listening to the talk of gatherings in which his presence was scarcely discernible; one constantly sees him being pointed at in the streets of New York as a curiosity, a queer old man, a gentleman who had "committed a terrible crime," the man who had killed Alexander Hamilton, the conspirator who would have betrayed his country, the guardian of many dreadful mysteries, the victim of many tragic griefs. Children were always told to look at him; and when they did, he often smiled at them, and they never forgot the gentle, patient face. . . .

But he was not entirely alone; there were friends who, unlike the Van Nesses, never abandoned him— the Swartwouts, Matthew Davis, Erich Bollmann, old army comrades, some of his relatives, the young men who worked in his office, a few charitable and kindly persons. And once the Duke of Saxe Weimar came to see him; and after many days John Vanderlyn came home, bringing with him, it is to be hoped, that copy of Theodosia's portrait which the Colonel had left him "with so much hesitation and regret." He had been a long time making up his mind, so that Colonel Burr was "weary of hearing that you are coming and shall not believe it until you do actually come. . . . Pay . . . half your passage and I will pay the rest on your arrival." And when he did come, "you may if you like [keep house] with me . . . but you are in this case to live on potatoes and maccaroni."

In politics he never lost interest, although the voicing of his opinions was necessarily restricted to that small circle of associates whose friendship justified his confidence. To them he expressed his views with energy and unfailing sagacity—in national affairs, as in the law, his mind was always clear and incisive—and some of his prophecies were not uninspired. "All that I have fought for has gone for naught," he once exclaimed. "The Legislature of New York has determined upon a speedy naturalization of all aliens, and they once having tasted of the sweets of liberty will flock to this country to be soon followed by hordes. . . . In time they will outnumber you two to one, will rule you and will demand an equal division of your property. Next, behold, you will have an elective judiciary!"

And on one occasion, at least, he sought to make his political influence felt beyond the limits of his study;

at the time of the presidential campaign which was
to elect James Monroe, when the Colonel wrote, in
November, 1815, to Mr. Alston that "a congressional
caucus will . . . nominate James Monroe. . . .
Whether we consider the measure itself, the character
and talents of the man, or the State whence he comes,
this nomination is equally exceptionable and odious.
. . . The man himself is one of the most improper
and incompetent that could be selected. Naturally
dull and stupid; extremely illiterate; indecisive . . .
pusillanimous, and, of course, hypocritical; has no
opinion on any subject. . . .

"If . . . there be a man in the United States of
firmness and decision, and having standing enough to
afford even a hope of success, it is your duty to hold
him up to public view; that man is Andrew Jackson.
. . . If this project should accord with your views
I could wish to see you prominent in the execution
of it. It must be known to be your work. . . .
This suggestion has not arisen from any exclusive
attachment to Jackson. The object is to break down
this vile combination [the Virginia Junto] which rules
and degrades the United States. If you should think
that any other man could be held up with better
prospects of success, name that man. I know of no
such. . . . Exhibit yourself, then, and emerge
from this state of nullity. You owe it to yourself,
you owe it to me, you owe it to your country, you
owe it to the memory of the dead."

And in December, again, "things are wonderfully
advanced. . . . These will require a written message (letter) from yourself and others . . . advising
Jackson what is doing; that communications have

been had with the northern States, requiring him only to be passive, and asking him for a list of persons in the western States to whom you may address your letters." Nothing was to come of it; Mr. Alston had only a few months to live; he was "too much alone, too entirely unconnected with the world, to take much interest in anything;" but Colonel Burr had not forgotten Andrew Jackson. . . .

And he had not forgotten Mexico. They were fighting for liberty out there during those years, and perhaps he understood that to many patriots throughout the Empire his name, and the memory of his adventure, were still an inspiration. As for the "conspiracy," he was reticent, and careful of its secrets, but once in a while the bitterness of old resentments flared up and found relief in speech. "Andrew Jackson dreads me in my decrepitude," he explained; "in the Blennerhassett case he was my general, Calhoun and McDuffie were my associates, but not a word has escaped my lips till now. Our idea was to take possession of Mexico and after a time annex it to the United States." But to a lady who wanted to be told what he had really meant to do in Mexico he replied that "I'd have made it a heaven for women, and you should have been there to enjoy it."

So Aaron Burr passed through the streets of New York, in his singlebreasted blue coat with the standing collar, his buff vest and dark pants, and in winter buckskin mittens and a fur cap under which his hair was "massed up on the top and held by a small shell comb, the whole head profusely powdered." His expression was "sad and melancholy," Mr. Burton T.

Beach was to report, "yet the features were mobile, and when addressing ladies . . . the smile around his mouth was literally beautiful, and his eyes would lose their piercing look, and become tender and gentle. His voice was not powerful, but round, full and crisp. . . . His elocution in conversation was perfect . . . his language was terse, almost epigrammatical . . . his words were always the most apt that could be used. . . . His manners were polished, his motions graceful and easy, yet he never . . . lost his noble and dignified bearing. . . . In a bearing and presence which you felt to be something beyond other men, with character in every motion and expression. . . . I have never seen his peer."

The years passed—twenty-one long, patient years. Colonel Burr was seventy-seven, life was very nearly done with—and then one morning, on Wednesday, July 3, 1833, Philip Hone wrote in his diary that "the celebrated Colonel Burr was married on Monday evening to the equally celebrated Mrs. Jumel, widow of Stephen Jumel. It is benevolent in her to keep the old man in his latter days. One good turn deserves another. . . ."

CHAPTER III

THE LADIES

I

COLONEL BURR's effect upon the ladies had always been devastating. "He seems passionately fond of female society," Judge Adams was writing in 1806, "and there is no being better calculated to succeed and shine in that sphere; to the ladies he is all attention—all attention—in conversation he gazes on them with complacency and rapture, and when he addresses them, it is with that smiling affability, those captivating gestures . . . those dissolving looks, that soft, sweet and insinuating eloquence. which takes the soul captive before it can prepare for defense. In short he is the most perfect model of an accomplished gentleman that could be formed, even by the wanton imagination of poetry and fiction."

Yes. Some of the captives of his charm and Chesterfieldian grace one has already seen. The young damsels of Litchfield and Fairfield, the nameless love whose brothers ducked him in the Kill von Kull, Margaret Moncrieffe who never forgot him, Heaven

knows how many belles of New York, Philadelphia
and Washington, Madeline, the Maid of Half Way
Hill, the ladies of London, and Copenhagen, and
Paris. There were others, without consulting Mr.
Cheetham's catalogue. There was, if tradition is
to be believed, an Indian squaw on the march to
Quebec. There was a middle-aged lady in New
York, who was silly and talkative but "certainly
good-tempered and cheerful; rather comely, abating
a flat chest," with whom, in 1804, "things are not
gone to extremities, but there is danger." There
were Clara—"that Clara you once loved"—and
Julia, who "won't do at all; sense without refinement,
passion without sentiment," and Leonora, who, the
Colonel admitted, "has claims on my recollection."

And in 1803 there was Celeste, a young French-
woman of Philadelphia. She was "pensive and
interesting," and "the plot thickens." In fact, the
Colonel proposed marriage, but "it is finished—concluded—forever abandoned—Celeste never means to
marry. . . . The parting was full of courtesy, and
there is a reason to hope there will be no hanging or
drowning." But Theodosia was of the opinion that
Celeste "meant from the beginning to say that awful word yes; but not choosing to say it immediately
. . . you took it as a plump refusal and walked
off. She called you back. What more could she do?
I would have seen you to Japan before I should have
done so much." And in 1804, just after the duel
with Mr. Hamilton, Celeste was more "pliant," and
"if any male friend of [Theodosia's] should be dying
of *ennui*, recommend to him to engage in a duel and
a courtship at the same time."

2

And there were other ladies, and some of them
bore him children.   Just how many is not clear, since
it seems to have become almost a national habit to
claim for nameless infants his illustrious fatherhood;
as in the case of that "Fearing Burr," born, in 1806,
on Blennerhassett's Island—and in all such instances
it was his practice to remark that "when a lady does
me the honor to name me as the father of her child, I
trust I shall always be too gallant to show myself
ungrateful for the favor."

But three of them, certainly. A son, Aaron
Columbus Burr, born in Paris of a French mother,
and sent at an early age to New York, where his
father received him, and provided for his education
until his entrance upon the silversmith's career.
And two daughters, sole legatees of his estate.
Elizabeth, described in the Colonel's will, dated April
21, 1834, as being "about the age of two years, now
residing with Mrs. Gayetta Conklin," and who died
not long after; and Frances Ann, referred to in the
same document as "aged about six years, now residing . . . under the immediate care of . . .
Mrs. Sarah Minthorne Tompkins,"and whose mother
was reported to have been a lady of Albany.

And perhaps another child, for one may not entirely ignore the rumors arising from a widespread
contemporary conviction.   The son, ostensibly, of a
New York State tavern keeper at whose inn Colonel
Burr had always been a constant visitor; who studied
in the office of William Van Ness and was frequently
associated in the courts with the Colonel, after the

MADAME JUMEL

latter's return from Europe; and who was reserved for a political career of the greatest distinction, during the course of which he gave evidence of qualities which could scarcely have been inherited from the tavern keeper. A man who did much to further the cause of Andrew Jackson's presidential aspirations, and of whom John Quincy Adams, in a comparison of him with Aaron Burr, did not hesitate to write that "there is much resemblance of character, manners and even person between the two men." And a master of intrigue and blandishment, who knew so well, too, how to please the ladies.

At all events, the world of 1830 thought it likely—indeed, thought it unquestionable. . . .

3

And in 1833, after all these other ladies, there was Eliza Jumel.

All legends to the contrary, she had been born at Providence, in 1775, the daughter of Phebe Kelley and the sailor, John Bowen, and christened Eliza, or Betsy, Bowen. She was a person of no education, sprung from the lowest origins, who for nineteen years led a vagrant and altogether disreputable existence, and then gave birth to a son—always known thereafter as George Washington Bowen—whom she promptly abandoned. Betsy went to New York; she was extremely beautiful; for a while there was a ship's captain, who took her to France; later on she was on the stage, calling herself Eliza Brown; and in 1800 Stephen Jumel, a Frenchman from Santo Domingo, one of the wealthiest merchants of the town, brought her to live with him in his fine house on Whitehall Street, and bought her a carriage in which she took a tactless pleasure in parading her good fortune.

At all events, society refused to have anything to do with her, and in 1804, by persuading him that she was dying, she bamboozled Mr. Jumel into marrying her. But society was still neglectful, and in 1810 the generous husband purchased for her the old Roger Morris house in Haarlem—which Colonel Burr had once thought of buying—and restored and furnished it in the most lavish and elegant manner to be the Jumel Mansion. Five years passed, no one came to see them, and finally they went to France. There, Madame Jumel was a great success; too much of a success, for she spent all of her husband's money, and in 1826, after various goings and comings, she was back in America with his power of attorney giving her authority to settle up his affairs "for his most benefit and advantage." When she had finished with them, his property was all safely in the hands of her niece, and he was an utterly ruined man. He came back to his mansion—to her mansion—in 1828, and in May, 1832, he was dead. Eliza Jumel was fifty-seven; she was an ill bred, ill tempered, ill minded old woman; she was eccentric to a degree which might have foretold her approaching insanity; she was, for her day, quite enormously wealthy.

Such was the lady whom, in his seventy-seventh year, Colonel Burr selected to be the successor to Theodosia Prevost. It was, in many ways, the greatest folly of his life, but the widow of a year had money and a beautiful home, and it was she—according to Mr. Craft, the last of Colonel Burr's law

partners—and not the Colonel, who conducted the
courtship in his office and proposed the match. It
may well be that Mr. Hone was right, and that she
had made up her mind "to keep the old man in his
latter days," since "one good turn deserves another."
For while Nelson Chase, her nephew by marriage,
was always to insist that his aunt had never met
Colonel Burr until 1832, as a result of his own introduction on a matter of business, contemporary gossip
had it otherwise. Betsy Bowen, or Eliza Brown, had
been well known as a beauty to all New York; her
affair with Jumel had been the talk of the town; her
name had frequently been mentioned in the same
whisper with those of many of the most prominent
gentlemen of the day, including Alexander Hamilton;
and Colonel Burr was not one to remain for long
unaware of the presence in his vicinity of such allur-
ing charms.

In fact, of all the legends which ornament both
their lives, the least credible is that which endeavors
to present Aaron Burr and Eliza Brown Jumel as
strangers until the death of her first husband. There
were those, indeed, who went around insisting that
the lady had had her share in sending Mr. Hamilton
and Colonel Burr to Weehawken; and it was with
this gossip in mind, no doubt, that John Randolph
wrote to Mr. Monroe, on July 20, 1804, that "Mr.
Hamilton's turbulent career has terminated by a
violent death, at the hands of a man whom he persisted in discountenancing, although his party wished
to take him up. This conduct of H. which at first
sight might be imputed to elevated principles, is I
fear for the honor of human nature to be referred to

personal pique against Mr. Burr, who is said to have injured him in a point which he, of all men in the world, could least brook—his vanity."

4

They were married at the Mansion, on July 1, 1833, by the Reverend David Bogart, and departed in Madame Burr's yellow carriage on a journey through Connecticut. Governor Edwards, a relative of the Colonel's, entertained them; they were received everywhere with a respect not unmixed, perhaps, with curiosity; they visited Hartford, where Colonel Burr succeeded in establishing his wife's right to sell certain disputed shares in the Bridge Company which he then disposed of for six thousand dollars; and when they returned home it developed that the Colonel had used the money in some speculation of his own. He was legally entitled to all her rents, goods and chattels, and "Madam," he is supposed to have informed her, "I would have you know that you now have a master, and I will care for your money hereafter."

He spent it, naturally, as fast as he could; the security of the entire estate was soon in jeopardy; even the carriage and horses were seized one day under a judgment against him; and husband and wife did nothing but wrangle over his financial extravagances. So much so that Colonel Burr left the Mansion within four months, although he was ill at the time, and went back to the city to live with his silversmith son in the Bowery, and later at Jersey City for a while. "I don't see him any more," Madame Burr told William Dunlap in June, 1834. "He got thirteen thousand of my property and spent it all or gave it away and had no money to buy him a dinner. I had a new carriage and a pair of horses cost me one thousand dollars., He took them and sold them for five hundred."

Whatever the defects of her upbringing, Betsy Bowen at least understood the value of money. She had worked too diligently to secure her first husband's fortune to have it squandered by her second. On July 12, 1834, she instituted a suit in chancery for an absolute divorce, and prayed for an injunction preventing the Colonel from interfering with her property, which was immediately granted.

5

Her bill of complaint—aside from its monetary grievances—alleged that Aaron Burr had recently committed matrimonial offences "at divers times with divers females," and specifically at Jersey City with one Jane McManus; that he had abandoned "the house, converse and society" of his wife; and that the "actings and doings of the said Aaron Burr are contrary to the duties he owes to your oratrix." Colonel Burr replied at great length to the complaint; he maintained his marital rights to the enjoyment of his wife's property; he denied her charges of infidelity and threatened to prove, in his turn, that she had misconducted herself "with one or more person or persons;" and he stated that the complainant had "behaved to [him] in a manner most undutiful, disobedient and insulting . . . at a time when [he] was in a very low state of health . . . in the month of

October or November, 1833," and that he had left
her house "in consequence of the violent and ferocious
temper of the same complainant and her abusive and
insulting conduct toward him." Very likely—for
she had once threatened Stephen Jumel with a pistol,
while treating him to a foul-mouthed harangue in the
presence of his butler.

The Colonel shortly after withdrew his answer,
however, and consented that a decree be entered
by the complainant, and the cause was referred
for proofs to Philo Ruggles, Master in Chancery.
Charles O'Conor represented the defendant at the
private hearing; a certain Maria Johnson recited her
dubious testimony, compromising Colonel Burr and
the absent Jane McManus whom she quoted as
having exclaimed "Oh la! Mercy save us;" Nelson
Chase gave the Master the benefit of his secret
ferretings; and Judge Ruggles reported in favor of a
decree, which, contrary to most subsequent accounts
of the case, was granted by Vice Chancelor McCoun,
on September 14, 1836, providing that—

". . . the marriage . . . be dissolved . . .
and it shall be lawful for the said Eliza B. Burr to
marry again as though the said Aaron Burr was actually dead, but it shall not be lawful for the said
Aaron Burr to marry again until the said Eliza B.
Burr shall be actually dead. And it is further ad-
judged and decreed that the said complainant shall
be entitled to retain, possess, have, hold, use and
employ all her real and personal property and estate
. . . free from any interference of any kind whatsoever of, by or from the said Aaron Burr."

It was a graceless episode in a life too far spent

AARON BURR

From the original portrait by Van Dyke in the possession of Dr. J. E. Stillwell.

for such sordid embarrassments; a disastrous ending to a long career of felicitous intimacy with women; a pitiful document to have filed on the very day— for so it turned out—of his death. . . .

CHAPTER IV

PORT RICHMOND

I

THERE had to be an end to it all some time, and the first warning had come already in 1830, at the age of seventy-four, when a stroke paralyzed the Colonel's right side.   Friends gathered, a doctor was sent for to experiment with electrical treatment, and as soon as she heard the news, Mrs. Howes—Cousin Kate— came from Brooklyn to the office at Gold and Fulton Streets in which he was then established.   And he wanted to be taken to her home, but they said he was not in a condition to be moved, and sent her away.   But the next day, the Reverend William Hague recorded, "a coach containing the Colonel and two strong men as attendants, who had arranged a mattress or pillows for his support, arrived at the dwelling of Mrs. Howes. . . .   He was cordially welcomed. . . .   A few weeks' assiduous care on the part of Mr. and Mrs. Howes, encouraging him with their help to rise, and by gentle exercise in the parlor, to learn to walk again, repeating the process at a set hour daily for a month, restored the old

warrior so that he resumed his office business with as
keen a zest as ever."

He went back to his affairs, and the following year
he was trying to persuade Mrs. Howes, who was now
living in Poughkeepsie, to come and keep house with
him in a "large elegant three story house in Duane
Street . . . adjoining the Furnace, which is an
inconvenience, for when the wind is eastwardly the
smoke and ashes are an annoyance, and is probabiy
the reason why the rent is so moderate—$550—
The house has 12 or 14 rooms." And two years
later he was getting married.

But in October and November of 1833 he was ill
again—in the midst of the fracas with Madame Burr
—and a second stroke paralyzed his legs for a time.
A few months later a third stroke crippled him. He
came back from Jersey City, and went to live in the
boarding house kept in the old Jay mansion, opposite
the Bowling Green, by Mrs. Newton, a Scotch lady
who took the greatest care of him, and every day
gave him luxuries and champagne; for a while he
insisted on receiving clients in his office, reclining
on a sofa; but his strength was gone, his handwriting
was terribly cramped, the old warrior had made his
last fight. There was nothing to do now but wait.

And the days passed pleasantly. He had a little
money, and a colored servant to look after him; he
had his books, of which he once said that "if I had
read Sterne more, and Voltaire less, I should have
known that the world was wide enough for Hamilton
and me;" Mrs. Newton was very kind; friends came
and sat with him—John Vanderlyn, Charles O'Con-
or, Matthew Davis who was to inherit his papers,

his cousin, Judge Ogden Edwards of Staten Island, the faithful Swartwouts. They sat there in his room, and talked of old times. . . .

2

But another move was necessary, for in the summer of 1836 they were getting ready to tear down the old Jay mansion, and Judge Edwards decided that it would be best to have the Colonel near him on Staten Island. So they packed him up, and put him on the little steam ferry, and took him over to Port Richmond, to Daniel Winant's Inn.

He was extremely weak now; toothless, and uncertain of his eyes; and so thin, just a little wisp of a man, tremulous and mumbly. They put him on the ferry, and perhaps he knew that he would never see New York again; perhaps along the dear, accustomed streets, in the windows of the little red brick houses, or at the columned threshold of those familiar doorways, he beheld a smiling vision of vanished faces, a friendly pageant of companionable figures gathered in kindly courtesy to speed his passage; perhaps there came to him in those last moments the echoes of all the busy years, the sound of forgotten voices calling to him in farewell above the tumult of the bustling wharves. Perhaps he understood that he must always be remembered, that legend must thenceforth adorn his name with a greater mystery than even he had fostered, and that the future must inevitably render him the homage of a fascinated interest, the justice, possibly, of a belated sympathy.

Or perhaps he was beyond regrets and hopes; perhaps his gaze fell wearily upon the disenchanted scene of many trivial vanities and turned with pleasure to the quiet woods and fields of Staten Island, where long ago Matthias Ogden and Aaron Burr, two Jersey lads, had tramped the hillsides and the golden meadows, in the sunlit days of youth. . . .

3

The Winants were Dutch folk, placidly oblivious of popular opinion and current prejudice; when even Judge Edwards, no doubt for the best of reasons, could not take Colonel Burr into his home at Dongan Manor, they received him without commotion or dismay, and surrounded him with thoughtful kindness, shielding him from the importunities of strangers.

A few months passed. Doctor Clark was in attendance; the Reverend P. J. Van Pelt came and went. The Scriptures, the Colonel assured him, were "the most perfect system of truth the world has ever seen." But the Colonel was not in need of religious consolation—although he had not always entirely neglected the observances of the Church; at all events, there exists an undated letter to him from Richard Platt, telling him that "I have not been successful as yet to find a pew in St. John's Church; but you can always find a seat in my pew, No. 107, and oftentimes your children in the afternoon." If, as is natural to suppose, the church in question was St. John's on St. John's Park, one wonders what children are referred to, as St. John's was not in fashionable use until some time after his return from Europe. Perhaps Mr. Platt had the Eden young ladies in mind. But at

Port Richmond, certainly, though ever patiently courteous with Mr. Van Pelt, Colonel Burr was not interested; and at the last, when the minister asked him, "in this solemn hour of your apparent dissolution, believing as you do in the sacred Scriptures [and] your accountability to God," whether he had "good hope, through grace, that all of your sins will be pardoned," the Colonel replied that "on that subject I am coy."

July, August, September. From his window on the second floor he might have looked across the Jersey marshes as far as Elizabethtown, nearly as far as Newark, where he had been born; but they had him in bed now most of the time, frail, and helpless, and almost childish. He was always better in the evenings, and people came to see him—the Judge, the Swartwouts, Mrs. Newton—and the two Winant girls, celebrated belles in their day, were always within call, so that until the very end he enjoyed the ministration of women. And on September 14, 1836, he whispered the word "Madame," and died. . . .

4

The good Mrs. Newton came one last time again, while Olando Buel was making his necessary preparations; on the morning of September 16, a service was conducted by Mr. Van Pelt in the inn parlor, and attended by Matthew Davis, Cornelius Vanderbilt, the Swartwouts, and one or two others besides the Edwards family; and the body was immediately taken by steamer to Amboy, thence by rail to Hightstown, and from there conveyed to Princeton. He had asked to be buried in Princeton, near his parents.

They arrived at one o'clock in the afternoon, and deposited him in the College chapel. "At half past three," the Princeton *Whig* recorded, "the Students of the College and Seminary, and a number of the citizens of Princeton, assembled in the [chapel]. The exercises commenced by reading the 90th Psalm, which was followed by prayer, by the Rev. Dr. Van Pelt. . . . An impressive discourse was pronounced by the Rev. Dr. Carnahan"—the President of Princeton.

"The Rev. Dr. B. H. Rice made the concluding prayer, after which the procession was formed. . . . The Military, the Hearse, the Pall Bearers"— Generals Robert Swartwout and Bogardus, Colonels Romeyn, Scott and Samuel Swartwout, Major Popham, Mr. Western and Mr. Corp—"the Clergy, Mourners, Professors, Students of the Colleges"— including the full roster of the Cliosophic Society wearing the bands of crape decreed "as a feeble testimony of our respect . . . for the space of thirty days"—"and Citizens. [The procession] proceeded to the Church yard, under the escort of one of our handsome volunteer corps, the Mercer Guards, who paid the customary honours of a military funeral in a manner highly creditable to them."

The grave was placed at the feet of his father and grandfather. It was a meet and decent burial, the last official honors "to the remains of this celebrated man," whose career had been "one of deep and thrilling interest and adventure. . . . At one time within one vote of being Chief Magistrate of the

United States; at another dragged as a felon to the
bar of a legal tribunal . . . and now . . . again
in his native town, and within the walls of his Alma
Mater; he is here, but the spirit has departed from
him. . . ." They had buried the Lieutenant Colonel, the ex-Vice President, with military honors—
but no monument was erected over the resting place
of Aaron Burr. It might, they feared in those hostile days, have drawn attention to the grave, and
invited insult. . . .

Twenty years later, only, was a stone provided by
Alfred Edwards, cut in Brown's marble yard at New
York. On it was inscribed—

AARON BURR

Born February 6th, 1756.

Died September 14th, 1836.

A Colonel in the Army of the Revolution.

Vice-President of the United States from

1801 to 1805.

A reticent inscription. . . .

5

Aaron Burr—there was something in the name itself that compelled attention, aside from the ingrati-
ating charm, the perfect manners, the tremendous
presence of that little man who caused so many big-
ger men to bow down to him, and the marvelous eyes.

Nature, heredity, the little accidents of voice, and
face, and gesture, had been so generous to him—in
compensation for his stature—had so conspired to

WINANT'S INN, PORT RICHMOND, STATEN ISLAND

make of him the peerless ornament of a not unfastidious age; he was so charged with grace, with intellect, with taste, so deft in utterance, so apt in courtesy, so rich in fascination; life should have been for him so brilliant an experiment, so fortunate an adventure, so superb an enterprise. If only, in the chambers of his mind, a door had not been ever so slightly, at first, ajar. . . .

All women adored him, and were by him beloved; young men admired him, and he welcomed them all. Flattery was his magic—the flattery of an adroitly daring eloquence poured into feminine ears; the flattery of a respectful silence offered to masculine vanity. He so seldom interrupted, he listened so eagerly, so attentively, so modestly. He made them feel so important, the young men who spoke to him, so absorbing, so indispensable. They never forgot; they idolized the man who so prized their thoughts. Women and boys, young lads and much older people; the divinely foolish sex—the ladies of his day were, for the most part, so delightfully unintelligent, so easily impressed, so readily responsive to the blandishments of those they called fine gentlemen—fatuous youth, diffident old age; in their presence he was supreme, magnificent, impeccable. Other men often disliked him, as men will usually dislike a too accomplished squire, a too successful recipient of tender favors. In spite of his soldiering and hardihood, there was in him a touch of effeminacy which exasperated. He was always whispering to a woman, and rolling those limpid eyes, and smiling that irresistible smile. They disliked him for these things more, perhaps, than for his hypocrisy, his trickery, his deceit.

But when he had them there before him, those same men, in the Senate or in the High Court of Impeachment, they respected him, they obeyed him, they could not deny his power and dignity, they wept to see him go. He was always to entrance, to captivate, to hypnotize. And to mystify. They believed him capable of every artifice, supposed him possessed of every guile, imagined him endowed with every skill—when really he was not so clever. He was not profound, he was not prudent, he was not learned with all his culture; for all his reputation as a lawyer he was not a great jurist; the politician in him was not a statesman; in the midst of all his imperial schemes he could not manage his own affairs, he was a poor judge of men, he never deceived another soul quite as much as he deceived himself. He never awoke from the wizardry of his own spells. He was, in many ways, astonishingly simple; one of the most fatal delusions of his mind was that which caused him to think himself a paragon of cunning.

He was an actor who never discarded his rôle, who was never out of character, whose features, and speech, and bearing were always attuned to the scene. He liked best to play those parts in which he portrayed the lavishly generous host, the patron of grateful protégés, the man of mysterious intrigues, the romantic lover, the exalted personage. In these rôles he excelled, in them he lived until they were become the realities of his existence, in them he dramatized himself to the utter dumbfounderment of his contemporaries, the entire bewitchment of his most intimate associates, the complete infatuation of himself. But the scene must always be prepared for him, and carefully restricted; when he improvised he floundered, and was trash.

He was, consequently, at his best when his mode of life, the requirements of his station, contributed most fully to the gratification of his theatrical nature, to the interpretation of his fondest impersonations. Mr. Hamilton was wrong; Aaron Burr was not dangerous in public life, in the chair of authority, hedged around with precedent and publicity, with the necessity of meticulous behavior, the opportunity of impressive self-display—on the contrary, there came to him then a harmony of purpose, an indulgence of conceit, a fulfilment of personal grandeur, which nourished him with repose, clothed him in content and anointed him with genius. Then, for a while, one saw what manner of man he might have been. It was only when he was cast adrift, when he was no longer given a stage upon which to play his rôles, when the reservoir of his energies began to overflow for lack of any appropriate outlet, it was then that he became dangerous. . . .

6

He lived thirty-one years too long. After 1805, they could find nothing to inscribe upon his epitaph —nothing but tragedy, and grief, and suffering, and these they did not consider worth recording. It has been said that the bullet which struck Alexander Hamilton killed Aaron Burr. That is not true; he had perished already in 1801, he had been marked for destruction, and the hand which was not raised to save him was that of Thomas Jefferson.

And after those thirty-one years, after a hundred

years, he remains tantalizing, challenging, disturbing. The central figure in a drama which can scarcely now be comprehended; for however faithfully one records the facts, however closely one follows him down the Mississippi, shadows fall upon the page, shadows of men who unexpectedly appear—Edward Livingston, John Adair, Daniel Clark, Andrew Jackson—men who shared a certain understanding, and kept silent. Shrouded in doubt, embalmed in secrecy, coffined in fantastic sorrows, entombed in mystery, Aaron Burr cannot rest in peace. And when his uneasy soul passes, one seems to hear a whispering of many great names inseparable from his, to catch a glimpse of countless honored shades aroused to ancient, private dread, to feel the presence of that host of choice spirits which were once, for good or evil, the witnesses of his venture.

A little man who felt, perhaps, that he must contradict his stature before the tall ones of his day, and raise his head above the shoulders of ordinary men.

"I am not a libertine," he said in his last years. "I am not a murderer; I am not a traitor. I never broke a promise to a woman in my life. I did not intend to kill Hamilton and did not shoot first. I never got within ten thousand leagues of a wish to break up the United States by a separatist or a secessionist movement, though I did hope to establish an empire in Mexico and to become its emperor."

Tormented spirit, sitting alone in a chamber filled with echoes, the door of which had swung quite open. . . .

INDEX

A

Adair, General John, ii, 43, 94, 95, 134, 143, 151, 155
Adams, Abigail, i, 122, 123, 151-2, 153, 154, 229
Adams, Henry, ii, 22, 26
Adams, John, i, 68, 122, 150; election to Presidency, i, 169; quoted on proposal for appointment of Burr to army in 1798, i, 174-5; his opinion of Hamilton, i, 175; criticism of, by Hamilton, i, 198-9; antagonizes members of his party, i, 200; attack on, by Hamilton in pamphlet, i, 201; defeated for reëlection in 1800, i, 203; suppression by Burr of John Wood's history of his administration, i, 242-3; letter concerning General Miranda, ii, 9-10; quoted on Burr's expedition, ii, 138, 139
Adams, John Quincy, i, 319, ii, 227, 228, 229, 323
Adams, Judge, description of Burr at time of his expedition, ii, 163-4
Alexander, James, ii, 133, 143
Alfred the Great, descent of Edwards family from, i, 4
Alien Bill, New York, and Holland Land Company affair, i, 178 ff.
Alien and Sedition Bills of 1798, i, 188, 189
Allbright, Jacob, testimony of, at the Burr trial, ii, 208-9
Allen, Colonel Ethan, capture of Fort Ticonderoga by, i, 43
Alston, Aaron Burr, son of Theodosia Burr Alston, i, 225, 226, 227, ii, 202, 242; death of, ii, 296

Alston, Joseph, marriage to Theodosia Burr, i, 222; letter of Burr to, preceding his duel with Hamilton, i, 286-7; subscribes to Burr's western enterprise, ii, 69; denies implication in Burr's projects, ii, 200; at Richmond at time of trial, ii, 202; letters of, to Burr on death of his son, and loss of Theodosia at sea, ii, 296, 298; Governor of South Carolina, ii, 296; attempts of Blennerhassett to collect money from, ii, 302-4; death of, ii, 304
Ames, Fisher, i, 156, 164, 257
Armstrong, John, American minister at Paris, ii, 27, 29; hostility to Burr, ii, 255, 256
Arnold, Benedict, expedition to Quebec, i, 42 ff.; wounded in attack on Quebec, i, 54; failure of assault, i, 54-5; retreat of, i, 55-6
Arnold, Mrs. Benedict, i, 86-7
Augusta, Me., Arnold's expedition at, i, 45

B

Back Countries, the, ii, 4 ff.
Baker, John, one of counsel for Burr in his trial, ii, 182
Baltimore, Md., congratulatory address to Burr by citizens of, in 1800, i, 236; demonstrations of populace in, after the Burr trial, ii, 224
Bartow, Theodosius, i, 89, 91
Bastrop project, the, ii, 69, 70, 71, 72, 87, 88, 96, 146, 152, 219
Bayard, Congressman Richard, i, 213, 214, 215, 237
Bayou Pierre, Burr at, ii, 160

Martin, Luther, i, 31; ii, 224; one of counsel for Judge Chase in impeachment trial, i, 318, 319; one of counsel for Burr in his trial, ii, 182, 189, 192, 200–1, 210, 214–15; Burr's care of, in old age, ii, 308

Martlings, the, part taken in New York election of 1800, i, 193–4

Massac, Fort, Burr's flotilla at, ii, 159–60

Mather, Cotton, i, 24

Maunsell, General, i, 90; co-trustee with Burr, and resulting litigation, i, 141

Meade, Cowles, ii, 161, 162, 266

Meigs, Jonathan, ii, 86

Merry, Anthony, British Minister at Washington, i, 230, ii, 32–3, 35, 48, 116, 236–7; proposals of Burr to, ii, 33, 34, 36–7, 39, 52–3; recall of, ii, 53

Mexican Association of New Orleans, ii, 46; statement of objects of, ii, 124 ff.

Mexico, Burr's purpose to invade, ii, 38–40, 96; suggestions of possible expedition against, ii, 44, 45, 46, 47, 48; previous plans for conquest of, ii, 97

"Midnight judges," the, i, 238

Minor, Stephen, ii, 48, 49, 50, 104, 122

Miranda, Don Francisco de, letter of John Adams concerning his purposes, ii, 9–10; plan for achieving independence of South America, ii, 10, 11; correspondence with Hamilton, ii, 11–13; reappearance in New York in 1805, ii, 60; his *Leander* expedition, ii, 61 ff.; resemblance of the expedition to Burr's so-called conspiracy, ii, 62–3

Miró, Governor, of Spanish Louisiana, ii, 5, 6

Mississippi River, difficulties with Spain over navigation of, ii, 4 ff.

Mitchill, Senator, quoted on Burr's last days as President of the Senate, i, 321, 322, 323

Mobile Act of 1804, ii, 25

Moncrieffe, Margaret, i, 61–3

Monmouth, battle of, 71–2

Monroe, James, i, 152, 156, 168, 184, 185; threatened duel between Hamilton and, i, 283; goes to France to purchase New Or-

leans and West Florida, ii, 21; with Livingston purchases Louisiana territory for United States, ii, 22; Burr's opinion of, at time of his election to Presidency, ii, 317

Montgomery, General Richard, capture of Montreal by, i, 44; before Quebec, i, 53; killed in assault on Quebec, i, 54–5

Montreal, capture of, by Montgomery, i, 44; mission of Franklin to, i, 55; American retreat from, i, 56

Mooney, William, reorganization of Tammany Society by, i, 190–1

Morgan, Colonel George, ii, 85–6

Morris, Gouverneur, i, 156, 229, 237, 239; opinion on merits of Jefferson and Burr in Presidential tie in 1800, i, 205; funeral oration for Hamilton, i, 298–9

N

Nashville, Tenn., Burr at, ii, 151; conflicting opinions as to the date of arrival of Jefferson's proclamation concerning Burr at, ii, 153 ff.

Nassau Hall, i, 16

National Gazette, organ of Jefferson, i, 158

Neutral Ground Treaty of Wilkinson with the Spaniards, ii, 107

New England, threatened separation of, from the Union, i, 256 ff.

New Haven, British attack on, i, 78

New Jersey, College of, beginnings of, i, 14 ff.

New Jersey Historical Society, i, 98

New Orleans, plans for capture of, in 1798, ii, 13, 14, 15; transfer of Louisiana territory at, from Spain to France and from France to the United States, ii, 24; deputies from, present grievances at Washington, ii, 34–5; Burr at, in 1805, ii, 45–7; Mexican Association of, ii, 46, 124 ff.; rumors in, in fall of 1806, ii, 123–4; acts of Wilkinson in, in December, 1806, ii, 129–36

New York, State of, abolishment of slavery in, i, 146; political affairs in, in 1791, and election of Aaron Burr to United States Senate from, i, 147–9; guberna-